GREAT SOURCE

Vocabulary for Achievement

Third Course

Margaret Ann Richek
Arlin T. McRae
Susan K. Weiler

Great Source Education Group
A Houghton Mifflin Company
Boston, Massachusetts

Authors

Margaret Ann Richek
Professor of Education, Northeastern Illinois University; consultant in reading and vocabulary study; author of *The World of Words*

Arlin T. McRae
Supervisor of English, Evansville-Vanderburgh School Corporation, Evansville, Indiana; Adjunct Instructor in English, University of Evansville

Susan K. Weiler
Teacher of Latin, Beaumont School for Girls, Cleveland Heights, Ohio

Classroom Consultants

Jack Pelletier
Teacher of English, Mira Loma High School, Sacramento, California

Valerie M. Webster
Teacher of English, Walnut Hill School, Natick, Massachusetts

Acknowledgments
Definitions for the three hundred words taught in this textbook are based on Houghton Mifflin dictionaries—in particular, the *Houghton Mifflin College Dictionary*—but have been abbreviated and adapted for instructional purposes. In the skill lessons, dictionary entries from the *Houghton Mifflin College Dictionary*, copyright © 1986, appear on pages 19–20; dictionary passages (some of them abridged) from the *American Heritage Dictionary, Second College Edition*, copyright © 1985 and *The American Heritage Dictionary of the English Language, Third Edition*, copyright © 1992, appear on pages 39–40. The pronunciation key on the inside front cover is adapted from the same sources. The reading passage on page 100 is adapted from *Reading for Results*, Second Edition, by Laraine E. Flemming and Sara C. Mansbach. Copyright © 1983 by Houghton Mifflin Company. Reprinted by permission of Houghton Mifflin Company.

Credits
Design and art production: Design Office, San Francisco

Illustration
Nanette Biers: pages 105, 137, 157; Keith Criss: pages 51, 65, 77, 177; Sylvia Giblin: pages 37, 85, 91, 97; Norman Nicholson: pages 25, 31, 45, 71

Copyright © 1994, 1988 by Houghton Mifflin Company. All rights reserved.

No part of this work may be reproduced or transmitted in any form or by any means, electronic or mechanical, including photocopying and recording, or by any information storage or retrieval system without prior written permission of Houghton Mifflin Company unless such copying is expressly permitted by federal copyright law. Address inquiries to School Permissions, Houghton Mifflin Company, 222 Berkeley Street, Boston, MA 02116.

Printed in the U.S.A.

ISBN: 0-395-67507-3

Contents

Lesson 1	Aspects of Language	1
Lesson 2	Words from Names	7
Lesson 3	Eating and Food	13
Dictionary Skills	Finding the Appropriate Definition	19
Lesson 4	Honesty and Deception	21
Lesson 5	Awareness	27
Lesson 6	The Roots *-polis-* and *-urb-*	33
Dictionary Skills	Usage Notes	39
Lesson 7	Completion	41
Lesson 8	The Usual and Unusual	47
Lesson 9	Puzzles	53
Test-Taking Skills	Antonym Tests	59
Lesson 10	Beginnings	61
Lesson 11	Stops and Delays	67
Lesson 12	The Roots *-pon-* and *-posit-*	73
Test-Taking Skills	Analogy Tests	79
Lesson 13	Size and Amount	81
Lesson 14	Medicine	87
Lesson 15	Damage and Deterioration	93
Test-Taking Skills	Reading Comprehension Tests	99
Lesson 16	Ability	101
Lesson 17	Pride	107
Lesson 18	Truth and Value	113
Reading Skills	Context Clues: Substitution	119
Lesson 19	Communication	121
Lesson 20	The Roots *-scribe-* and *-script-*	127
Lesson 21	Words from Spanish	133
Reading Skills	The Prefixes *ex-* and *e-*	139
Lesson 22	Boldness	141
Lesson 23	Accident and Purpose	147
Lesson 24	Words from the Latin Word *Facere*	153
Reading Skills	The Prefixes *ab-*, *a-*, and *abs-*	159
Lesson 25	Praise and Criticism	161
Lesson 26	Ignoring and Paying Attention	167
Lesson 27	The Root *-tract-*	173
Reading Skills	The Suffixes *-ful* and *-ous*	179
Lesson 28	Thinking and Believing	181
Lesson 29	Argument and Debate	187
Lesson 30	The Roots *-gno-* and *-sci-*	193
Reading Skills	Four Verb Suffixes	199
Flash cards		201

Complete Word List

- abnormal, 47
- accolade, 161
- adept, 101
- adulation, 161
- affectation, 153
- aficionado, 133
- ambiguous, 53
- anathema, 161
- apologist, 187
- appraisal, 113
- appreciable, 81
- aptitude, 101
- arbitrary, 147
- archaic, 1
- argot, 1
- arrogant, 107
- ascribe, 127
- assert, 141
- assess, 167
- astute, 101

- baffle, 53
- base, 113
- behold, 27
- beneficiary, 153
- bland, 13
- blight, 93
- bonanza, 133
- boycott, 7
- bravado, 133
- breadth, 81
- broach, 61

- candid, 113
- capillary, 87
- cataclysm, 93
- cessation, 67
- circumlocution, 121
- circumscribe, 127
- cognizant, 193
- coincidental, 147
- commence, 67
- commend, 161
- composite, 73
- comprehensive, 41
- connoisseur, 193
- connotation, 1
- conscientious, 193
- consciousness, 193
- contend, 187
- contract, 173
- contrive, 147
- convene, 61
- conventional, 47
- convoluted, 53
- copious, 81
- cosmopolitan, 33
- criterion, 113
- culinary, 13

- dauntless, 141
- dearth, 41
- debut, 61

- decimate, 93
- decomposition, 93
- defect, 153
- deficient, 41
- deficit, 41
- delectable, 13
- deliberation, 147
- denotation, 1
- deter, 67
- detract, 173
- devious, 21
- devour, 13
- dexterity, 101
- diagnosis, 193
- diffident, 107
- dilemma, 53
- discernment, 27
- discourse, 121
- disposition, 73
- disregard, 167
- dissuade, 187
- distraction, 173
- dogmatic, 181
- duplicity, 21

- edible, 13
- efficacy, 153
- egocentric, 107
- embargo, 133
- embark, 61
- enervate, 87
- enigma, 53
- enthrall, 167
- entreaty, 173
- envision, 27
- epicure, 13
- epidemic, 87
- epidermis, 87
- eradication, 93
- esteem, 107
- eulogy, 161
- euphemism, 121
- exhaustive, 41
- exponent, 73
- extol, 161
- extract, 173

- faction, 153
- factor, 153
- fallacy, 187
- falter, 121
- ferocity, 141
- fictitious, 21
- finesse, 101
- flotilla, 133
- flout, 141
- foresee, 27
- fortuitous, 147

- galvanize, 7
- gape, 27
- gargantuan, 81
- generate, 61

- geopolitics, 33
- gloat, 107
- guileless, 21
- gullible, 21

- hacienda, 133
- hamper, 67
- haphazard, 147
- havoc, 93
- headstrong, 141
- heedless, 167
- homage, 161
- humility, 107
- hypocritical, 21
- hypothesis, 187

- idiom, 1
- idiosyncrasy, 47
- impolitic, 33
- impostor, 73
- impressionistic, 27
- incipient, 61
- incisive, 141
- indifferent, 167
- indisputable, 187
- inference, 187
- infirmity, 87
- initiative, 61
- innovation, 61
- innumerable, 81
- inordinate, 81
- inscribe, 127
- insight, 27
- inspiration, 101
- integral, 41
- intent, 147
- intricate, 53

- jargon, 1
- jovial, 7
- junta, 133
- juxtaposition, 73

- labyrinth, 53
- laudable, 161
- legitimate, 113
- literate, 121

- macadam, 7
- malady, 87
- mar, 93
- masquerade, 21
- maverick, 7
- mediocre, 113
- megalopolis, 33
- mentor, 7
- meritorious, 113
- metropolitan, 33
- modest, 107
- morsel, 13
- myopia, 27

- negligible, 81
- nemesis, 7
- nondescript, 127
- notoriety, 193

- novice, 61
- nutrient, 87

- obliterate, 93
- oblivious, 167
- obstruction, 67
- odyssey, 7
- officiate, 153
- officious, 153
- omniscient, 193
- opposition, 73
- orthodox, 47
- outspoken, 141
- overt, 21
- overture, 61

- pallor, 87
- paltry, 41
- paucity, 81
- peccadillo, 133
- pensive, 181
- peon, 133
- perceptive, 27
- philosophy, 181
- pittance, 81
- plausible, 181
- plethora, 41
- policy, 33
- politico, 33
- pompous, 107
- ponder, 181
- portray, 173
- postulate, 181
- prattle, 121
- precedent, 47
- preclude, 67
- precocious, 101
- premeditated, 147
- preoccupy, 167
- prescribe, 127
- prevalent, 47
- procrastinate, 67
- prodigy, 101
- prognosis, 193
- proliferate, 81
- prolific, 153
- proposition, 73
- propound, 73
- prosaic, 47
- proscribe, 127
- protracted, 173
- pulverize, 93
- pungent, 13

- quaff, 13
- quaint, 47
- quandary, 53
- quixotic, 7

- raconteur, 121
- rarity, 47
- rational, 181
- ravenous, 13
- receptive, 167

- recognition, 193
- red herring, 187
- refute, 187
- reiterate, 121
- renegade, 133
- replenish, 41
- repository, 73
- reproach, 161
- reputable, 21
- resourceful, 101
- retract, 173
- reverence, 161
- reverie, 181

- scant, 41
- scripture, 127
- scrutinize, 167
- scuttle, 67
- semantics, 1
- singular, 47
- skeptical, 181
- slang, 1
- soluble, 53
- speculation, 181
- spontaneous, 147
- stagnant, 93
- standard, 1
- subscribe, 127
- subscript, 127
- subside, 67
- substantiate, 187
- subtle, 113
- suburban, 33
- suffice, 153
- supposition, 73
- survey, 27
- susceptible, 87
- swagger, 107

- tactic, 53
- tantalize, 7
- temerity, 141
- thwart, 67
- tract, 173
- trait, 173
- transcribe, 127
- truism, 113

- unconscionable, 193
- unwitting, 147
- urban, 33
- urbane, 33
- utterance, 121

- validate, 113
- vaunt, 107
- vehement, 141
- veracity, 21
- verbose, 121
- vernacular, 1
- vibrant, 141
- vigilant, 167
- virtuoso, 101
- virulent, 87

Lesson 1

Aspects of Language

When you write a letter to a friend or call an acquaintance on the telephone, the casual language that you use suits the informality of the situation. On the other hand, when you write a job application letter or prepare a speech for a debate, you choose words, sentence structures, and expressions that are much more formal. The occasion dictates your manner of writing or speaking.

Levels of language are only one area of a fascinating subject, however. In this lesson you will learn words that introduce you to wide-ranging aspects of language and help you to become an informed user of English.

WORD LIST
archaic
argot
connotation
denotation
idiom
jargon
semantics
slang
standard
vernacular

DEFINITIONS

After you have studied the definitions and example for each vocabulary word, write the word on the line to the right.

1. **archaic** (är-kā′ĭk) *adjective* **a.** Referring to words and language that were once common but are now rarely used. **b.** Ancient. **c.** No longer applicable: *archaic laws*. (From the Greek word *arkhaikos*, meaning "old-fashioned")

    EXAMPLE Many historical documents, such as the Declaration of Independence, contain *archaic* words.

    1. _____

2. **argot** (är′gō, är′gət) *noun* The informal vocabulary used by a particular class or group, such as criminals; a secret language. (From the French word *argot*, meaning "slang")

    EXAMPLE *The Beggar's Opera*, a humorous play written in the 1700s, is rich in thieves' *argot*.

    2. _____
    SEE *jargon*.

3. **connotation** (kŏn′ə-tā′shən) *noun* The mental connections or associations suggested by a word that go beyond its literal meaning or its dictionary definition.

    RELATED WORDS **connotative** *adjective*; **connote** *verb*

    EXAMPLE The word *crowd* has a more favorable *connotation* than the word *mob*.

    3. _____
    SEE *denotation*.

4. **denotation** (dē′nō-tā′shən) *noun* The exact meaning of a word. (From the Latin word *denotare*, meaning "to specify")

    RELATED WORDS **denotative** *adjective*; **denote** *verb*

    EXAMPLE The word *nice* usually has the *denotation* of "attractive" or "pleasant," but it can also have the connotation of "fussy" or "finicky."

    4. _____
    MEMORY CUE *Denotation* means "the exact dictionary *definition*," and *connotation* means "the ideas and feelings *connect*ed with a word."

Aspects of Language   1

5. **idiom** (ĭd′ē-əm) *noun* **a.** An expression having a special meaning that is not clear from the usual meaning of the individual words in the expression. **b.** The specific grammatical and structural characteristics of a language; the accepted pattern of word usage. **c.** Speech that is characteristic of a particular region. (From the Greek word *idios*, meaning "one's own")

   RELATED WORDS **idiomatic** *adjective;* **idiomatically** *adverb*

   EXAMPLE The *idiom* "to have an ax to grind" refers to having a selfish aim or motive.

6. **jargon** (jär′gən) *noun* **a.** The specialized technical vocabulary used by people in the same profession or field. **b.** Confusing, meaningless talk.

   EXAMPLE The patient asked the doctor to explain what she meant without using confusing medical *jargon*.

7. **semantics** (sĭ-măn′tĭks) *noun* **a.** The study of historical changes in the meanings of words. **b.** The study of the relation of words to the objects they stand for. (From the Greek word *sēma*, meaning "sign")

   RELATED WORDS **semantic** *adjective;* **semantically** *adverb;* **semanticist** *noun*

   EXAMPLE Thelma, who is fascinated by *semantics*, told us that the word *silly* once meant "holy."

8. **slang** (slăng) *noun* Highly informal language that occurs most often in casual conversation.

   EXAMPLE When Ned described Robinson Crusoe as a "together person," Mr. Cummings asked him to express the same idea without using *slang*.

9. **standard** (stăn′dərd) *adjective* **a.** Conforming to established usage in speech or writing. **b.** Commonly used and accepted as an authority. *noun* **a.** A rule or model used to judge the quality or correctness of something; criterion. **b.** A level of requirement, excellence, or attainment. (From the Old French word *estandard*, meaning "a rallying place")

   RELATED WORD **standardize** *verb*

   EXAMPLE Correct use of *standard* English requires an understanding of grammar and usage.

10. **vernacular** (vər-năk′yə-lər) *noun* The normal spoken language of a country or region as distinct from the literary or learned language; everyday speech. *adjective* Native to or commonly spoken by residents of a particular country or region. (From the Latin word *vernaculus*, meaning "of home-born slaves")

    EXAMPLE Mark Twain is well known for his use of Southern *vernacular* in his writing.

---

5. _____

6. _____
USAGE NOTE *Jargon* refers to a specialized vocabulary. *Argot* is jargon used for secret communication.

7. _____
USAGE NOTE The word *semantics* is always used with a singular verb.

8. _____
SEE *vernacular.*

9. _____

10. _____
USAGE NOTE The *vernacular* is the everyday speech of the general population. Within the vernacular is *slang*, which is specific to groups within the general population (such as teenagers) and is short-lived in its use.

Aspects of Language

Name _____ Date _____

Exercise 1 Writing Correct Words

On the answer line, write the word from the vocabulary list that fits each definition.

1. An expression having a meaning different from the meaning of the individual words in it
2. The secret language used by a particular group or class
3. The mental associations suggested by a word
4. The study of changes in the meanings of words
5. The everyday spoken language of a country or region
6. The technical vocabulary of those in the same occupation or field
7. The exact meaning of a word
8. Highly informal language
9. Referring to formerly common words that are now rarely used
10. Conforming to established usage in speech or writing

1. _____
2. _____
3. _____
4. _____
5. _____
6. _____
7. _____
8. _____
9. _____
10. _____

Exercise 2 Using Words Correctly

Each of the following questions contains an italicized vocabulary word. Choose the correct answer to the question, and write *Yes* or *No* on the answer line.

1. Are the *connotations* of the word *inexpensive* more favorable than the connotations of the word *cheap*?
2. Is a *hit* the same thing in the *jargons* of baseball and football?
3. If you want to make a good impression at a job interview, will you use *slang*?
4. Might two spies use *argot* so that others could not understand them?
5. Is the *denotation* of a word its range of suggested meanings?
6. Does *semantics* deal with the alterations of meanings in a language?
7. Would you expect a scholarly book to be written in the *vernacular*?
8. Do newspapers contain many *archaic* terms?
9. Is being "down in the dumps" an *idiom*?
10. In a term paper, would you use *standard* English?

1. _____
2. _____
3. _____
4. _____
5. _____
6. _____
7. _____
8. _____
9. _____
10. _____

Exercise 3 Choosing the Best Word

Decide which vocabulary word or related form best completes the sentence, and write the letter of your choice on the answer line.

1. If your teacher asks for the __?__ of a word, he or she wants you to furnish an exact definition.
   a. semantics   b. idiom   c. connotation   d. denotation

1. _____

Copyright © 1988 Houghton Mifflin Company. All rights reserved.   Aspects of Language   3

2. Many dictionaries contain words that are no longer used, but they are labeled as ___?___ .
   a. connotative b. vernacular c. archaic d. standard

3. The jury could not understand the testimony of the jockey because he used so much ___?___ .
   a. argot b. idiom c. connotation d. vernacular

4. If Lucy had followed ___?___ rules of punctuation, her letter would have been easier to understand.
   a. vernacular b. standard c. archaic d. connotative

5. The novelist captured the ___?___ of the mountain people.
   a. connotation b. semantics c. jargon d. vernacular

6. *Thin* and *scrawny* mean the same, but each has a different ___?___ .
   a. idiom b. connotation c. argot d. semantic

7. Compiling a dictionary of current ___?___ is difficult because most of the terms are used only a short time.
   a. slang b. denotation c. semantics d. connotation

8. Saying that someone is going to "hit the deck" is one of several ___?___ that people use to express preparing for action.
   a. semantics b. connotations c. idioms d. jargons

9. The study of ___?___ has proven that language undergoes gradual change.
   a. idioms b. connotation c. argot d. semantics

10. The ___?___ of computer experts is often difficult for people outside the field to understand.
    a. slang b. vernacular c. denotation d. jargon

Exercise 4 Using Different Forms of Words

Decide which form of the vocabulary word in parentheses best completes the sentence. The form given may be correct. Write your answer on the answer line.

1. Pam used less ___?___ as she got older. *(slang)*

2. To appreciate ___?___ speech, one must hear it spoken by a native. *(vernacular)*

3. *Thy* is an ___?___ pronoun. *(archaic)*

4. The ___?___ of *argument* and *quarrel* are almost the same. *(denotation)*

5. Although Gretchen does well on ___?___ tests, she always gets nervous before taking them. *(standard)*

6. Dale is sensitive to the ___?___ aspects of language. *(connotation)*

7. ___?___ expressions cannot be understood from the meanings of the individual words. *(Idiom)*

8. Sometimes people will disagree about wording when there is really only a small ___?___ difference. *(semantics)*

9. When used for a general audience, ___?___ can be confusing and meaningless. *(jargon)*

10. Michael could not understand the ___?___ of the prisoners. *(argot)*

4 Aspects of Language

Name _____ Date _____

Reading Comprehension

Each numbered sentence in the following passage contains an italicized vocabulary word or related form. After you read the passage, you will complete an exercise.

Levels of Usage

(1) According to *semanticists,* English is a vigorous language that is constantly changing. (2) Words like *forsooth, belike,* and *parlous,* though commonly used during Shakespeare's time, are considered *archaic* today.

(3) In the same way, specialized terms that are currently limited to the *jargon* of a particular profession may become part of ordinary usage tomorrow.

With the amount of change that occurs, the English language is highly flexible. (4) It includes everything from the private *argot* of special groups to the more formal language used for serious occasions. We learn that to communicate effectively we must use the level of language that is appropriate to a given situation.

(5) Formal English is the kind of *standard* English that is used for serious writing and for ceremonial speeches. (6) Formal English is sometimes known as "literary" English because the term *denotes* the kind of writing found in some works of literature and in scholarly publications. In formal English, writers and speakers use complex, precisely structured sentences and conservative grammar. (7) Users of formal English choose sophisticated vocabulary with a concentration on the *connotations* of words. (8) When formal English is required, people avoid using both *slang* and contractions.

(9) Informal English, the second kind of standard English, is closer to the *vernacular.* It is widely used in conversation, broadcasting, and informal speeches, and in many newspapers, magazines, and books. It is characterized by sentence length and variety that are typical of conversation. Sentences are shorter and have fewer clauses than in formal English. (10) Usage is more relaxed than in formal English, and contractions and *idioms* may be common.

Nonstandard English is composed of words, expressions, and grammatical constructions that do not conform to accepted usage. Although many authors use nonstandard English to create realistic dialogue, sentences like Eugene O'Neill's "Well, you got to watch out, that's all I says" should be avoided when you communicate with a general audience.

Choosing words and sentence structures appropriate to a topic and a situation is similar to choosing clothing suitable for a particular occasion. Just as you would not wear your best outfit to clean the attic, you would not want to choose language that could not be understood. In speaking and writing, you want the clearest and most effective way to convey your meaning.

Reading Comprehension Exercise

Each of the following statements corresponds to a numbered sentence in the passage. Each statement contains a blank and is followed by four answer choices. Decide which choice fits best in the blank. The word or phrase that you choose must express roughly the same meaning as the italicized word in the passage. Write the letter of your choice on the answer line.

1. __?__ claim that English is a constantly changing language.
   a. Those who study architecture
   b. Journalists
   c. Those who study changes in meaning
   d. Dictionary writers

   1. _____

2. Words like *forsooth* and *belike* are __?__ today.
   a. rarely used   b. common   c. literary   d. humorous

   2. _____

Copyright © 1988 Houghton Mifflin Company. All rights reserved.

Aspects of Language 5

3. Terms that are limited to the ___?___ of particular professions may be in ordinary usage tomorrow.
   a. experts
   b. specialized vocabularies
   c. lives
   d. rare examples

4. English includes everything from ___?___ to formal language.
   a. phrases
   b. associations
   c. improved pronunciation
   d. secret language

5. Formal English is the ___?___ English used for serious writing and speaking.
   a. commonly accepted
   b. informal
   c. ordinary
   d. commonly discussed

6. The term *literary* ___?___ the writing of literature and scholarship.
   a. classifies   b. does not apply to   c. describes   d. improves

7. Users of formal English concentrate on the ___?___ meanings of words.
   a. rare   b. rough   c. interesting   d. suggested

8. In formal English, people avoid contractions and ___?___.
   a. grammar
   b. long sentences
   c. highly informal language
   d. punctuation

9. Informal English is closer to ___?___.
   a. written language
   b. everyday speech
   c. suggested language
   d. correct grammar

10. ___?___ are common in informal English.
    a. Expressions with special meanings
    b. Confusing words
    c. Formal structures
    d. Rare words

3. _____
4. _____
5. _____
6. _____
7. _____
8. _____
9. _____
10. _____

Writing Assignment

Choose a piece of writing such as a newspaper or magazine article or a passage from a work by an author whom you admire. Using at least five vocabulary words from this lesson, write a paragraph in which you discuss the author's use of language. Underline each vocabulary word that you use.

Vocabulary Enrichment

Vernacular, which comes from the Latin word *vernaculus*, meaning "of home-born slaves," has an interesting connection with Roman history. In ancient times it was common for wealthy Roman families to own many slaves. These slaves and their families often lived in the house with their owners. A slave child born in the master's house was known as a *verna*. As centuries passed, people forgot that *verna* meant "home-born slave" and associated the word solely with "home-born." Our word *vernacular*, referring to the home-born, or native, speech of a country, comes from the Latin word.

ACTIVITY Using your dictionary, look up the following words and write their meanings and Latin roots. Then write an explanation of the connection between the root and the meaning.

1. ancillary   2. servitude   3. menial   4. domestic

Lesson 2

Words from Names

Many of the words we use today are derived from the names of famous people in history or characters in literature. For example, the word *sandwich* was inspired by an Englishman, John Montagu, the fourth Earl of Sandwich (1718–1792). The word originated after Montagu spent twenty-four hours at a gambling table, eating only pieces of cold beef *sandwiched* between slices of toast.

Each word in this lesson has its own interesting history with an entertaining story from the past. You can discover these stories for yourself in the reading passage of this lesson.

WORD LIST
boycott
galvanize
jovial
macadam
maverick
mentor
nemesis
odyssey
quixotic
tantalize

DEFINITIONS

After you have studied the definitions and example for each vocabulary word, write the word on the line to the right.

1. **boycott** (boi′kŏt′) *trans. verb* To take part in an organized group refusal to use a product or service as a means of protest. *noun* An organized group refusal.
   RELATED WORD **boycotter** *noun*
   EXAMPLE A group of concerned environmentalists *boycotted* the store that sold pesticides.

2. **galvanize** (găl′və-nīz′) *trans. verb* **a.** To stir to action or awareness. **b.** To stimulate or shock with an electric current. **c.** To put a coating of zinc on iron or steel as protection against rust.
   RELATED WORD **galvanization** *noun*
   EXAMPLE A persuasive speech *galvanized* the audience into donating money to a worthy cause.

3. **jovial** (jō′vē-əl) *adjective* Full of fun and good cheer; sociable.
   RELATED WORDS **joviality** *noun*; **jovially** *adverb*
   EXAMPLE Because of his *jovial* personality, Mark was usually the life of the party.

4. **macadam** (mə-kăd′əm) *noun* **a.** A paving material made of layers of small stones that are packed together with asphalt or tar. **b.** A road surface that has been paved with layers of small stones.
   RELATED WORD **macadamize** *verb*
   EXAMPLE The road leading through the country village was paved with *macadam*.

5. **maverick** (măv′ər-ĭk) *noun* **a.** A person who refuses to go along with the policies or views of his or her group; someone who is independent-minded; a nonconformist. **b.** An unbranded calf or colt. **c.** A horse or steer that has escaped from the herd.
   EXAMPLE Club members called Jessica a *maverick* after she criticized their new rules.

6. **mentor** (měn′tôr′) *noun* A person depended upon for wise advice and guidance; a trusted counselor.
   EXAMPLE The professional athlete was a valuable *mentor* to the struggling high school football player.

7. **nemesis** (něm′ĭ-sĭs) *noun* **a.** Someone or something that is the source of just punishment. **b.** Just punishment for wrongdoing. **c.** An unbeatable rival.
   EXAMPLE Freezing weather was the *nemesis* of the invading army.

8. **odyssey** (ŏd′ĭ-sē) *noun* **a.** A long, adventurous, wandering journey. **b.** An intellectual or spiritual quest.
   EXAMPLE In the 1800s explorers went on *odysseys*, hoping to discover unknown islands in the Pacific Ocean.

9. **quixotic** (kwĭk-sŏt′ĭk) *adjective* Full of impractical ideas; idealistic.
   RELATED WORD **quixotically** *adverb*
   EXAMPLE Ted's *quixotic* aunt encouraged her nephew to quit his job and travel through Europe.

10. **tantalize** (tăn′tə-līz′) *trans. verb* To tease or torment by presenting something desirable while it is out of reach.
    RELATED WORD **tantalizingly** *adverb*
    EXAMPLE Because Sarah was very hungry, the picture of the delicious meal *tantalized* her.

Words from Names

Name _____ Date _____ **Words from Names**

Exercise 1 Completing Definitions

On the answer line, write the word from the vocabulary list that best completes each definition.

1. To tempt but deny satisfaction is to __?__ .
2. To rouse to action is to __?__ .
3. To refuse to do business with so as to force change is to __?__ .
4. An independent-minded person or a nonconformist is a(n) __?__ .
5. The source of just punishment is a(n) __?__ .
6. A sociable, fun-loving person is __?__ .
7. An idealistic but impractical person is __?__ .
8. A wise adviser or trusted counselor is a(n) __?__ .
9. Layers of small stones used as a paving material are __?__ .
10. An adventurous, wandering journey is a(n) __?__ .

1. _____
2. _____
3. _____
4. _____
5. _____
6. _____
7. _____
8. _____
9. _____
10. _____

Exercise 2 Using Words Correctly

Decide whether the italicized vocabulary word has been used correctly in the sentence. On the answer line, write *Correct* for correct use and *Incorrect* for incorrect use.

1. "We'll *boycott* that store so effectively that business will be booming," promised the protesters.
2. At 6:00 A.M. a ringing alarm clock *galvanizes* me into action.
3. The twins wear yellow *macadams* on rainy days.
4. The French emperor Napoleon I met his *nemesis* in the English Duke of Wellington at Waterloo in 1815.
5. In a fable by Aesop, a fox is *tantalized* by a bunch of ripe grapes that is slightly out of reach.
6. The editor was an inspiring *mentor* for the reporter.
7. Tommy's *odyssey* took him into the next room.
8. Pam, the class *maverick*, acts like everyone else.
9. The clowns at the circus are very *jovial*.
10. Joan's *quixotic* personality enabled her to work at the same job for twenty years.

1. _____
2. _____
3. _____
4. _____
5. _____
6. _____
7. _____
8. _____
9. _____
10. _____

Exercise 3 Choosing the Best Word

Decide which vocabulary word or related form best completes the sentence, and write the letter of your choice on the answer line.

1. The cowhands searched the canyon for the missing __?__ .
   a. nemesis   b. mentor   c. boycotter   d. maverick

1. _____

2. Bob hoped his editorial would __?__ the indifferent community. 2. _____
   a. galvanize   b. macadamize   c. boycott   d. tantalize

3. The reformer suggested a(n) __?__ of the company that had unsafe 3. _____
   working conditions.
   a. nemesis   b. boycott   c. maverick   d. odyssey

4. Waving and laughing as he greeted us, Grandpa was as __?__ as ever. 4. _____
   a. quixotic   b. tantalizing   c. galvanizing   d. jovial

5. Larry's __?__ ideas about working kept him from getting a job. 5. _____
   a. quixotic   b. jovial   c. tantalizing   d. galvanizing

6. Janet skinned her knee on the __?__ surface of the playground. 6. _____
   a. nemesis   b. maverick   c. mentor   d. macadam

7. The philosopher Socrates was the teacher and __?__ of Plato. 7. _____
   a. nemesis   b. mentor   c. macadam   d. odyssey

8. Carla's summer __?__ took her around the world. 8. _____
   a. nemesis   b. boycott   c. odyssey   d. maverick

9. "Too bad you can't come to Florida with me!" exclaimed Lee as he 9. _____
   __?__ his brother.
   a. boycotted   b. macadamized   c. tantalized   d. galvanized

10. Susanne, a champion runner, finally met her __?__ at the Olympics. 10. _____
    a. odyssey   b. nemesis   c. maverick   d. mentor

Exercise 4 Choosing the Best Word

Decide which vocabulary word or related form best expresses the meaning of the italicized word or phrase in the sentence. On the answer line, write the letter of the correct choice.

1. The *sociable* child made friends quickly. 1. _____
   a. quixotic   b. jovial   c. tantalized   d. boycotted

2. Workers hurried to finish the road paved with *layers of compacted 2. _____
   stones*.
   a. boycott   b. odyssey   c. macadam   d. nemesis

3. Intense heat was the *just punishment* of the thieves who hid in the 3. _____
   desert.
   a. mentor   b. nemesis   c. maverick   d. odyssey

4. The coach's pep talk was responsible for the baseball team's being 4. _____
   stirred to action.
   a. quixotic   b. boycotted   c. tantalized   d. galvanized

5. The *people refusing to buy in order to force change* publicized their 5. _____
   campaign through posters.
   a. odysseys   b. mavericks   c. boycotters   d. mentors

6. In a Jules Verne novel, the main characters undertake a *long, 6. _____
   adventurous journey* by balloon.
   a. odyssey   b. maverick   c. boycott   d. nemesis

7. Critics called the unconventional playwright a *nonconformist*. 7. _____
   a. boycott   b. mentor   c. maverick   d. nemesis

8. The novelist's *wise adviser* introduced her to a literary agent. 8. _____
   a. nemesis   b. mentor   c. maverick   d. macadam

10 Words from Names

Name _____ Date _____

9. Always *impractical*, Sarah suggested, "Let's build a cabin and live off the land!"
   a. jovial   **b.** macadamized   **c.** galvanized   **d.** quixotic

   9. _____

10. Sally *tormented* her little sister by not giving her a favorite toy.
    a. tantalized   **b.** boycotted   **c.** galvanized   **d.** macadamized

    10. _____

Reading Comprehension

Each numbered sentence in the following passage contains an italicized vocabulary word. After you read the passage, you will complete an exercise.

Words from Names

All of the words in this lesson have something in common: they come from peoples' last names. Some of these people are historical figures. Others are fictional personalities, and a few are mythological characters.

Two of the words in this lesson are based on historical incidents. In the late 1870s, the Englishman Charles C. Boycott managed Lord Erne's Irish estate and collected rents from tenant farmers. Because of a serious food shortage, the farmers asked Boycott for a reduction in rent. **(1)** After Boycott denied their request, the farmers then refused to work for him, joining in the first **boycott**.

A refusal of a different kind led to the creation of the word *maverick*. The Texan Samuel A. Maverick (1803–1870) was a strong nonconformist who refused to brand his cattle. **(2)** His position resulted in the word **maverick**, which is used to describe an independent-minded person.

Some historical figures have made scientific contributions that led to new words. For example, in 1827 a Scottish civil engineer named John Loudon Macadam published a successful essay that detailed the advantages of paving a road with small, broken stones. **(3)** The engineer's last name was then used for this type of road and **macadam** paving material. **(4)** The Italian physicist Luigi Galvani (1737–1798) conducted electrical experiments on frogs and thus inspired the verb **galvanize**.

A fictional character can often become as real in people's minds as a historical figure. Don Quixote de la Mancha, the main character in the Spanish author Miguel de Cervantes's sixteenth-century novel, is a good example of this. **(5)** From this colorful, impractical character came the word **quixotic**.

Two of the words in this lesson come from Homer's Greek epic poem, the *Odyssey* (written around 850 B.C.). In this poem the main character, Odysseus, attempts to sail home after a long battle at the city of Troy. **(6)** The return trip becomes a long **odyssey** as Odysseus faces obstacle after obstacle. **(7)** Also from the *Odyssey* comes the inspiration for the word **mentor**. In the classic story, Mentor is the wise adviser to Odysseus' son, Telemachus.

Just as fictional characters have endured through the centuries, giving the language new words, so have the ancient mythological figures. The word *jovial*, for example, comes from Jove (Jupiter), the king of the gods in Roman mythology. **(8)** People born under his influence were expected to be **jovial**, or full of fun like Jove. **(9)** The word **nemesis**, on the other hand, reflects a darker mood. Nemesis was a Greek goddess who judged humans, punishing those who dared to be too happy.

The Greek mythological figure King Tantalus is the source of another English word. Because Tantalus displeased the gods, Nemesis condemned him to stand forever in a pool of water beneath a fruit tree. Thirsty and hungry, Tantalus reached for water and fruit, but Nemesis caused both to recede from his grasp. **(10)** Tantalus' punishment was to be **tantalized** forever by the sight of what he could not have.

These words have unique stories behind them, but then so do you. Perhaps your own last name may someday become a new word.

Please turn to the next page.

Copyright © 1988 Houghton Mifflin Company. All rights reserved.

Words from Names 11

Reading Comprehension Exercise

Each of the following statements corresponds to a numbered sentence in the passage. Each statement contains a blank and is followed by four answer choices. Decide which choice fits best in the blank. The word or phrase that you choose must express roughly the same meaning as the italicized word in the passage. Write the letter of your choice on the answer line.

1. An Irish tenant farmers' __?__ was the source of a new word.
   a. party   b. protest   c. estate   d. relocation

2. Another word came from the name of a man with a(n) __?__ personality.
   a. conformist   b. pleasing   c. nonconformist   d. antisocial

3. Another man's last name came to mean __?__ .
   a. rare stones   c. an essay
   b. a paving material d. civil service

4. Through experiments with frogs, an inventor originated a verb that came to mean __?__ .
   a. to become conscious   c. to wire for electricity
   b. to socialize   d. to stir to action

5. A fictional character who is colorful and __?__ gave the language another word.
   a. unrealistic   b. nearsighted   c. practical   d. militaristic

6. Another fictional character who undertakes a(n) __?__ inspired a new word.
   a. new job   c. adventurous journey
   b. long battle   d. long vacation

7. Still another fictional character, a(n) __?__ , was the source of a new word.
   a. warrior   b. student   c. adviser   d. adventurer

8. To be __?__ is a characteristic associated with the Roman god Jove.
   a. powerful   b. serious   c. reckless   d. merry

9. A Greek goddess inspired the expression that means __?__ .
   a. just punishment   c. undeserved punishment
   b. irrational punishment   d. unintentional punishment

10. A Greek king's dilemma created a word that means __?__ .
    a. having too much   c. being stranded
    b. to tempt and deny   d. hunger and thirst

1. _____
2. _____
3. _____
4. _____
5. _____
6. _____
7. _____
8. _____
9. _____
10. _____

Writing Assignment

Included in this lesson are several words, such as *maverick*, *quixotic*, and *jovial*, that suggest a certain type of personality. For example, someone with a *jovial* personality might constantly crack jokes or try to be the life of the party. Imagine that you have been asked to write a personality sketch for a magazine. Choose someone, real or imaginary, whose personality could be described by one of the three words. Write an opening paragraph for the profile that shows how your featured personality is *quixotic* or *jovial* or a *maverick*.

Lesson 3

Eating and Food

One of the joys of life is eating well. There are so many varieties of food and so many delicious ways to prepare it that most people look forward to meals eagerly. Whether one is having a fancy six-course dinner in an elegant restaurant, a quick bite in a café, or a festive meal prepared at home for a holiday, eating can be a delight. In this lesson you will learn words that refer to eating and food.

WORD LIST
bland
culinary
delectable
devour
edible
epicure
morsel
pungent
quaff
ravenous

DEFINITIONS

After you have studied the definitions and example for each vocabulary word, write the word on the line to the right.

1. **bland** (blănd) *adjective* **a.** Mild; soothing; not irritating: *a bland diet.* **b.** Dull; lacking in interest: *a bland personality.* (From the Latin word *blandus*, meaning "soothing")

   RELATED WORDS **blandly** *adverb;* **blandness** *noun*

   EXAMPLE Joaquin's chili is so *bland* that I have to add pepper to make it tasty.

2. **culinary** (kŭl'ə-nĕr'ē, kyōō'lə-nĕr'ē) *adjective* Pertaining to cooking or the kitchen. (From the Latin word *culina*, meaning "kitchen")

   EXAMPLE Boris is improving his *culinary* skills by fixing breakfast for his family each morning.

3. **delectable** (dĭ-lĕk'tə-bəl) *adjective* Greatly pleasing, especially to the sense of taste; delicious; delightful. (From the Latin word *delectare*, meaning "to delight")

   EXAMPLE The Philbricks enjoyed the *delectable* food in the Virgin Islands.

4. **devour** (dĭ-vour') *trans. verb* **a.** To eat up greedily; swallow; engulf. **b.** To consume enthusiastically: *to devour books.* (From the Latin word *devorare*, meaning "to swallow up")

   EXAMPLE Hungry animals *devour* their food.

Eating and Food 13

5. **edible** (ĕd'ə-bəl) *adjective*   Suitable for eating; capable of being eaten. (From the Latin word *edere,* meaning "to eat")

   EXAMPLE   A cashew nut is *edible;* a wing nut is not.

6. **epicure** (ĕp'ĭ-kyŏŏr') *noun*   A person with refined tastes in food and drink; a gourmet. (From *Epicurus,* the name of an early Greek philosopher)

   RELATED WORD   **epicurean** *adjective*

   EXAMPLE   Eloise is a notable *epicure* with a particular fondness for pheasant and wild rice.

7. **morsel** (môr'səl) *noun*   **a.** A bite or small amount of food. **b.** A small piece; a tidbit. (From the Latin word *morsum,* meaning "a piece bitten off")

   EXAMPLE   Brian's mother always has a few choice *morsels* for us to nibble on after school.

8. **pungent** (pŭn'jənt) *adjective*   Sharp; strong; penetrating; producing a sharp sensation, usually of taste or smell. (From the Latin word *pungere,* meaning "to sting")

   RELATED WORDS   **pungency** *noun;* **pungently** *adverb*

   EXAMPLE   Garlic, cayenne pepper, and coriander are *pungent* spices.

9. **quaff** (kwŏf, kwăf, kwôf) *trans. verb*   To drink heartily and deeply of.

   EXAMPLE   The thirsty girls *quaffed* the water happily after their three-mile run.

10. **ravenous** (răv'ə-nəs) *adjective*   Extremely hungry. (From the Old French word *raviner,* meaning "to take by force")

    RELATED WORD   **ravenously** *adverb*

    EXAMPLE   Dr. von der Vogelweide tells me that teen-agers are often *ravenous* because they are growing so fast.

5. _____

6. _____

7. _____

8. _____

9. _____

10. _____

Name _____   Date _____

Exercise 1 Matching Words and Definitions

Match the definition in Column B with the word in Column A. Write the letter of the correct definition on the answer line.

Column A	Column B
1. epicure	a. delicious; greatly pleasing
2. devour	b. mild
3. pungent	c. to drink heartily and deeply of
4. edible	d. one with refined taste in food and drink
5. culinary	e. a small piece or a bite of food
6. delectable	f. suitable for eating
7. ravenous	g. to eat up greedily
8. quaff	h. sharp; biting
9. morsel	i. pertaining to cooking
10. bland	j. extremely hungry

1. _____
2. _____
3. _____
4. _____
5. _____
6. _____
7. _____
8. _____
9. _____
10. _____

Exercise 2 Using Words Correctly

Decide whether the italicized vocabulary word has been used correctly in the sentence. On the answer line, write *Correct* for correct use and *Incorrect* for incorrect use.

1. The mustard Johanna ate was so *bland* that she had to drink two glasses of water to cool her mouth.
2. Red pepper is a *pungent* spice.
3. The *ravenous* two-year-old whined all during dinner and only picked at her food.
4. The *epicure* preferred to eat meals cooked by her own chef because she knew that they would be delicious.
5. The slops in the farmer's pail must look *delectable* to the pigs.
6. Baking, broiling, and frying are three *culinary* techniques.
7. At dinner the guests *quaffed* their salads with gusto.
8. We ate every *morsel* that Vera prepared.
9. Rob admitted that his peanut butter, mustard, and sardine sandwich was barely *edible*.
10. Showing off her best table manners, Monique *devoured* her cucumber soup.

1. _____
2. _____
3. _____
4. _____
5. _____
6. _____
7. _____
8. _____
9. _____
10. _____

Exercise 3 Choosing the Best Definition

For each italicized vocabulary word in the following sentences, write the letter of the best definition on the answer line.

1. The name of Caspar Milquetoast, a character in a comic strip, was derived from a *bland* dish of toast served in warm milk.
   a. sweet   b. tasty   c. healthful   d. mild

1. _____

Copyright © 1988 Houghton Mifflin Company. All rights reserved.   Eating and Food

2. The *pungent* taste of coriander overwhelmed Maria's roast.
   a. hot   b. biting   c. fragrant   d. mild

   2. _____

3. Three *ravenous* teen-agers drank two quarts of milk and ate seven tuna salad sandwiches and six peaches for lunch.
   a. overweight   b. hungry   c. ravaging   d. thirsty

   3. _____

4. Leilani's grandmother makes a Thanksgiving feast that would satisfy the most demanding *epicure*.
   a. gourmet   b. chef   c. critic   d. guest

   4. _____

5. In the Old English poem *Beowulf*, the monster Grendel *devours* many warriors before being killed.
   a. prepares   b. hunts for   c. eats greedily   d. frightens

   5. _____

6. In the wilderness one should be able to recognize *edible* plants.
   a. easy to eat   b. healthful   c. fit to eat   d. tasty

   6. _____

7. The thirsty gardener *quaffed* an entire glass of orange juice before sitting down to lunch.
   a. sipped   b. drank heartily   c. poured   d. choked on

   7. _____

8. The hikers agreed that after three days in the wild even their freeze-dried turnips were *delectable*.
   a. delicious   b. wholesome   c. tempting   d. nutritious

   8. _____

9. Victor is studying to be a chef at the Pacific School of *Culinary* Arts.
   a. pertaining to restaurants   c. concerning uniforms
   b. concerning cooking   d. pertaining to dining rooms

   9. _____

10. Eating Swiss fondue involves dipping a *morsel* of bread into a pot of melted cheese.
    a. large chunk   b. crumb   c. small bite   d. loaf

    10. _____

Exercise 4   Using Different Forms of Words

Decide which form of the vocabulary word in parentheses best completes the sentence. The form given may be correct. Write your answer on the answer line.

1. Tonight the restaurant is offering a __?__ chicken dish. *(delectable)*

   1. _____

2. The __?__ of the mustard made Nguyen sneeze when he opened the jar. *(pungent)*

   2. _____

3. Hilary surprised her brother by saying __?__, "I'll go to whatever movie you want to see." *(bland)*

   3. _____

4. Not one __?__ of food was left after our Fourth of July picnic. *(morsel)*

   4. _____

5. Roger eats __?__ after his diets and gains back in a week the weight he has lost. *(ravenous)*

   5. _____

6. With poached salmon as the main dish, Aunt Ruth's tailgate picnic before the big football game was an __?__ delight. *(epicure)*

   6. _____

7. After ice-skating on the pond for two hours, the children sat before the fire and __?__ cider. *(quaff)*

   7. _____

8. St. George, the patron saint of England, is said to have slain a dragon that was about to __?__ a princess. *(devour)*

   8. _____

Name _____ Date _____

9. The __?__ knowledge of Brillat-Savarin can be found in his book *The Physiology of Taste.* (culinary)

9. _____

10. The __?__ of cream cheese contrasts nicely with smoked salmon. (bland)

10. _____

Reading Comprehension

Each numbered sentence in the following passage contains an italicized vocabulary word. After you read the passage, you will complete an exercise.

Dining in Rome

(1) It is an **epicure's** delight to dine in Italy, a country with 182 different ways of preparing pizza and 245 different kinds of pasta. (2) Although nearly every Italian city has superb restaurants to satisfy a **ravenous** appetite, Rome is an especially fine place to sample a wide variety of outstanding Mediterranean foods. (3) A Roman meal often begins with a hearty serving of pasta topped with a **pungent** sauce of tomatoes and meat, cheese and pepper, or garlic and olive oil. A sprinkling of freshly grated cheese makes the steaming sauces even more tempting. (4) Because hot spices and seasonings are sometimes used to create these authentic dishes, it is frequently necessary to **quaff** beverages while partaking of the meal. (5) A meat dish flavored with delicate herbs is the next delicious course one will be eager to **devour.** (6) What a mouth-watering experience it is to inhale the aroma of veal, ham, and sage cooking together; beef slices stuffed with sweet peppers; or chicken **morsels** simmered with garlic, onion, and tomatoes. (7) Fluffy omelettes laced with vegetables, cheese, and pieces of bacon are not as hearty as the meat dishes, but neither are they **bland.** They might be served in place of meat. (8) In addition to creating crisp salads, the Romans have a talent for creating **delectable** vegetables. (9) Hearts of artichokes, the most **edible** parts, are often flavored with ham, anchovies, and cheese. Tomatoes are stuffed with herbed rice, and eggplants and zucchini are filled with ground meat and spices. Cheeses, such as bel paese, always find a welcome place on the table.

To end the meal, there may be fresh fruit from the farms near Rome. Ripe strawberries, juicy peaches, and sweet watermelon are favorites. It is a genuine treat to experience a typical Roman meal. (10) One can always rely on its being of high quality and deeply rooted in the region's noteworthy **culinary** traditions.

Reading Comprehension Exercise

Each of the following statements corresponds to a numbered sentence in the passage. Each statement contains a blank and is followed by four answer choices. Decide which choice fits best in the blank. The word or phrase that you choose must express roughly the same meaning as the italicized word in the passage. Write the letter of your choice on the answer line.

1. To dine in Italy is a delight for a __?__ .
   a. pasta and meat expert   c. wine and cheese expert
   b. food and drink expert   d. pastry and fruit expert

1. _____

2. Any Italian restaurant would delight a person with a __?__ appetite.
   a. hearty   b. dull   c. moderate   d. picky

2. _____

Copyright © 1988 Houghton Mifflin Company. All rights reserved.   Eating and Food   17

3. Pasta is served with __?__ sauces.   3. _____
   a. mild   b. tasty   c. cooked   d. biting

4. Sometimes it becomes necessary to __?__ beverages during the meal.   4. _____
   a. order   b. sip   c. enjoy   d. gulp

5. Next, one will __?__ the delicious meat course dish.   5. _____
   a. chew on   b. taste   c. smell   d. eat greedily

6. __?__ of chicken are simmered in a tomato sauce.   6. _____
   a. Large chunks   c. Tasty shreds
   b. Medium slices   d. Small pieces

7. The omelettes are not __?__ .   7. _____
   a. spicy   b. hot   c. mild   d. flavorful

8. The Romans have a knack for creating __?__ vegetables.   8. _____
   a. unusual   b. spicy   c. crisp   d. delicious

9. The most __?__ part of the artichoke is its heart.   9. _____
   a. suitable for eating   c. suitable for planting
   b. suitable for cooking   d. suitable for tasting

10. One can rely on Roman __?__ traditions.   10. _____
    a. pasta   b. cooking   c. holiday   d. restaurant

Writing Assignment

Imagine creating your own restaurant. You can serve whatever you like to whomever you like. Write a report describing to your friends what and how you intend to serve them in your new restaurant. Use at least five of the words from this lesson and underline each one.

Vocabulary Enrichment

Epicure, a word in this lesson on eating and food, comes from the name Epicurus, a Greek philosopher who lived from 342 to 270 B.C. Epicurus taught moderation in all things, believing that excess brings pain and unhappiness. According to his philosophy, pleasure was the highest good, pleasure being freedom of the body from pain and of the soul from anxiety. After Epicurus died, his philosophy was interpreted in different ways. Some people, forgetting his teachings about moderation, thought it meant that they should base their lives on the principle of indulging themselves in sensuous pleasures. The English word *epicure* is loosely related to pleasure, but only in the sense of appreciating fine food and drink. It has, however, lost any connection with Epicurus' philosophy of life.

ACTIVITY In your dictionary look up the following words and write their meanings and their Greek roots. Then write an explanation of the connection between the root and the meaning.

1. stentorian   2. Pyrrhic victory   3. laconic   4. draconian

Dictionary Skills

Finding the Appropriate Definition

Suppose that you are unfamiliar with the word *dock* as it is used in this sentence:

> The boss said that he would *dock* my pay if I was late.

One dictionary gives thirteen definitions divided among four separate entries for the word *dock*. How can you determine which definition is the appropriate one—that is, the one that best fits the word as it is used in the sentence? The following strategies will guide you to the right choice.

STRATEGIES

1. *If there is more than one entry for a word, be sure to look at each one.* Words that are spelled alike but differ in origin and meaning are called **homographs.** They have separate entries in the dictionary and are distinguished by small raised numbers. There are four homographs spelled *dock:*

dock[1] (dŏk) *n.* [MDu. *docke*, prob. < Lat. *ductia*, act of leading < *ducere*, to lead.] **1.** The area of water between two piers or alongside a pier that receives a ship for loading, unloading, or repairs. **2.** A wharf or pier. **3.** *often* **docks.** A group of piers on a protected basin or other waterway serving as a general landing area for watercraft. **4.** A loading platform for trucks or trains. —*v.* **docked, dock·ing, docks.** —*vt.* **1.** To maneuver (a vessel or other vehicle) into or next to a dock. **2.** *Aerospace.* To couple (e.g., two or more spacecraft) in space. —*vi.* To move or come into a dock.

dock[2] (dŏk). *n.* [ME *dok.*] **1.** The fleshy part of an animal's tail. **2.** The tail of an animal after it has been clipped or bobbed. —*vt.* **docked, dock·ing, docks. 1.** To clip or bob (e.g., an animal's ears or tail). **2.** To withhold or deprive of a benefit or a part of the wages, esp. as a punitive measure. **3.** To subject (e.g., wages) to a deduction.

dock[3] (dŏk) *n.* [Flem. *docke,* cage.] An enclosure where the defendant stands or sits in a criminal court.

dock[4] (dŏk) *n.* [ME < OE *docce.*] A weedy plant of the genus *Rumex,* with small greenish or reddish flower clusters.

2. *Determine the part of speech of the unfamiliar word.* In the sentence above, *dock* is a verb. This information eliminated *dock*[3] and *dock*[4] entirely, since they are nouns only. *Dock*[1] can be used as either a transitive *(vt.)* or an intransitive *(vi.)* verb. *Dock*[2] can only be a transitive verb.

3. *Read all the definitions of the word for the appropriate part of speech.* Since *dock* is a transitive verb in the sentence, read all the transitive verb definitions for *dock*[1] and *dock*[2].

4. *Read the sentence to yourself, substituting each of the possible definitions for the word. Decide which one best fits the sentence.* The third definition of *dock*[2] best fits the sentence:

> The boss said that he would *subject* my pay *to a deduction* if I was late.

Please turn to the next page.

Exercise Finding the Appropriate Definition

Using the dictionary entries at the end of this exercise, write the part of speech and the appropriate definition of the italicized word in each sentence. Then write a sentence of your own in which you use the word with the same definition.

1. As *earnest* for the house that she was buying, Beatrice gave the owner two thousand dollars.

   PART OF SPEECH _____
   DEFINITION _____
   SENTENCE _____

2. The Schusters have a collection of *miniature* dolls.

   PART OF SPEECH _____
   DEFINITION _____
   SENTENCE _____

3. His *earnest* expression convinced us that he was telling the truth.

   PART OF SPEECH _____
   DEFINITION _____
   SENTENCE _____

4. Josh gave Aunt Clara a *miniature* of his mother and father.

   PART OF SPEECH _____
   DEFINITION _____
   SENTENCE _____

5. Melissa *plumed* herself on having the highest average in her class.

   PART OF SPEECH _____
   DEFINITION _____
   SENTENCE _____

ear·nest[1] (ûr′nĭst) *adj.* [ME *ernest* < OE *eornoste*.] **1.** Characterized by or showing deep sincerity or seriousness <an *earnest* expression of regret> **2.** Important: grave. —**in earnest.** With a serious or purposeful intent. —**ear′nest·ly** *adv.* —**ear′nest·ness** *n.*

ear·nest[2] (ûr′nĭst) *n.* [ME *ernest* < OFr. *erres*, pl. of *erre*, pledge < Lat. *arra*, short for *arrabo* < Gk. *arrabōn* < Heb. ʹ*ārabh*, he pledged.] **1.** Money paid in advance as part payment to bind a contract or bargain. **2.** A token of something to come: PROMISE.

min·i·a·ture (mĭn′ē-ə-choŏr′, mĭn′ə-, -chər) *n.* [Ital. *miniatura*, illumination of manuscripts < *miniare*, to illuminate < Lat., to color red < *minium*, red lead.] **1.a.** A copy or model that reproduces or represents something in a greatly reduced size. **b.** Something small of its class. **2.a.** A small painting done with great detail, often on a surface such as ivory or vellum. **b.** A small portrait, picture, or decorative letter on an illuminated manuscript. **c.** The art of painting miniatures. —*adj.* Greatly reduced in size or scale: TINY <*miniature* houses>

plume (ploōm) *n.* [ME < OFr. < Lat. *pluma*.] **1.** A feather, esp. a large and ornamental one. **2.** A large feather or cluster of feathers worn as an ornament or symbol of rank, as on a helmet. **3.** A token of achievement or honor. **4.** A featherlike structure, form, or object <smoke rising in *plumes*> **5.** *Geol.* A column of molten rock hypothesized to rise from the earth's lower mantle and held to be the driving force in plate tectonics. —*vt.* **plumed, plum·ing, plumes. 1.** To cover, decorate, or provide with or as if with plumes. **2.** To smooth (feathers) in preening. **3.** To pride or congratulate (oneself).

Lesson 4

Honesty and Deception

As society grows more complex, we become more dependent on others for our information. We tend to accept as true whatever reaches us through ordinary communication channels. Perhaps because only a small number of people have specialized knowledge of what is going on in a particular field, it is sometimes easy to fool others. Therefore, we need to learn to distinguish between fact and opinion in the news media and to become aware of deceptive advertising techniques. With effort, we can become informed citizens and consumers.

The words in this lesson describe different aspects of honesty and deception. By studying these words and the concepts they express, you may be better able to recognize truth and detect dishonesty.

WORD LIST
devious
duplicity
fictitious
guileless
gullible
hypocritical
masquerade
overt
reputable
veracity

DEFINITIONS

After you have studied the definitions and example for each vocabulary word, write the word on the line to the right.

1. **devious** (dē′vē-əs) *adjective* **a.** Done in an underhanded manner; tricky; shifty. **b.** Straying from a straight or direct course. **c.** Departing from the correct or proper way; erring. (From the Latin *de-*, meaning "away from," and *via*, meaning "road")

   RELATED WORDS **deviously** *adverb;* **deviousness** *noun*

   EXAMPLE The young child quickly learned *devious* methods for getting attention.

   1. _____
   SEE *duplicity.*

2. **duplicity** (do͞o-plĭs′ĭ-tē, dyo͞o-plĭs′ĭ-tē) *noun* Deliberate deception or trickery by speaking or acting in two different ways concerning the same matter. (From the Latin word *duplex*, meaning "twofold")

   RELATED WORD **duplicitous** *adjective*

   EXAMPLE *Duplicity* is often referred to as "double dealing" or "bad faith."

   2. _____
   USAGE NOTE *Devious* and *duplicitous* are close in meaning, but *duplicitous* suggests treachery and is more extreme than *devious.*

3. **fictitious** (fĭk-tĭsh′əs) *adjective* **a.** Adopted or assumed in order to deceive; false. **b.** Of fiction; imaginary; unreal. (From the Latin word *fictus*, meaning "made up" or "untrue")

   RELATED WORD **fictitiousness** *noun*

   EXAMPLE The spy gave a *fictitious* chronology of his activities in the city.

   3. _____

4. **guileless** (gīl′lĭs) *adjective* Free of slyness or craftiness; simple and innocent.
   RELATED WORDS **guile** *noun;* **guilelessly** *adverb*
   EXAMPLE The children's *guileless* account of the incident was accepted as true.

   4. _____

5. **gullible** (gŭl′ə-bəl) *adjective* Easily deceived or fooled.
   RELATED WORD **gullibly** *adverb*
   EXAMPLE Cary was so *gullible* that he believed that striped paint came in spray cans.

   5. _____

6. **hypocritical** (hĭp′ə-krĭt′ĭ-kəl) *adjective* Pretending to have some desirable or publicly approved attitude; insincere. (From the Greek word *hypokrinesthai,* meaning "to pretend")
   RELATED WORDS **hypocrisy** *noun;* **hypocrite** *noun;* **hypocritically** *adverb*
   EXAMPLE Tartuffe is a *hypocritical* character who pretends to be kind and generous.

   6. _____

7. **masquerade** (măs′kə-rād′) *intrans. verb* To have or put on a deceptive appearance; to wear a mask or disguise.   *noun* **a.** A dance or party at which masks and fancy costumes are worn. **b.** A disguise or false outward show; pretense. **c.** An involved scheme. (From the Arabic word *maskharah,* meaning "buffoon")
   EXAMPLE The stowaway *masqueraded* as a member of the ship's crew.

   7. _____

8. **overt** (ō-vûrt′, ō′vûrt′) *adjective* Open and observable; apparent. (From the Old French word *ovrir,* meaning "to open")
   RELATED WORDS **overtly** *adverb;* **overtness** *noun*
   EXAMPLE The cat hissed when the child made an *overt* attempt to grab it.

   8. _____

9. **reputable** (rĕp′yə-tə-bəl) *adjective* Having a good name; well thought of; honorable. (From the Latin word *reputare,* meaning "to think over")
   RELATED WORDS **reputably** *adverb;* **reputation** *noun*
   EXAMPLE A *reputable* company should guarantee its products.

   9. _____

10. **veracity** (və-răs′ĭ-tē) *noun* **a.** Devotion to the truth; honesty. **b.** Conformity to truth or fact; accuracy and precision. (From the Latin word *verax,* meaning "true")
    EXAMPLE The *veracity* of his testimony was supported by other witnesses.

    10. _____

Name _____ Date _____

Exercise 1 Completing Definitions

On the answer line, write the word from the vocabulary list that best completes each definition.

1. Deliberate deception by acting in two different ways concerning the same matter is __?__ .
2. To be simple and innocent or free of craftiness is to be __?__ .
3. An action that is open and observable is __?__ .
4. Being honorable or well thought of is being __?__ .
5. Something that is done in an underhanded way is __?__ .
6. Something that is not real or is adopted in order to deceive is __?__ .
7. To pretend to have a publicly approved attitude is to be __?__ .
8. Someone who is easily fooled is __?__ .
9. To put on a deceptive appearance is to __?__ .
10. Devotion to the truth is __?__ .

1. _____
2. _____
3. _____
4. _____
5. _____
6. _____
7. _____
8. _____
9. _____
10. _____

Exercise 2 Using Words Correctly

Each of the following questions contains an italicized vocabulary word. Decide the answer to the question, and write *Yes* or *No* on the answer line.

1. If something is *overt*, is it kept hidden?
2. Is an act of *duplicity* free of pretense?
3. If you question the *veracity* of a statement, do you question its truthfulness?
4. Is a *devious* person honest and straightforward?
5. If you *masquerade* as a knight, do you try to look and act like one?
6. If one is *gullible*, is one easily fooled?
7. If someone is considered *reputable*, is that person well thought of?
8. Is a *guileless* individual sly?
9. Is something that is not real *fictitious*?
10. To be accepted by others, might a *hypocritical* person pretend to be something he or she is not?

1. _____
2. _____
3. _____
4. _____
5. _____
6. _____
7. _____
8. _____
9. _____
10. _____

Exercise 3 Choosing the Best Definition

For each italicized vocabulary word or phrase in the following sentences, write the letter of the best definition on the answer line.

1. In Mark Twain's story "The Man That Corrupted Hadleyburg," a stranger reveals the *hypocritical* nature of the townspeople.
   a. insincere b. erring c. open d. hollow

1. _____

Copyright © 1988 Houghton Mifflin Company. All rights reserved.   Honesty and Deception

2. In Aesop's fable about the fox and the crow, the fox flatters the *gullible* crow into singing so that she will drop her piece of cheese. 2. _____
   a. stubborn   c. easily fooled
   b. easily stopped   d. untrustworthy

3. In the television program about organized crime, *fictitious* names were used to protect the innocent. 3. _____
   a. false   b. difficult   c. unusual   d. special

4. Some people *masquerade as* fierce lions when they are really gentle lambs. 4. _____
   a. have the true character of   c. mistakenly identify
   b. put on the deceptive appearance of   d. would like to be

5. The *guileless* look on Latham's face was misleading. 5. _____
   a. secretive   b. surprised   c. guilty   d. innocent

6. Aunt Katy claims that her children specialize in *overt* acts of mischief. 6. _____
   a. terrible   b. humorous   c. open   d. hidden

7. Mrs. Roman fired the employee who was guilty of *duplicity*. 7. _____
   a. misconduct   b. deception   c. arrogance   d. foolishness

8. Michael put the first step of his *devious* plan into action. 8. _____
   a. cruel   b. ugly   c. underhanded   d. creative

9. Dr. Amy Dwight, a *reputable* zoologist, was named director of the zoo. 9. _____
   a. thoughtful   b. respected   c. previous   d. deceptive

10. The editor's dedication to *veracity* made him check each fact in the manuscript. 10. _____
    a. accuracy   b. numbers   c. humor   d. writing

Exercise 4   Using Different Forms of Words

Decide which form of the vocabulary word in parentheses best completes the sentence. The form given may be correct. Write your answer on the answer line.

1. When asked about the party, John answered __?__, not wanting to spoil the surprise. *(devious)*   1. _____

2. The treasury agent discovered the __?__ of the forger. *(guileless)*   2. _____

3. The __?__ of the spy's behavior tricked the surveillance team. *(overt)*   3. _____

4. Films taken at the track meet proved the __?__ of the athlete's story. *(fictitious)*   4. _____

5. Gene __?__ encourages others to contribute to charity but makes no contributions himself. *(hypocritical)*   5. _____

6. Dina had lied so often that __?__ was now very difficult for her. *(veracity)*   6. _____

7. The diplomat always acted __?__. *(reputable)*   7. _____

8. Kyle __?__ as an astronaut on Halloween. *(masquerade)*   8. _____

9. Maggie's __?__ behavior cost her her best friend's trust. *(duplicity)*   9. _____

10. Nance __?__ accepted her friend's story that two major-league baseball teams may occasionally decide not to keep score. *(gullible)*   10. _____

24   Honesty and Deception

Reading Comprehension

Each numbered sentence in the following passage contains an italicized vocabulary word or related form. After you read the passage, you will complete an exercise.

An Art Hoax

(1) Regarded as a crook by some and a genius by others, Hans van Meegeren was an obscure Dutch painter who succeeded in fooling **reputable** museum directors, art dealers, critics, and collectors. (2) Although van Meegeren is best remembered for his creations of **fictitious** Jan Vermeer paintings, many people believe that he might have achieved fame in his own right if only he had put his efforts into his own artwork.

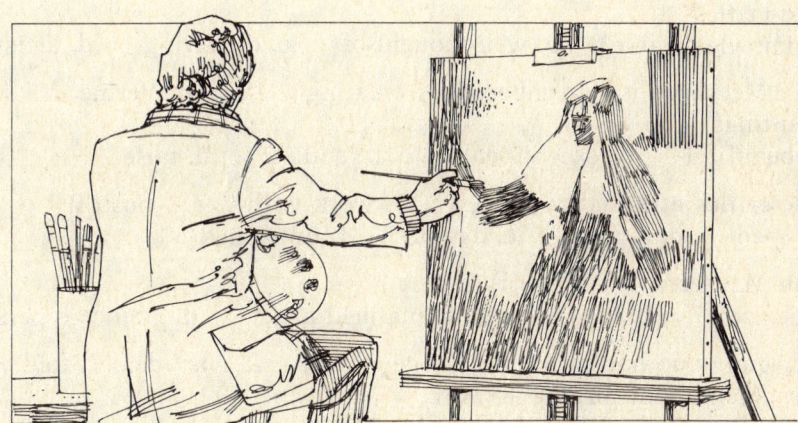

Hans van Meegeren was born in the Netherlands in 1889. As a young man, he studied art in Delft, the birthplace of Jan Vermeer, a famous seventeenth-century painter. Van Meegeren's early paintings won prizes at several exhibitions. Despite his growing reputation, however, he had difficulty making a living until he discovered that he could do better by painting what the public wanted. Although he would always include in each exhibit a few paintings that represented his best work, these were overlooked. (3) The critics attacked his superficial work with **overt** hostility. (4) By 1930 van Meegeren was making a lot of money on his commercialized paintings and his portraits of nobility, but he felt like a **hypocrite**. He wanted critical approval as well as financial success.

(5) One day a friend told van Meegeren how he had taken advantage of a **gullible** art dealer. (6) The friend had allowed one of his paintings to **masquerade** as a Rembrandt and had made a fantastic sum of money from the forgery. (7) This tale was the trigger for Hans van Meegeren's **devious** plan.

Van Meegeren chose to copy Jan Vermeer because Vermeer, too, had been mistreated by the critics. Van Meegeren spent months practicing Vermeer's techniques. He studied seventeenth-century accounts of the artist to learn what materials Vermeer had used and even developed a procedure to make his forgeries appear 250 years old. (8) Van Meegeren fully absorbed the spirit and style of Vermeer in order to carry out his **duplicitous** scheme.

Originally Hans van Meegeren intended to forge only one Vermeer and then admit his hoax. (9) At first he wanted only to teach a lesson to the **guileless** critics who had accused him of a lack of talent and imagination. The opportunity for financial gain was irresistible, however. Van Meegeren continued to forge Vermeer paintings that were sold for large sums of money.

At the end of World War II, Hans van Meegeren was accused of collaborating with the enemy and arrested for selling a Vermeer to a German officer. He confessed to forgery, a lesser offense than collaboration. (10) When officials refused to accept the **veracity** of his confession, van Meegeren proved himself by producing another superb Vermeer copy in the presence of the police.

In 1947 Hans van Meegeren was prosecuted for deception and sentenced to one year in prison. He died before he could serve his term. By giving in to the frustration caused by the critics and to his ambitions for money and fame, Hans van Meegeren had betrayed his real talent.

Please turn to the next page.

Reading Comprehension Exercise

Each of the following statements corresponds to a numbered sentence in the passage. Each statement contains a blank and is followed by four answer choices. Decide which choice fits best in the blank. The word or phrase that you choose must express roughly the same meaning as the italicized word in the passage. Write the letter of your choice on the answer line.

1. Hans van Meegeren succeeded in fooling __?__ museum directors and critics.
   a. knowledgeable   b. well-thought-of   c. deserving   d. artistic

2. Van Meegeren is remembered for creating __?__ Jan Vermeer paintings.
   a. beautiful   b. exceptional   c. legendary   d. false

3. The critics attacked van Meegeren's work with __?__ hostility.
   a. open   b. sincere   c. careful   d. untrained

4. Van Meegeren felt like a(n) __?__ .
   a. success   b. failure   c. unqualified artist   d. insincere person

5. A friend, who had taken advantage of a(n) __?__ art dealer, told van Meegeren about forging artwork.
   a. easily fooled   b. expert   c. guilty   d. easily depressed

6. The friend had allowed a painting to __?__ a Rembrandt.
   a. have critical acclaim as
   b. be signed as
   c. have the deceptive appearance of
   d. be framed as

7. This tale was the trigger for van Meegeren's __?__ plan.
   a. final   b. underhanded   c. outlandish   d. gracious

8. Van Meegeren absorbed the style of Vermeer to carry out his __?__ plans.
   a. artistic   c. apparently genuine
   b. creative   d. deliberately deceptive

9. He wanted to teach the __?__ critics a lesson.
   a. innocent   b. dishonest   c. major   d. art

10. Officials refused to accept the __?__ of his confession.
    a. facts   b. form   c. spirit   d. truthfulness

Writing Assignment

Suppose that you are an elementary school aide. The teacher whom you assist has asked you to introduce myths or tall tales to third graders. In addition to reading several stories that you have located in the library, you decide to write an original story. Using five words from this lesson, write a myth or a tall tale about a character who deceives others. Be sure to develop the situation, the reason for the deception, and the effect on others of the character's dishonesty. Underline each vocabulary word that you use.

Lesson 6

The Roots *-polis-* and *-urb-*

The roots *-polis-* (and its related form *-polit-*) and *-urb-* derive from two ancient words for "city." *Polis* was the ancient Greek word for city-state, that is, a self-governing city such as Athens or Sparta. *Urbs* was the Latin word for city. Both *polis* and *urbs* have been sources for many newer words in English, ten of which you will learn in this lesson.

WORD LIST
cosmopolitan
geopolitics
impolitic
megalopolis
metropolitan
policy
politico
suburban
urban
urbane

DEFINITIONS

After you have studied the definitions and example for each vocabulary word, write the word on the line to the right.

1. **cosmopolitan** (kŏz′mə-pŏl′ĭ-tn) *adjective* Sophisticated in an international way. (From the Greek words *kosmos*, meaning "universe," and *polis*, meaning "city")
   EXAMPLE With students from seventeen different countries, the school has a *cosmopolitan* atmosphere.

   1. _____

2. **geopolitics** (jē′ō-pŏl′ĭ-tĭks) *noun* The study of the relationship between geography and politics. (From the Greek words *gē*, meaning "earth," and *polis*)
   RELATED WORD **geopolitical** *adjective*
   EXAMPLE Someone doing work in *geopolitics* might study the relationship between oil production and per-capita income in the nations of the world.

   2. _____

3. **impolitic** (ĭm-pŏl′ĭ-tĭk) *adjective* Unwise; not exhibiting good judgment. (From the Latin *in-*, meaning "not," and the Greek word *polis*)
   EXAMPLE It is *impolitic* to insult those from whom you expect favors.

   3. _____

4. **megalopolis** (mĕg′ə-lŏp′ə-lĭs) *noun* A unified urban region comprising several large cities and their surrounding areas. (From the Greek *megalo-*, meaning "large," and *polis*)
   EXAMPLE The "San-San" *megalopolis* extends from San Diego to San Francisco, California.

   4. _____

Copyright © 1988 Houghton Mifflin Company. All rights reserved.

The Roots *-polis-* and *-urb-*

5. **metropolitan** (mĕt′rə-pŏl′ĭ-tən) *adjective* Pertaining to a major city: *A metropolitan area usually includes a large city and its suburbs.*   *noun* A high-ranking bishop. (From the Greek words *mētēr*, meaning "mother," and *polis*)

   RELATED WORD   **metropolis** *noun*

   EXAMPLE   The Los Angeles *metropolitan* area is the center of film and television production in the United States.

5. _____

6. **policy** (pŏl′ĭ-sē) *noun* A general plan, principle, or course of action followed by an organization or an individual. (From the Greek word *polis*)

   EXAMPLE   This store has a *policy* of allowing returns for cash.

6. _____

7. **politico** (pə-lĭt′ĭ-kō′) *noun* An informal or journalistic term for a politician. (From the Italian word *politico*, meaning "political")

   EXAMPLE   In the capital many of the *politicos* meet for lunch at the Longworth Grill.

7. _____

8. **suburban** (sə-bûr′bən) *adjective* Characteristic of the suburbs, the mainly residential areas surrounding large cities. (From the Latin words *sub*, meaning "secondary," and *urbs*, meaning "city")

   RELATED WORDS   **suburb** *noun;* **suburbanite** *noun*

   EXAMPLE   When a *suburban* region grows in population, a shopping center usually follows.

8. _____

9. **urban** (ûr′bən) *adjective* Like a city; characteristic of cities. (From the Latin word *urbs*)

   EXAMPLE   *Urban* transport in Boston consists of trains, trolleys, buses, subways, and taxis.

9. _____

10. **urbane** (ûr-bān′) *adjective* Elegantly polite and sophisticated. (From the Latin word *urbs*)

    RELATED WORD   **urbanity** *noun*

    EXAMPLE   The *urbane* couples danced the mambo until dawn.

10. _____

Name _____ Date _____

Exercise 1   Matching Words and Definitions

Match the definition in Column B with the word in Column A. Write the letter of the correct definition on the answer line.

Column A

1. megalopolis
2. urbane
3. impolitic
4. metropolitan
5. geopolitics
6. politico
7. cosmopolitan
8. policy
9. suburban
10. urban

Column B

a. a course of action followed by an individual or organization
b. polite and sophisticated
c. pertaining to a major city
d. a politician, informally
e. characteristic of residential areas near cities
f. unwise or not exhibiting good judgment
g. a region comprising several large cities
h. characteristic of cities
i. sophisticated in an international way
j. study of the relationship between geography and politics

1. _____
2. _____
3. _____
4. _____
5. _____
6. _____
7. _____
8. _____
9. _____
10. _____

Exercise 2   Using Words Correctly

Each of the following questions contains an italicized vocabulary word. Decide the answer to the question, and write *Yes* or *No* on the answer line.

1. Does an *urban* area have many orchards?
2. Might a *politico* run for public office?
3. Does a *megalopolis* have small, isolated villages?
4. Might *geopolitics* deal with international fishing rights?
5. Is it *impolitic* to make rude remarks about your employer to others?
6. Is a small village in New England *cosmopolitan*?
7. Do *urbane* people make a habit of interrupting people?
8. Is Tokyo a *suburban* town?
9. Does keeping a budget indicate good financial *policy*?
10. Is Mobile, Alabama, a part of *metropolitan* Seattle?

1. _____
2. _____
3. _____
4. _____
5. _____
6. _____
7. _____
8. _____
9. _____
10. _____

Exercise 3   Choosing the Best Definition

For each italicized vocabulary word in the following sentences, write the letter of the best definition on the answer line.

1. The candidate for mayor emphasized *suburban* growth.
   a. of shopping centers   c. of a city
   b. of transportation   d. of a community near a city

2. The *politico* was frequently accused of trading favors for votes.
   a. politician   c. sales representative
   b. business person   d. intern

1. _____

2. _____

Copyright © 1988 Houghton Mifflin Company. All rights reserved.   The Roots *-polis-* and *-urb-*   35

3. The ambassador felt it was *impolitic* to intervene in the negotiations.
   a. impolite   b. important   c. nonpolitical   d. unwise

3. _____

4. When a computer company moved its headquarters to a small Utah community, residents feared that their town would become *urban*.
   a. out of date   c. full of machinery
   b. like a park   d. like a city

4. _____

5. The *megalopolis* of Hong Kong boasts the highest population density in the world.
   a. forested region   c. huge urban area
   b. island cluster   d. constellation

5. _____

6. Large numbers of people from many different countries help to make New York a *cosmopolitan* city.
   a. internationally sophisticated   c. varied
   b. crowded   d. multilingual

6. _____

7. *Geopolitics* played a role in the organization of the United Nations.
   a. Campaign strategies
   b. Unrealistic expectations
   c. Geographical and political relationships
   d. Fears about flying

7. _____

8. The *metropolitan* planning commission considered a proposal for a new shopping center in the downtown area.
   a. of a city and its suburbs   c. of fuel and lighting
   b. of transportation   d. economic

8. _____

9. Wanting to appear *urbane* to his prospective in-laws, Terence wore a red carnation in his lapel and bowed deeply as he was introduced.
   a. colorful   b. sophisticated   c. artistic   d. older

9. _____

10. Senator O'Donoghue has a *policy* of responding personally to the mail received by her office.
    a. belief   b. principle   c. recommendation   d. pretense

10. _____

Exercise 4 Using Different Forms of Words

Decide which form of the vocabulary word in parentheses best completes the sentence. The form given may be correct. Write your answer on the answer line.

1. When Paula returned to her hometown after being away for twenty years, she found that it had become a bustling __?__ . *(metropolitan)*

1. _____

2. Stan and Donna Troost are __?__ now that they have moved from New Orleans to the nearby residential area of Metairie. *(suburban)*

2. _____

3. Because of the large number of checks returned by the bank, the store adopted a cash-only __?__ . *(policy)*

3. _____

4. Steven hoped that during his work in the state capital he would find some dedicated leaders among the bureaucrats and __?__ . *(politico)*

4. _____

5. The President invited leaders of several Latin American nations to discuss some of the __?__ concerns of the hemisphere. *(geopolitics)*

5. _____

6. Because Beth was in a rush, she was __?__ and failed to say good-by to Mrs. Poindexter. *(impolitic)*

6. _____

7. Oakland, Berkeley, and San Francisco form a __?__ . *(megalopolis)*

7. _____

Name _____ Date _____

8. At the party I met Manuel from Honduras, Fawzia from Morocco, and Daisy from New Zealand — a very ? group. *(cosmopolitan)*

8. _____

9. Unhappy with the fast pace of ? life, Flo and Bucky Jensen bought an old farm and moved to the country. *(urban)*

9. _____

10. Despite his ? , Benedict still enjoys spending Saturday mornings in the country lounging around in old clothes. *(urbane)*

10. _____

Reading Comprehension

Each numbered sentence in the following passage contains an italicized vocabulary word or related form. After you read the passage, you will complete an exercise.

Megalopolis: Our Growing Cities

(1) During the past two centuries, the United States has become increasingly **urban**. (2) According to the 1990 census, over 75 percent of United States citizens live in **metropolitan** areas.

Some of these areas are enormous. (3) The **megalopolis** that extends from Boston, Massachusetts, to Washington, D.C., is approximately five hundred miles long and thirty to one hundred miles wide. More than forty million people live and work in this area sometimes called "Bos-Wash" by population experts. Lands that were wilderness areas in George Washington's time now bustle with activity.

The size and complexity of such a vast region call for intergovernmental cooperation. (4) The **policies** of one state or city may have an impact on another. For example, sewage treatment in Maryland might affect Virginia. (5) Representatives of a state, city, or **suburban** area may consult with others when planning projects such as water systems, energy production, or highways. (6) Should they be so **impolitic** as to fail to consult all affected parties, a lawsuit could result.

This interdependence of cities and states within the same megalopolis can lead to unusual situations. Some areas in New Jersey, for example, are actually suburbs of New York City. Many people who live in New Jersey work in New York. (7) Thus, the New York **politicos** who want to win the support of the business community, for example, might find themselves addressing New Jersey residents, who cannot vote for them.

The consequences of what takes place in this particular northeastern megalopolis are not limited to the states and cities that compose it. (8) The Boston-to-Washington megalopolis has a highly developed industrial base, the world's foremost financial community, and **cosmopolitan** cultural centers. (9) These factors have contributed to the **geopolitical** influence of this region throughout the world. (10) **Urbane** individuals from around the world have settled there and contributed to the sophistication of the region. New people are continually attracted to the area, and its growth is likely to continue; experts foresee a population in excess of one hundred million during the twenty-first century.

Please turn to the next page.

Reading Comprehension Exercise

Each of the following statements corresponds to a numbered sentence in the passage. Each statement contains a blank and is followed by four answer choices. Decide which choice fits best in the blank. The word or phrase that you choose must express roughly the same meaning as the italicized word in the passage. Write the letter of your choice on the answer line.

1. The United States has grown more and more __?__ .
   a. citified   b. interesting   c. sophisticated   d. dirty

2. Almost three out of every four Americans live in __?__ areas.
   a. growing   b. poor   c. cultured   d. city

3. The Boston-to-Washington __?__ is enormous.
   a. coastline   c. multicity area
   b. multistate area   d. urbane population

4. The __?__ of one state or city may affect another.
   a. way of thinking   c. public officials
   b. course of action   d. political structure

5. Representatives of a state, a city, or a __?__ may consult with others on certain projects.
   a. rural area   c. park area
   b. rich area   d. community near a city

6. Lawsuits can result if the representatives of one governmental division are __?__ .
   a. lacking in good judgment   c. well staffed with lawyers
   b. particularly aggressive   d. involved in politics

7. The New York __?__ may appeal to New Jersey residents.
   a. politics   b. politicians   c. polity   d. police

8. The Boston-to-Washington megalopolis is __?__ cultural center.
   a. an elegantly polite   c. an internationally sophisticated
   b. a politically sophisticated d. a politically elegant

9. Industry, finance, and culture enhance American __?__ influence.
   a. economic and geological   c. geographic and political
   b. geological and political   d. economic and psychological

10. Many __?__ people have settled in this megalopolis.
    a. urban and rich   c. political and chic
    b. pretty and smart   d. sophisticated and polite

1. _____
2. _____
3. _____
4. _____
5. _____
6. _____
7. _____
8. _____
9. _____
10. _____

Writing Assignment

It is election time, and you are running for mayor of Metropolis. The biggest problem your city faces is that a large number of people from Suburbia, a small town in an adjoining state, work in Metropolis, using its services, such as transportation systems, but do not pay taxes to support the city. Using five words from this lesson and underlining them, write a brief campaign speech about the Suburbia issue for the citizens of Metropolis.

The Roots *-polis-* and *-urb-*

Name _____ Date _____

Dictionary Skills

Usage Notes

Most dictionaries contain usage notes. These notes are given within an entry or in a separate paragraph at the end of an entry. Usage notes provide information on the correct use of words. They describe the acceptable and unacceptable uses of a word, distinguish easily confused words, and discuss points of grammar. Notes are given only for words likely to cause uncertainty. Here are some examples of information provided by usage notes.

1. *Usage notes explain acceptable and unacceptable uses of a word.* This note appears at the end of an entry for *how*.

   Usage: *How* is often used in informal speech where strict grammar would require *that*, as in *He told us how he was an orphan and needed the money.* The use of *as how* for *that* in sentences like *he said as how he would go* is informal and should be avoided in writing. Similarly, one should avoid in writing the expressions *seeing as how* and *being as how*.

   The note says that *how* and *as how* should not be used as substitutes for the conjunction *that*. The italicized sentences in the note should be revised to read: *He told us that he was an orphan and needed the money* and *He said that he would go.*

2. *Usage notes explain the correct usage of frequently confused words.* The following note discusses the different meanings of two verbs that are often confused, *affect* and *effect*.

   Usage: *Affect*[1] and *effect* have no senses in common. As a verb, *affect*[1] is most commonly used in the sense of "to influence" (*how smoking affects health*). *Effect* means "to bring about or execute": *layoffs designed to effect savings.*

   The usage note can help you remember the difference between the two verbs. You can check whether you have used the verbs correctly in a sentence with these substitutions.

   The weather may *affect* (influence) our weekend plans.
   We will *effect* (accomplish) the schedule change in the fall.

3. *Usage notes explain points of grammar.* The usage note is given at the end of an entry for the noun *number*. The note provides a rule for deciding whether to use a singular or plural verb.

   Usage: As a collective noun, *number* may take either a singular or a plural verb. It takes a singular verb when it is preceded by the definite article *the*: *The number of skilled workers is small.* It takes a plural verb when preceded by the indefinite article *a*: *A number of the workers are unskilled.*

   Please turn to the next page.

Exercise Using Usage Notes

Read the dictionary entries and usage notes at the end of this exercise. *Step 1:* Decide whether the italicized word in each of the following sentences is used correctly. *Step 2:* On the "USAGE" line, write *Correct* or *Incorrect*. *Step 3:* Write a sentence of your own in which you use the word correctly.

1. During the nineteenth century, many people *immigrated* from Europe.

   USAGE _____
   SENTENCE _____

2. The construction company hasn't *scarcely* made any progress on the bridge.

   USAGE _____
   SENTENCE _____

3. Mrs. Hayashi has always wanted to visit Japan, the country from which her grandparents had *emigrated*.

   USAGE _____
   SENTENCE _____

4. Sue wanted to be alone for *awhile* so she could work on her math problem.

   USAGE _____
   SENTENCE _____

5. It was so foggy we could *scarcely* see across the street.

   USAGE _____
   SENTENCE _____

6. Lenny rested *a while* before continuing his climb up the mountain.

   USAGE _____
   SENTENCE _____

a·while (ə-hwīl′) *adv.* For a short time. **Usage:** *Awhile,* an adverb, is never preceded by a preposition such as *for,* but the two-word form *a while* may be preceded by a preposition. In writing, each of the following is acceptable: *stay awhile; stay for a while; stay a while* (but not *stay for awhile*).

em·i·grate (ĕm′ĭ-grāt′) *intr. v.* **-grat·ed, -grat·ing, -grates.** To leave one country or region to settle in another. —See Usage note at **immigrate.** [Lat. *emigrare, emigrat-: ex-,* away + *migrare,* to move.] —**em′i·gra′tion** (ĕm′ĭ-grā′shən) *n.*

im·mi·grate (ĭm′ĭ-grāt′) *v.* **-grat·ed, -grat·ing, -grates.** —*intr.* To enter and settle in a country or region to which one is not native. —*tr.* To send or introduce as immigrants. [Lat. *immigrare, immigrat-,* to go into: *in-,* in + *migrare,* to depart.] —**im′mi·gra′tion** *n.*
Usage: *Emigrate* pertains to a single move by persons, and implies permanence. It has specific reference to the place of departure and emphasizes movement from that place. If the place is mentioned, the preposition is *from: Since many people have emigrated from France, the population is declining. Immigrate* also pertains to a single move by persons and likewise implies permanence. But it refers to destination, emphasizes movement there, and is followed by *to: Since many people have immigrated to the United States, its population is increasing.*

scarce·ly (skârs′lē) *adv.* **1.** By a small margin; barely. **2.** Almost not; hardly. **3.** Certainly not.
Usage: *Scarcely* has the force of a negative; therefore it is not properly used with another negative: *I could scarcely believe it* (not *I couldn't scarcely believe it*). A clause following *scarcely* is introduced by *when* or, less often, by *before* but not by *than: The meeting had scarcely begun when* (or *before* but not *than*) *it was interrupted.*

40 Usage Notes   Copyright © 1988 Houghton Mifflin Company. All rights reserved.

Test-Taking Skills

Antonym Tests

Antonym items are a common feature of most standardized tests. They are also frequently used in classroom vocabulary tests. **Antonyms** are words with opposite or nearly opposite meanings. *Black* and *white*, and *slow* and *fast* are examples of antonyms. Most antonym test items are not so simple, however. They usually require you to distinguish slight differences in the meanings of words. The following procedure will help you answer antonym test items.

PROCEDURE

1. *Read all of the choices before selecting an answer.* To determine which word is most nearly opposite in meaning to the given word, you must study all of the choices.

2. *Eliminate synonym choices.* **Synonyms**—words similar in meaning to the given word—are frequently given as answer choices. Study the following test item.

   FASTIDIOUS:
   (A) careful   (B) discriminating   (C) casual   (D) slovenly
   (E) particular

   A fastidious person pays careful or excessive attention to detail. The word is most often used to refer to personal appearance, work habits, manners, or housekeeping. Of the answer choices given, *careful*, *discriminating*, and *particular* are more nearly synonyms than antonyms of *fastidious*.

3. *Watch for other misleading choices and eliminate them.* For example, eliminate any answer choice that is not the same part of speech as the given word. Then look for other misleading answer choices. In the test item above, *casual* is misleading. You might think that a casual person—one who is informal and easygoing—is the opposite of a fastidious individual. However, of the choices given, *slovenly* is more nearly opposite to *fastidious*. *Slovenly* is correct because it means "careless in personal appearance or work." Antonym test items often contain two possible antonyms as answer choices. You must select the better of the two.

4. *Increase your awareness of how words are used.* The best way to prepare for any test of verbal skills is to expand your vocabulary. The more you know about the meaning and use of words, the better you will do on such tests.

Please turn to the next page.

Exercise   Identifying Antonyms

Select the word or phrase that is most nearly opposite in meaning to the word in capital letters. Write the letter of your choice on the answer line. Use your dictionary as needed.

1. GENIAL :
   (A) hostile   (B) friendly   (C) spirited   (D) somber   (E) agile

2. OUST :
   (A) say loudly   (B) throw out   (C) gather together   (D) allow in   (E) express regret

3. HAUGHTY :
   (A) regal   (B) poor   (C) wistful   (D) stingy   (E) humble

4. ERRATIC :
   (A) undependable   (B) loving   (C) foreign   (D) eccentric   (E) steady

5. HARMONY :
   (A) unmusical   (B) radiance   (C) ruse   (D) discord   (E) petulance

6. DECIDUOUS :
   (A) evergreen   (B) botanical   (C) leafy   (D) seasonal   (E) oak

7. TRANSIENT :
   (A) permanent   (B) mobile   (C) short-lived   (D) long-lasting   (E) fugitive

8. LAUD :
   (A) contend   (B) enlist   (C) extol   (D) condemn   (E) whisper

9. MEAGER :
   (A) bountiful   (B) scanty   (C) clean   (D) lively   (E) ill

10. GARRULOUS :
    (A) taciturn   (B) decent   (C) voluntary   (D) agile   (E) respected

11. AUDACITY :
    (A) folly   (B) power   (C) meekness   (D) sacrilege   (E) bleakness

12. CONCISE :
    (A) false   (B) succinct   (C) similar   (D) generous   (E) wordy

13. ACCLAIM :
    (A) applaud   (B) avow   (C) conflict   (D) ignore   (E) ignite

14. UNSCATHED :
    (A) safe   (B) injured   (C) unaware   (D) alert   (E) perjured

15. PRODIGIOUS :
    (A) overgrown   (B) minuscule   (C) magnificent   (D) glamorous   (E) abundant

1. _____
2. _____
3. _____
4. _____
5. _____
6. _____
7. _____
8. _____
9. _____
10. _____
11. _____
12. _____
13. _____
14. _____
15. _____

Lesson 12

The Roots *-pon-* and *-posit-*

More than forty English words are derived from the Latin verb *ponere*, which means "to place" or "to put," and its past participle, *positus*, which means "placed" or "put." Among the common words in English derived from *ponere* or *positus* are *opponent* and *opposite*, *proponent* and *preposition*. These derivatives have a wide range of applications, so mastery of them can aid one's oral and written expression in many different ways.

WORD LIST
composite
disposition
exponent
impostor
juxtaposition
opposition
proposition
propound
repository
supposition

DEFINITIONS

After you have studied the definitions and example for each vocabulary word, write the word on the line to the right.

1. **composite** (kəm-pŏz′ĭt) *adjective* **a.** Put together from various parts: *a composite photograph.* **b.** In mathematics, having factors: *a composite number.* *noun* Something made up of various parts; a combination.
   RELATED WORDS **compose** *verb;* **composition** *noun*
   EXAMPLE Some computers can now create *composite* portraits, combining the features of several people.

2. **disposition** (dĭs′pə-zĭsh′ən) *noun* **a.** One's usual mood or temperament. **b.** Arrangement. (From the Latin word *dispositio*, meaning "arrangement")
   RELATED WORD **dispose** *verb*
   EXAMPLE Monica's cheerful *disposition* makes her popular at Van Buren.

3. **exponent** (ĭk-spō′nənt, ĕk′spō′nənt) *noun* **a.** A person who speaks for something; a representative or interpreter of. **b.** A superscript number indicating how many times a given number is multiplied by itself. (From the Latin word *exponere*, meaning "to put forth")
   RELATED WORDS **exponential** *adjective;* **exponentially** *adverb*
   EXAMPLE The movie star was a leading *exponent* of the Stanislavski method of acting.

Copyright © 1988 Houghton Mifflin Company. All rights reserved.

The Roots *-pon-* and *-posit-*

4. **impostor** (ĭm-pŏs′tər) *noun* A person who assumes a false identity for the purpose of deceiving others.

   EXAMPLE The seemingly innocent man at the embassy party was an *impostor*, for he was in fact a high-level spy.

   4. _____

5. **juxtaposition** (jŭk′stə-pə-zĭsh′ən) *noun* Placement side by side or close together, often producing an unusual effect. (From the Latin words *juxta*, meaning "close by," and *positio*, meaning "situation")

   RELATED WORD **juxtapose** *verb*

   EXAMPLE When the paintings were placed in *juxtaposition*, I could see that the Corot was more skillfully executed.

   5. _____

6. **opposition** (ŏp′ə-zĭsh′ən) *noun* **a.** The condition of being against, contrary to, or in conflict with. **b.** A rival. (From the Latin word *oppositus*, meaning "put against")

   RELATED WORDS **oppose** *verb;* **opposite** *adjective*

   EXAMPLE The new plan for traffic control around the school met with *opposition* from both students and teachers.

   6. _____

7. **proposition** (prŏp′ə-zĭsh′ən) *noun* **a.** A statement or plan suggested for acceptance; a proposal. **b.** An issue put before voters. (From the Latin word *propositus*, meaning "put forth")

   RELATED WORDS **proposal** *noun;* **propose** *verb*

   EXAMPLE The board members discussed the vice president's *proposition* for increasing trade in the Middle East.

   7. _____
   SEE *propound.*

8. **propound** (prə-pound′) *trans. verb* To offer or set forth for consideration. (From the Latin word *proponere*, meaning "to put forth")

   RELATED WORD **proponent** *noun*

   EXAMPLE When Galileo first *propounded* his theory of the universe, few people believed him.

   8. _____
   USAGE NOTE *Propound* is a synonym of *propose.*

9. **repository** (rĭ-pŏz′ĭ-tôr′ē) *noun* **a.** A place for safe storage; a storehouse. **b.** A source.

   EXAMPLE The museum was a *repository* for ancient Mesopotamian artifacts.

   9. _____

10. **supposition** (sŭp′ə-zĭsh′ən) *noun* An assumption.

    RELATED WORDS **suppose** *verb;* **supposed** *adjective;* **supposedly** *adverb*

    EXAMPLE His *supposition* that the course would be dull proved to be incorrect.

    10. _____

Name _____ Date _____

Exercise 1 Writing Correct Words

On the answer line, write the word from the vocabulary list that fits each definition.

1. A deceitful person who assumes a false identity   1. _____
2. Made up of a variety of parts   2. _____
3. Something that is assumed   3. _____
4. A person who represents or speaks for something   4. _____
5. A proposal   5. _____
6. One's usual mood   6. _____
7. To set forth for consideration   7. _____
8. Condition of being in conflict with or contrary to   8. _____
9. Placement side by side or close together   9. _____
10. A place for safekeeping   10. _____

Exercise 2 Using Words Correctly

Each of the following questions contains an italicized vocabulary word. Decide the answer to the question, and write *Yes* or *No* on the answer line.

1. If two people were in *opposition*, would they agree with each other?   1. _____
2. Can a person be an *exponent* of a particular scientific theory?   2. _____
3. Would you consider a shoe box to be a suitable *repository* for a diamond necklace?   3. _____
4. Is a picture of one's face superimposed on another's body a *composite*?   4. _____
5. Are the North and South poles in *juxtaposition*?   5. _____
6. If a scientist does not consider any possibilities, is she making any *suppositions*?   6. _____
7. If someone remarked on another person's *disposition*, would he be discussing the person's posture?   7. _____
8. If you suggested a new school rule to be adopted by the student body, would you be making a *proposition*? 8. _____
9. If someone were an *impostor*, would he assume a false identity?   9. _____
10. If you *propound* a theory, do you reject it?   10. _____

Exercise 3 Choosing the Best Definition

For each italicized vocabulary word or related form in the following sentences, write the letter of the best definition on the answer line.

1. Teddy always thinks of Janet as a *repository* of sports statistics.   1. _____
   a. storehouse   b. purveyor   c. enemy   d. columnist

The Roots *-pon-* and *-posit-*   75

2. Before taking the picture, the photographer *juxtaposed* the bowl of fruit and the basket of flowers.
   a. placed far away from each other
   b. placed in a natural setting
   c. placed close together
   d. placed opposite each other

   2. _____

3. Our math teacher, Mrs. Fredricks, has a good *disposition*.
   a. outlook   b. usual mood   c. sense of humor   d. class

   3. _____

4. The school board voted on a *proposition* that the library be expanded and improved.
   a. demand   b. contrary statement   c. proposal   d. rule

   4. _____

5. A book is a *composite* of ink and paper.
   a. unification of similar elements
   b. container in which something is kept
   c. uniform pattern
   d. something made up of various distinct parts

   5. _____

6. At the meeting the delegates from Zimbabwe expressed their *opposition*.
   a. agreement   b. disagreement   c. approval   d. confusion

   6. _____

7. The pianist Artur Rubinstein was an *exponent* of the romantic school.
   a. representative   b. opponent   c. expert   d. leader

   7. _____

8. The economist *propounded* her theory of inflation.
   a. organized   c. offered for consideration
   b. wrote about   d. analyzed

   8. _____

9. Amelia Earhart made the *supposition* that she could fly across the Atlantic.
   a. absolute denial   c. doubtful statement
   b. assumption   d. arrogant statement

   9. _____

10. The *impostor* wore a mask.
    a. person who wears funny disguises   c. thief
    b. person who assumes a false identity   d. ceremonial dancer

    10. _____

Exercise 4   Using Different Forms of Words

Each sentence contains an italicized vocabulary word in a form that does not fit the sentence. On the answer line, write the form of the word that does fit the sentence.

1. When a number is multiplied by itself, it increases *exponent*.

   1. _____

2. If you *juxtaposition* the model and the flowers, you will have a more attractive painting.

   2. _____

3. The answer is not *fewer* but *more*, its *opposition*.

   3. _____

4. I am a *propound* of First Amendment rights.

   4. _____

5. *Disposition* of your litter properly!

   5. _____

6. Despite Angela's *supposition* knowledge about rockets, her scale model certainly did not fly very well.

   6. _____

7. Your final *composite* shows a more sophisticated writing style.

   7. _____

76   The Roots *-pon-* and *-posit-*

Name _____   Date _____

8. Vincent Wainwright is *supposition* the brightest student in the country.

9. I *proposition* that we reduce the prices on all winter clothes.

10. Ladies and gentlemen, we must all *opposition* tyranny.

8. _____

9. _____

10. _____

Reading Comprehension

Each numbered sentence in the following passage contains an italicized vocabulary word. After you read the passage, you will complete an exercise.

Harry Houdini: Escape Artist

A warmly dressed crowd watched as a slender man, stripped to bathing trunks and tightly handcuffed by police experts, leaped from a bridge into a freezing river through a hole cut in the ice. Two minutes later Harry Houdini emerged, free and smiling, to the cheers of the spectators.

(1) Harry Houdini is recognized as history's leading **exponent** of the art of escape. Born in 1874, he began his career with a circus at the age of nine and continued to give public performances for forty-three years. His physical endurance and remarkable dexterity enabled him to escape from handcuffs and ropes, from jail cells and sealed chests, from vaults buried underground, and from packing cases hurled into the sea.

(2) Many people made the **supposition** that his escapes were mere trickery. To disprove this, he would often invite people to inspect his equipment. **(3)** Once they had found that the apparatus had no secret devices, the **opposition** would die down. Houdini even won a German lawsuit by demonstrating his ability to open locks and safes.

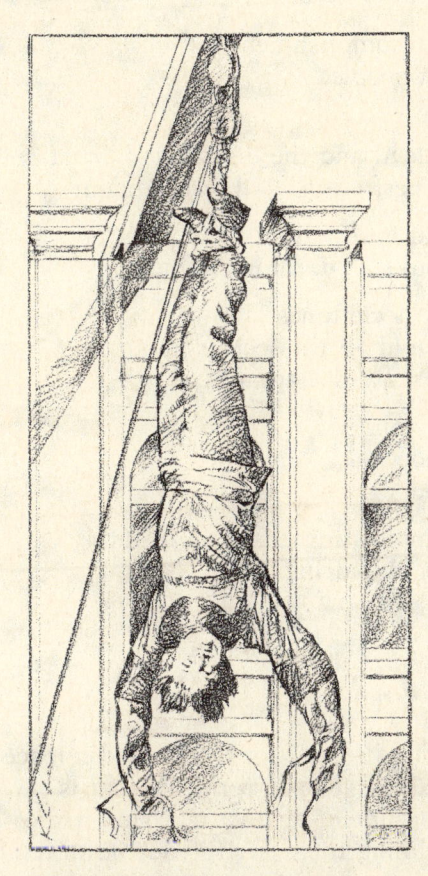

(4) After he had been performing for years, no one could deny the **proposition** that Houdini was the greatest escape artist of the day. **(5)** Frequently **impostors** from all over the world posed as "The Great Houdini" and tried to imitate his feats. But no one could match Houdini.

(6) Houdini was a **composite** of the daredevil and the superbly disciplined escape artist. He generated interest in his shows by publicizing them and then by accepting challenges from the audiences that came to see him. Houdini was also a careful student of his art. **(7)** His mind was a **repository** of technical information about locks and handcuffs. He trained his body to endure cold, to use a minimum of oxygen in breathing, and to make toes do the work of fingers. **(8)** He wrote books that **propounded** the techniques involved in the art of escape.

(9) Although Houdini's public image was theatrical, his private **disposition** was far from temperamental. **(10)** Harry Houdini's life reveals an interesting **juxtaposition** of the quiet family man and the flamboyant magician.

Please turn to the next page.

Reading Comprehension Exercise

Each of the following statements corresponds to a numbered sentence in the passage. Each statement contains a blank and is followed by four answer choices. Decide which choice fits best in the blank. The word or phrase that you choose must express roughly the same meaning as the italicized word in the passage. Write the letter of your choice on the answer line.

1. Houdini is recognized as history's leading __?__ the art of escape.
   a. interpreter of   b. student of   c. opponent of   d. writer on

2. People made the __?__ that Houdini's escapes were tricks.
   a. complaint   b. statement   c. assumption   d. claim

3. When his equipment was proved legitimate, the __?__ ended.
   a. publicity   b. interest   c. criticism   d. magic

4. In time everyone accepted the __?__ that Houdini was the best.
   a. decision   b. statement   c. news   d. lie

5. __?__ tried to imitate Houdini's accomplishments.
   a. Deceivers   c. Show-business people
   b. Opponents   d. Children

6. Houdini was a __?__ of the daredevil and the disciplined artist.
   a. result   b. combination   c. perfection   d. great talent

7. His mind was a __?__ of technical information.
   a. library   b. safe   c. storehouse   d. filing cabinet

8. He wrote books that __?__ escape techniques.
   a. established theories of   c. told all the secrets about
   b. offered for consideration   d. showed diagrams of

9. His __?__ was controlled and disciplined.
   a. usual mode   c. unusual mood
   b. unusual mode   d. usual mood

10. Houdini's personality reveals an interesting __?__ of traits.
    a. set   b. range   c. conflict   d. pairing

1. _____
2. _____
3. _____
4. _____
5. _____
6. _____
7. _____
8. _____
9. _____
10. _____

Writing Assignment

Imagine that you have interviewed a scientist for a televised science program in your area. This scientist has developed a theory that is very controversial and has aroused much argument against it. Using five of the words from this lesson and underlining them, write your news report of this controversial theory as you will present it on your program, "Scientific Frontiers: Conflict or Consensus?"

Test-Taking Skills

Analogy Tests

Analogy items are sometimes the most difficult part of standardized examinations such as the Preliminary Scholastic Aptitude Test (PSAT). An **analogy** is a similarity between things that are otherwise dissimilar. Analogy test items require you to understand relationships between pairs of words. The strategies that follow will assist you when you take an analogy test.

STRATEGIES

1. *Determine the relationship between the given pair of words.* An analogy test item asks you to choose a pair of words that best express a relationship similar to that expressed by the given pair. Therefore, you must first understand the relationship between the given words. Here is an example of an analogy item.

    COPSE : FOREST : :
    (A) bark : tree (B) palm : jungle (C) pond : lake
    (D) asphalt : wood (E) mountain : knoll

    A copse is a small group of trees and other plants. A forest is many trees and plants covering a large area. The relationship between the two words is a small group of something to a large group of the same thing.

2. *Say a sentence to yourself that expresses the relationship between the given words: eliminate answer choices that are obviously incorrect.* For the test item above, you could say, "A small group of trees and plants is to a large group of trees and plants as...." You should then complete the sentence with each of the answer choices. In this way you could rule out three answers— *bark : tree, palm : jungle,* and *asphalt : wood.* Bark is a part of a tree, and a palm can be part of a jungle. Asphalt is an artificial material, while wood is a natural material.

3. *Watch for reversed elements in answer choices.* The last choice above, *mountain : knoll*, is similar to the given pair of words because a knoll is a small hill. However, the *copse : forest* relationship is small to large, and *mountain : knoll* is large to small. Thus, the correct answer is *pond : lake.* A pond is a small body of water and a lake is a larger body of water.

Please turn to the next page.

Exercise Identifying Analogies

In each of the following items, select the lettered pair of words that best expresses a relationship similar to that expressed by the two capitalized words. Write the letter of your choice on the answer line. Use your dictionary as needed.

1. NASTURTIUM : FLOWER : :
   (A) nasty : sweet   (B) artichoke : fruit   (C) hornet : insect
   (D) education : school   (E) goal : soccer

2. TACT : DIPLOMAT : :
   (A) lesson : teacher   (B) baker : bread   (C) wit : comedian
   (D) astronaut : courage   (E) ambassador : embassy

3. PURLOIN : THIEF : :
   (A) jacket : waiter   (B) sew : tailor   (C) money : beggar
   (D) kindness : librarian   (E) clever : intricate

4. EQUILIBRIUM : IMBALANCE : :
   (A) scale : uncoordinated   (B) magenta : purple
   (C) rain : snow   (D) peace : truce   (E) concord : strife

5. CHUCKLE : GUFFAW : :
   (A) ovation : clapping   (B) smile : grin   (C) clown : comedian
   (D) affection : disfavor   (E) rim : surface

6. INERTIA : MOMENTUM : :
   (A) motor : car   (B) delay : traffic   (C) vigor : exhaustion
   (D) standstill : movement   (E) motion : silence

7. RADIANT : SUN : :
   (A) moon : stars   (B) solar : lunar   (C) luminous : moon
   (D) set : rise   (E) dark : night

8. TADPOLE : FROG : :
   (A) larva : butterfly   (B) egg : bird   (C) stone : rock
   (D) early : late   (E) ugly : pretty

9. PURGE : CLEANSE : :
   (A) defile : soil   (B) stain : spotless   (C) politics : housekeeping
   (D) wash : dry   (E) bleach : soap

10. CLEMENT : MERCIFUL : :
    (A) brutal : mild   (B) free : easy   (C) vivacious : lively
    (D) plague : disease   (E) sentry : watchful

11. PROFESSOR : TEACHES : :
    (A) doctor : heals   (B) lawyer : courtroom
    (C) testimony : witness   (D) athlete : sports
    (E) actor : memorizes

12. DAWN : DUSK : :
    (A) noon : midnight   (B) sunrise : sunset   (C) light : darkness
    (D) morning : afternoon   (E) evening : night

13. COSTLY : EXPENSIVE : :
    (A) thankful : ungrateful   (B) frugal : extravagant
    (C) valuable : cheap   (D) free : gratis   (E) priceless : worthless

14. POISON : ARSENIC : :
    (A) gold : mineral   (B) bread : food   (C) nutrient : vitamin
    (D) food : water   (E) mushroom : toxic

1. _____
2. _____
3. _____
4. _____
5. _____
6. _____
7. _____
8. _____
9. _____
10. _____
11. _____
12. _____
13. _____
14. _____

Analogy Tests

Lesson 14

Medicine

Current medical knowledge and technology make it possible to cure, control, or prevent hundreds of diseases. Illnesses, such as tetanus and polio, that once disabled or killed people now can be prevented by vaccination. New methods of diagnosing illness, such as computerized x-rays and sound-wave pictures of different parts of the body, permit early detection of disease. The efforts of laboratory scientists and doctors lead daily to possible cures for serious illnesses.

The words in this lesson will help you to understand the medical advances that are reported in newspapers and magazines and on television. These words may also help you to appreciate the combination of art and science that enables us to lead longer and healthier lives.

WORD LIST
capillary
enervate
epidemic
epidermis
infirmity
malady
nutrient
pallor
susceptible
virulent

DEFINITIONS

After you have studied the definitions and example for each vocabulary word, write the word on the line to the right.

1. **capillary** (kăp′ə-lĕr′ē) *noun* Any of the tiny blood vessels that connect the smallest arteries to the smallest veins. *adjective* Of or like a capillary. (From the Latin word *capillus*, meaning "hair")

   EXAMPLE When you cut your finger, the walls of the *capillaries* contract to help stop the bleeding.

2. **enervate** (ĕn′ər-vāt′) *trans. verb* To deprive someone of strength or vitality; weaken; sap. (From the Latin *ex-*, meaning "out," and *nervus*, meaning "nerve" or "muscle")

   RELATED WORD **enervation** *noun*

   EXAMPLE Strenuous exercise may *enervate* someone who is not physically fit.

3. **epidemic** (ĕp′ĭ-dĕm′ĭk) *noun* **a.** An outbreak of a contagious disease that spreads rapidly. **b.** A rapid spread, growth, or development: *an epidemic of new dance steps.* *adjective* **a.** Spreading rapidly and widely by infection among many individuals in an area. **b.** Widespread. (From the Greek *epi-*, meaning "on," and *dēmos*, meaning "people")

   RELATED WORD **epidemiology** *noun*

   EXAMPLE *Epidemics* of the Black Plague killed almost one quarter of the population of Europe during the 1300s.

USAGE NOTE *Pandemic*, a closely related word, means "an epidemic over an especially wide geographic area."

Medicine 87

4. **epidermis** (ĕp′ĭ-dûr′mĭs) *noun* **a.** The outer protective layer of skin. **b.** The outer layer of cells or the protective covering of a plant. (From the Greek *epi-*, meaning "on," and *derma*, meaning "skin")

RELATED WORD **epidermal** *adjective*

EXAMPLE Too much exposure to the sun causes damage to the *epidermis* in the form of sunburn.

4. _____

5. **infirmity** (ĭn-fûr′mĭ-tē) *noun* **a.** A physical disability. **b.** A lack of power; frailty. (From the Latin *in-*, meaning "not," and *firmus*, meaning "strong")

RELATED WORDS **infirm** *adjective;* **infirmary** *noun*

EXAMPLE Loss of mobility is an *infirmity* sometimes suffered by accident victims.

5. _____
SEE *malady*.

6. **malady** (măl′ə-dē) *noun* **a.** A disease, ailment, or disorder. **b.** An unwholesome condition: *the malady of discontent*. (From the Latin phrase *male habitus*, meaning "in poor condition")

EXAMPLE Malaria is a *malady* caused by the bite of an infected anopheles mosquito.

6. _____
USAGE NOTE A *malady* is an illness or disorder. An *infirmity* is a physical disability.

7. **nutrient** (no͞o′trē-ənt, nyo͞o′trē-ənt) *noun* Something that nourishes, especially an ingredient in food. (From the Latin word *nutrire*, meaning "to feed")

RELATED WORDS **nutrition** *noun;* **nutritious** *adjective*

EXAMPLE Whole-grain products, such as cereal and bread, provide many important *nutrients*.

7. _____

8. **pallor** (păl′ər) *noun* Extreme or unnatural paleness. (From the Latin word *pallere*, meaning "to be pale")

RELATED WORD **pallid** *adjective*

EXAMPLE Anemia, a condition that occurs because of a lack of red blood cells, often produces *pallor*.

8. _____

9. **susceptible** (sə-sĕp′tə-bəl) *adjective* **a.** Likely to be stricken or infected with or by: *susceptible to illness*. **b.** Easily influenced or affected; sensitive: *susceptible to flattery*. (From the Latin word *suscipere*, meaning "to receive")

RELATED WORD **susceptibility** *noun*

EXAMPLE Young children and the elderly were particularly *susceptible* to the new virus.

9. _____

10. **virulent** (vîr′yə-lənt, vîr′ə-lənt) *adjective* **a.** Having a strong tendency to cause harm; very severe; poisonous. **b.** Intensely irritating, hostile, obnoxious, or harsh: *virulent criticism*. (From the Latin word *virus*, meaning "poison")

RELATED WORDS **virulence** *noun;* **virulently** *adverb*

EXAMPLE Children are often vaccinated to prevent *virulent* diseases.

10. _____

Name _____ Date _____ Medicine

Exercise 1 Writing Correct Words

On the answer line, write the word from the vocabulary list that fits each definition.

1. A disease, ailment, or disorder
2. Likely to be stricken or infected with or by
3. An outbreak of contagious disease that spreads rapidly
4. Something that nourishes, especially an ingredient in food
5. Having a strong tendency to cause harm; very severe
6. A tiny blood vessel
7. To deprive of strength or vitality
8. Extreme or unnatural paleness
9. The outer protective layer of skin
10. A physical disability

1. _____
2. _____
3. _____
4. _____
5. _____
6. _____
7. _____
8. _____
9. _____
10. _____

Exercise 2 Using Words Correctly

Each of the following questions contains an italicized vocabulary word. Decide the answer to the question, and write *Yes* or *No* on the answer line.

1. Is a *nutrient* a part of a beehive?
2. Is a disease well controlled during an *epidemic*?
3. Is a portion of a person's *epidermis* visible to people around him or her?
4. Could an *infirmity* prevent a person from playing tennis or golf?
5. Might a doctor use *pallor* to treat a patient's cough?
6. Does blood flow through a healthy person's *capillaries*?
7. Are people who often brush their teeth less *susceptible* to tooth decay than those who never brush their teeth?
8. Might a person be *enervated* by a good night's sleep?
9. Would you be likely to consult a doctor if you had a *virulent* illness?
10. Is a *malady* an instrument used by a surgeon?

1. _____
2. _____
3. _____
4. _____
5. _____
6. _____
7. _____
8. _____
9. _____
10. _____

Exercise 3 Choosing the Best Word

Decide which vocabulary word or related form best completes the sentence, and write the letter of your choice on the answer line.

1. The surgery on Jerry's leg made him temporarily __?__ to infection.
   a. susceptible   b. virulent   c. epidemic   d. epidermal

2. Raymond felt __?__ after his first hour-long aerobics class.
   a. susceptible   b. epidermal   c. virulent   d. enervated

1. _____
2. _____

3. The medical illustrator prepared accurate drawings of human ___?___ .
   a. infirmities   b. pallor   c. capillaries   d. nutrition

4. The ___?___ that had kept Gillian bedridden after her accident disappeared gradually.
   a. pallor   b. epidemic   c. nutrient   d. infirmity

5. Nicole lost her tan when her ___?___ peeled.
   a. capillary   b. epidermis   c. pallor   d. malady

6. Maintaining careful sterilization, medical researchers grew new cultures of the ___?___ bacteria.
   a. pallid   b. nutritious   c. infirm   d. virulent

7. Mark's ___?___ lessened when he lay down and raised his feet.
   a. pallor   b. epidermis   c. epidemic   d. nutrient

8. Doctors could find no cause for Li-Ming's ___?___ .
   a. nutrient   b. malady   c. capillary   d. epidermis

9. Before the development of certain medicines, ___?___ could greatly reduce the population of small towns.
   a. nutrients   b. infirmities   c. epidemics   d. enervation

10. To remain healthy, people must get sufficient ___?___ in their diets.
    a. pallor   b. nutrients   c. infirmities   d. capillaries

1. _____
2. _____
3. _____
4. _____
5. _____
6. _____
7. _____
8. _____
9. _____
10. _____

Exercise 4   Using Different Forms of Words

Decide which form of the vocabulary word in parentheses best completes the sentence. The form given may be correct. Write your answer on the answer line.

1. Father believes in large, ___?___ breakfasts. *(nutrient)*
2. The number of cases of influenza reached ___?___ proportions during that very cold winter. *(epidemic)*
3. Rachel was unaware of the ___?___ of Ellen's temper. *(virulent)*
4. Grandmother's ___?___ vanished once her broken hip healed. *(infirmity)*
5. The campers' ___?___ to the cold increased when the sudden rain soaked their clothes. *(susceptible)*
6. Looking at the chart that compared the sizes of blood vessels, I was surprised by the smallness of the ___?___ . *(capillary)*
7. The burn had affected only the ___?___ layer of the child's skin. *(epidermis)*
8. After his first ride on a roller coaster, Eric was ___?___ and trembling. *(pallor)*
9. Jeremiah's ___?___ did not prevent him from attending school. *(malady)*
10. Marcella and Guy rested after their ___?___ ten-mile run. *(enervate)*

1. _____
2. _____
3. _____
4. _____
5. _____
6. _____
7. _____
8. _____
9. _____
10. _____

Medicine

Reading Comprehension

Each numbered sentence in the following passage contains an italicized vocabulary word or related form. After you read the passage, you will complete an exercise.

The Conquest of Scurvy

(1) Sailors once feared scurvy, a *malady* caused by a lack of vitamin C in the diet, more than they feared the unpredictability of oceans. **(2)** In its mildest form, scurvy caused *enervation* and aching muscles. **(3)** The disease, however, could become *virulent,* resulting in death.

Scurvy was once quite common because during their long voyages sailors lived on a diet of dried, salted, and preserved foods. **(4)** Although practical to store and carry for months at a time, these foods lacked the *nutrients* found in fresh fruits and vegetables.

Vasco da Gama, the Portuguese explorer, furnished the earliest description of scurvy. **(5)** He wrote in his ship's log in 1497 about an *infirmity* accompanied by loss of appetite that plagued his men. **(6)** The illness reached *epidemic* proportions when one hundred of da Gama's 170 men died by the time he had reached the Cape of Good Hope.

In 1536 Jacques Cartier, while on a winter expedition in Canada, lost twenty-six members of his exploration party to scurvy. **(7)** Cartier noted the extreme *pallor,* fever, swollen joints, and bleeding gums of his men before they died. Several members of the party and Cartier himself recovered from the disease, however, following treatment with an Indian remedy, a water extract of pine needles.

It was not until 1749 that James Lind, a Scottish naval surgeon, began experiments that proved scurvy was caused by a dietary deficiency. **(8)** Lind was initially concerned about scurvy victims' *susceptibility* to other diseases. **(9)** He also observed that people with scurvy healed poorly and were prone to severe bruising of the *epidermis.* **(10)** Lind concluded that the walls of the *capillaries* became so weak that the slightest pressure could cause them to break. Lind administered different combinations of foods to scurvy patients, noting which foods seemed to bolster resistance to disease and which promoted faster healing.

In 1753 James Lind published his "Treatise on the Scurvy," detailing the wide range of symptoms and recommending that lemons and limes be included in all ships' rations. Since sailors from Great Britain were the first to benefit from Lind's recommendations, people often referred to them as "limeys." We now know that these fruits as well as strawberries, tomatoes, and lettuce contain vitamin C, essential in human nutrition.

Please turn to the next page.

Reading Comprehension Exercise

Each of the following statements corresponds to a numbered sentence in the passage. Each statement contains a blank and is followed by four answer choices. Decide which choice fits best in the blank. The word or phrase that you choose must express roughly the same meaning as the italicized word in the passage. Write the letter of your choice on the answer line.

1. Scurvy is a(n) __?__ caused by a lack of vitamin C in the diet.
   a. accident   b. disease   c. misfortune   d. problem

2. Scurvy caused __?__ and aching muscles.
   a. illness   b. loss of life   c. weakness   d. digestive problems

3. The disease could become __?__.
   a. uncomfortable   c. very severe
   b. slightly painful   d. common

4. Dried and salted foods lacked the __?__ found in fresh fruits and vegetables.
   a. nourishing ingredients   c. water content
   b. value   d. essential taste

5. Vasco da Gama wrote about the __?__ that afflicted members of his crew.
   a. anxiety   b. poor sight   c. infection   d. frailty

6. The illness reached __?__ proportions when the majority of da Gama's crew died.
   a. unbelievable   b. rapidly spreading   c. low   d. unforgivable

7. Jacques Cartier noted the __?__ of his men.
   a. unnatural paleness   b. bleeding   c. rashes   d. fever

8. James Lind was concerned about scurvy victims' __?__ other diseases.
   a. understanding of   c. likelihood of contracting
   b. familiarity with   d. likelihood of ignoring

9. Lind also observed that people with scurvy had severe bruising of the __?__.
   a. body   b. outer layer of skin   c. inner layer of skin   d. limbs

10. Lind concluded that the walls of the __?__ became weak.
    a. small blood vessels   b. stomach   c. ship   d. skin

1. _____
2. _____
3. _____
4. _____
5. _____
6. _____
7. _____
8. _____
9. _____
10. _____

Writing Assignment

To emphasize the importance of a nutritious diet, your health teacher has asked you to prepare a report on a vitamin-deficiency disease. Choose a topic such as rickets, beriberi, or pellagra, and do library research on the cause of the disease, its symptoms, and its treatment. Use at least five of the words from this lesson and underline each one.

Lesson 15

Damage and Deterioration

Sometimes damage or destruction is the result of a natural phenomenon, such as a flood or tornado. At other times, human carelessness or ignorance causes harm or ruin, as when improperly handled chemical products or sewage pollute water. In this lesson you will learn words associated with damage and deterioration.

WORD LIST
blight
cataclysm
decimate
decomposition
eradication
havoc
mar
obliterate
pulverize
stagnant

DEFINITIONS

After you have studied the definitions and example for each vocabulary word, write the word on the line to the right.

1. **blight** (blīt) *trans. verb* **a.** To cause to decline or decay; to ruin or destroy. **b.** To cause a plant to be affected with disease. *noun* **a.** Any of several diseases that cause plants to wither and deteriorate. **b.** Unfavorable environmental conditions.
   EXAMPLE   Weevils *blighted* the cotton crops in 1946.

2. **cataclysm** (kăt′ə-klĭz′əm) *noun* **a.** A violent upheaval; a disaster. **b.** A violent, sudden change in the earth's crust. **c.** A destructive flood. (From the Greek word *kataklysmos*, meaning "deluge" or "flood")
   RELATED WORD   **cataclysmic** *adjective*
   EXAMPLE   When the *cataclysm* struck Putney Corners at 3:00 A.M., the earth began to shake like a maraca.

3. **decimate** (dĕs′ə-māt′) *trans. verb* To destroy or kill a large part of.
   RELATED WORD   **decimation** *noun*
   EXAMPLE   The Black Plague *decimated* the population of western Europe during the Middle Ages.

   ETYMOLOGY NOTE *Decimate*, from the Latin word for ten, originally meant "to destroy or kill one out of ten."

4. **decomposition** (dē-kŏm′pə-zĭsh′ən) *noun* The process of decaying, rotting, or breaking down.
   RELATED WORD   **decompose** *verb*
   EXAMPLE   The *decomposition* of the eggs caused a foul odor.

Damage and Deterioration

5. **eradication** (ĭ-răd′ĭ-kā′shən) *noun* Elimination, as if by tearing out by the roots; ridding. (From the Latin *ex-*, meaning "out," and *radix*, meaning "root")
   RELATED WORD **eradicate** *verb*
   EXAMPLE The mayor's goal is the *eradication* of poverty in Millwood.

6. **havoc** (hăv′ək) *noun* **a.** Widespread destruction. **b.** Confusion; disorder.
   EXAMPLE The sudden windstorm created *havoc* at the Fourth of July picnic.

7. **mar** (mär) *trans. verb* To damage; spoil the quality of.
   EXAMPLE A scratch can *mar* the beauty of fine furniture.

8. **obliterate** (ə-blĭt′ə-rāt′, ō-blĭt′ə-rāt′) *trans. verb* To do away with completely; to wipe out. (From the Latin word *oblitterare*, meaning "to erase")
   RELATED WORD **obliteration** *noun*
   EXAMPLE I can't wait to *obliterate* your sand castle when you finish it!

9. **pulverize** (pŭl′və-rīz′) *trans. verb* **a.** To pound, crush, or grind into a powder. **b.** To destroy, as if by crushing into powder. (From the Latin word *pulvis*, meaning "dust")
   EXAMPLE In order to make flour, one must *pulverize* grains of wheat.

10. **stagnant** (stăg′nənt) *adjective* **a.** Foul from standing still; stale. **b.** Lacking in freshness, liveliness, or originality. (From the Latin word *stagnum*, meaning "swamp")
    RELATED WORDS **stagnancy** *noun;* **stagnate** *verb*
    EXAMPLE Fish could not live in the *stagnant* pond because it lacked oxygen.

94 *Damage and Deterioration*

Name _____   Date _____

Reading Comprehension

Each numbered sentence in the following passage contains an italicized vocabulary word. After you read the passage, you will complete an exercise.

The Borers are Back!

(1) For a long time, the *decomposition* of organic and inorganic matter has polluted the waters of New York Harbor. (2) An unlikely benefit of this pollution has been the *eradication* of the troublesome mollusk known as the marine borer. (3) This shelled creature, once a familiar resident, could not live in the harbor's *stagnant* waters and departed in search of a healthier and cleaner environment.

The borer's destructive life cycle had been a major problem in the harbor. Its free-swimming larvae would fasten onto the harbor's wooden pilings, which support the piers. (4) After the larvae changed into adult form, they *pulverized* the wood with their sharp, filelike shells and devoured the wooden shreds for food. Piers became dangerously shaky, and pilings had to be replaced constantly.

(5) New York Harbor, *marred* by pollution for the past forty years, has recently experienced a renewal.

(6) The filthy pollutants that had fouled the harbor for so long have largely been *obliterated*. (7) The only problem is that the *decimated* population of marine borers has returned in full force. (8) They are again wreaking *havoc*. (9) Like a *cataclysm*, they are leaving behind a trail of destruction.

To test the renewed activity of these creatures, scientists submerged panels of pine in the harbor. When the panels were removed after several months, they looked like sponges. (10) Up to 90 percent of the wood had been *blighted*.

So far, in an effort to control this disaster, researchers have used the chemical obtusaquinone, a natural substance derived from rosewood. When injected into the pilings, it seems to prevent the mollusks from growing shells sturdy enough to drill deep into the wood. Scientists are hopeful that obtusaquinone will aid the harbor by finally controlling this annoying and costly pest.

Reading Comprehension Exercise

Each of the following statements corresponds to a numbered sentence in the passage. Each statement contains a blank and is followed by four answer choices. Decide which choice fits best in the blank. The word or phrase that you choose must express roughly the same meaning as the italicized word in the passage. Write the letter of your choice on the answer line.

1. New York Harbor has been damaged by the __?__ of pollutants.
   a. addition   b. breaking down   c. combination   d. building up

1. _____

Copyright © 1988 Houghton Mifflin Company. All rights reserved.   Damage and Deterioration   97

2. Pollution had brought about the ___?___ of the marine borer from the harbor.
   a. birth   b. growth   c. departure   d. elimination

3. Marine borers cannot live in ___?___ waters.
   a. muddy   b. foul   c. cloudy   d. soiled

4. With their shells the borers ___?___ the wood of the pilings.
   a. sawed   b. ate   c. ground   d. slept in

5. New York Harbor was long ___?___ by pollution.
   a. attacked   b. spoiled   c. marked   d. scarred

6. Filthy pollutants in the harbor have largely been ___?___ .
   a. eliminated   b. checked   c. chopped up   d. removed

7. The ___?___ population of the borer is back.
   a. largely destroyed   c. ever-increasing
   b. vastly multiplying   d. partially destroyed

8. The troublesome borers are causing ___?___ .
   a. waste   b. panic   c. destruction   d. disease

9. The destruction caused by the borers can be compared to a ___?___ .
   a. post   b. disaster   c. harbor   d. disease

10. In an experiment borers ___?___ up to 90 percent of the wood.
    a. ruined   b. submerged   c. filed   d. consumed

2. _____
3. _____
4. _____
5. _____
6. _____
7. _____
8. _____
9. _____
10. _____

Practice with Analogies

DIRECTIONS On the answer line, write the vocabulary word that completes each analogy.

See page 79 for some strategies to use with analogies.

1. ORDER : TRANQUILLITY : : chaos : ___?___
2. DYNAMIC : FLOWING : : ___?___ : motionless
3. OXIDATION : RUST : : ___?___ : compost
4. BUFF : POLISH : : disfigure : ___?___
5. MISSPELLING : MISTAKE : : earthquake : ___?___

1. _____
2. _____
3. _____
4. _____
5. _____

Vocabulary Enrichment

The word *decimate*, which is also in this lesson, is based on the Latin word *decimus*, meaning "one tenth," and has its roots in Roman history. When Roman military commanders conquered a tribe or group, they sometimes inflicted a punishment of killing every tenth person. The word *decimate* arose as a description of this practice, meaning "to kill one out of every ten." Later in history *decimate* lost its penal association and its ratio of one out of ten. Today it simply means "to destroy a large proportion of a group."

ACTIVITY In your dictionary look up the following words and write their definitions and their Latin etymologies. Then write an explanation of the connection between the root and the definition.

1. decimeter   2. decimal   3. decade   4. dime   5. December

98   Damage and Deterioration

Test-Taking Skills

Reading Comprehension Tests

A section on reading comprehension is part of the Preliminary Scholastic Aptitude Test (PSAT) and other standardized tests. In a reading comprehension test, you read one or more paragraphs and then answer questions about them. The following strategies will help you when you take a reading comprehension test.

STRATEGIES

1. *As you read, determine the main idea.* The main idea of a passage is the principal point that the author is making. It may or may not be stated in a topic sentence. A common test question requires you to select a title for the passage. The best answer is always the one that expresses the main idea.

2. *Identify sentences that support the main idea.* Such sentences contain reasons and examples. As you read, try to remember each piece of information and where it occurs in the passage. Reading comprehension questions often require you to answer with specific information.

3. *Identify sentences that state conclusions.* Conclusions are different from support sentences. Conclusions are general statements that summarize the ideas presented in earlier sentences. Words such as *therefore, hence,* and *thus* signal a sentence that states a conclusion. Tests often ask you to select the correctly stated conclusion in a group of possible conclusions.

4. *Make inferences about what you read.* An inference is an unstated conclusion that can be drawn from one or more statements in the passage. Suppose, for example, that you read the following. "At first glance Harrison was not an impressive person." From the sentence you can infer that in time Harrison proved to have some memorable qualities after all. Tests often ask you to draw inferences from the reading passage.

5. *Read as fast as you can and still understand what you are reading.* Do not be tempted to look at the questions before reading. Read the passage first; then answer the questions. Check each answer by glancing at the appropriate part of the passage. Your first reading should have acquainted you with the general way in which the author develops his or her main idea. Finally, do not attempt to answer the questions by recalling what you already know about the subject; answer strictly in terms of what the passage clearly states.

Please turn to the next page.

Exercise Taking Tests of Reading Comprehension

Read the passage carefully and then answer the questions about it. For each question write the letter of your choice on the answer line.

The Africanized bees, or so-called *killer bees*, are scheduled to appear in the United States sometime around 1990, and their projected arrival has aroused much speculation and fear. However, a lot of the anxiety surrounding the killer bees is unfounded. In many ways, they resemble the familiar honeybee. Their venom, for example, is no more toxic than that of the honeybee. In fact, it is less toxic than the venom of a yellow jacket or wasp. Although movies have tended to play up the vicious nature of the bees, they are actually no more destructive than bees that now inhabit American gardens. What does distinguish the Africanized bee from the ordinary honeybee is its determined defense of territory. Disturbed, the bees will mount an attack that can continue for days, and they will pursue an intruder whereas honeybees will quickly give up.

1. Which of the following titles best fits the passage?
   (A) The Truth About Killer Bees
   (B) The Menace of Killer Bees
   (C) Killer Bees Versus Honeybees
   (D) Killer Bees As Portrayed in Films
   (E) Killer Bees: Defenders of Territory

   1. _____

2. The venom of a killer bee is
   (A) less poisonous than a honeybee's
   (B) more poisonous than a wasp's
   (C) about as poisonous as a honeybee's
   (D) about as poisonous as a yellow jacket's
   (E) more poisonous than any other bee's

   2. _____

3. The arrival of killer bees has caused which of the following?
     I. scientific studies
    II. fear
   III. unnecessary worry
    IV. curiosity
   (A) II only   (B) III only   (C) IV only   (D) II and IV only
   (E) II, III, and IV

   3. _____

4. Which of the following phrases could best be substituted for "to play up"?
   (A) to depict accurately
   (B) to minimize
   (C) to discuss
   (D) to emphasize
   (E) to explain in an entertaining way

   4. _____

5. The destructiveness of killer bees is
   (A) no worse than that of American bees
   (B) worse than that of American bees
   (C) less pronounced than that of American bees
   (D) minimal
   (E) extreme

   5. _____

Think for a moment about how varied the skills and talents of your friends are. You may know someone who is a wonderful athlete, another who is a fine mechanic, and a third who can speak several languages. We all have been given or have developed certain skills, while we lack others. For those we lack, we can sometimes rely on our friends who possess them to help us out. The words in this lesson will add to your understanding of the different ways in which people may be gifted.

WORD LIST
adept
aptitude
astute
dexterity
finesse
inspiration
precocious
prodigy
resourceful
virtuoso

DEFINITIONS

After you have studied the definitions and example for each vocabulary word, write the word on the line to the right.

1. **adept** (ə-dĕpt′) *adjective* Very skilled or capable. (From the Latin word *adeptus*, meaning "achieved" or "acquired")
   RELATED WORD **adeptly** *adverb*
   EXAMPLE Paloma Picasso is an *adept* jewelry designer.

2. **aptitude** (ăp′tĭ-tōōd′, ăp′tĭ-tyōōd′) *noun* **a.** A talent or natural ability. **b.** Ease in learning; intelligence.
   EXAMPLE Lazarus does well on essay examinations because he has an *aptitude* for writing.

3. **astute** (ə-stōōt′, ə-styōōt′) *adjective* Shrewd in judgment; possessing a keen mind. (From the Latin word *astus*, meaning "craftiness" or "guile")
   RELATED WORD **astuteness** *noun*
   EXAMPLE Millicent Paige is an *astute* financier.

4. **dexterity** (dĕk-stĕr′ĭ-tē) *noun* Skill in the use of the hands, the body, or the mind; adroitness. (From the Latin word *dexter*, meaning "on the right" or "skillful")
   RELATED WORDS **dexterous** *adjective;* **dexterously** *adverb*
   EXAMPLE He showed amazing *dexterity*, assembling the puzzle in record time.

Ability 101

5. **finesse** (fə-něs′) *noun* Delicacy and refinement of performance, execution, or workmanship. (From the French word *finesse*, meaning "refinement")

   EXAMPLE Isadora Duncan showed such *finesse* in her dancing that she became a highly regarded artist throughout Europe.

6. **inspiration** (ĭn′spə-rā′shən) *noun* **a.** A creative stimulus for the mind or the emotions. **b.** A sudden insight or creative idea. (From the Latin *in-*, meaning "into," and *spirare*, meaning "to breathe")

   RELATED WORDS **inspirational** *adjective;* **inspire** *verb*

   EXAMPLE A woman named Laura served as the *inspiration* for most of the poems of the Italian writer Petrarch.

7. **precocious** (prĭ-kō′shəs) *adjective* Having unusual mental development at an early age. (From the Latin word *praecox*, meaning "premature")

   RELATED WORDS **precociously** *adverb;* **precociousness** *noun*

   EXAMPLE Anna and John Franklin's *precocious* daughter mastered algebra at the age of eight.

8. **prodigy** (prŏd′ə-jē) *noun* A person who is exceptionally gifted, usually at a young age. (From the Latin word *prodigium*, meaning "omen")

   EXAMPLE Sonja Franklin is a mathematical *prodigy*.

9. **resourceful** (rĭ-sôrs′fəl, rĭ-zôrs′fəl) *adjective* Capable; effective; able to meet most situations effectively.

   RELATED WORDS **resource** *noun;* **resourcefully** *adverb;* **resourcefulness** *noun*

   EXAMPLE Martin de la Rochefoucauld is so *resourceful* that he can make attractive party favors out of paper towels.

10. **virtuoso** (vûr′cho͞o-ō′sō, vûr′cho͞o-ō′-zō) *noun* One skilled in the technique of an art, especially music. (From the Latin word *virtus*, meaning "manliness" or "excellence")

    RELATED WORD **virtuosity** *noun*

    EXAMPLE Constance Ward is a *virtuoso* of the viola da gamba.

5. _____

6. _____

7. _____

8. _____

9. _____

10. _____

Name _____ Date _____

Exercise 1 Matching Words and Definitions

Match the definition in Column B with the word in Column A. Write
the letter of the correct definition on the answer line.

Column A	Column B
1. inspiration	a. a talent or ability
2. adept	b. delicacy of execution
3. astute	c. highly developed intellectually while young
4. dexterity	d. shrewd in judgment
5. aptitude	e. the creative stimulation of the mind
6. virtuoso	f. very skilled or capable
7. prodigy	g. skill in the use of the hands
8. precocious	h. an unusually gifted young person
9. finesse	i. able to deal with any situation
10. resourceful	j. one skilled in music

1. _____
2. _____
3. _____
4. _____
5. _____
6. _____
7. _____
8. _____
9. _____
10. _____

Exercise 2 Using Words Correctly

Each of the following questions contains an italicized vocabulary
word. Decide the answer to the question, and write *Yes* or *No* on the
answer line.

1. Is *dexterity* mental sharpness?
2. If one is *adept*, is one lacking in skill?
3. Is *aptitude* either a natural ability or an ease in learning?
4. If a child is *precocious*, does this mean that he or she is large?
5. Does *virtuoso* mean morally upright?
6. Is a *prodigy* a highly gifted or talented person?
7. Is an *astute* person keen of mind?
8. Is *inspiration* a dulling of the mind?
9. Is a *finesse* the end of a race?
10. Is a *resourceful* person likely to be capable of handling a difficult situation?

1. _____
2. _____
3. _____
4. _____
5. _____
6. _____
7. _____
8. _____
9. _____
10. _____

Exercise 3 Choosing the Best Definition

For each italicized vocabulary word in the following sentences, write
the letter of the best definition on the answer line.

1. Pablo Casals, a cello *virtuoso*, is considered one of the greatest cellists
   of the twentieth century.
   a. inspiration
   b. one gifted, usually at an early age
   c. one skilled in the technique of an art
   d. a proper and well-mannered person

1. _____

Copyright © 1988 Houghton Mifflin Company. All rights reserved.

Ability 103

2. Casals was a *prodigy*, beginning his concert career at fifteen. 2. _____
   a. one gifted, usually at an early age
   b. one skilled in the technique of an art
   c. a youth with many talents
   d. a great performer

3. Many a musician has found *inspiration* in the art of Pablo Casals. 3. _____
   a. emotional solitude   c. technical excellence
   b. mental stimulation   d. mental ability

4. Casals's *dexterity* helped him to develop his expressive playing technique. 4. _____
   a. strong hands   c. musical ability
   b. skilled hands   d. ambition

5. The *finesse* with which Casals played brought him international acclaim. 5. _____
   a. finality   b. beauty   c. originality   d. refinement

6. Casals was *adept* at playing not only the cello but the piano as well. 6. _____
   a. good   b. busy   c. skilled   d. famous

7. Casals's *aptitude* for music extended to composition as well. 7. _____
   a. love   b. interest   c. talent   d. recognition

8. Casals as a teacher was *astute* in his choice of students. 8. _____
   a. gifted   b. shrewd   c. odd   d. obvious

9. Most of his students had a *precocious* interest in music. 9. _____
   a. early   b. talented   c. unhealthy   d. shrewd

10. A *resourceful* disciple could learn much about the cello from Casals. 10. _____
    a. organized   b. attentive   c. confident   d. capable

Exercise 4   Using Different Forms of Words

Decide which form of the vocabulary word in parentheses best completes the sentence. The form given may be correct. Write your answer on the answer line.

1. The graduation speaker hoped to __?__ the students to enter the computer industry. *(inspiration)* 1. _____

2. Although he began school a month late, Gregory showed high __?__ and soon caught up with his class. *(aptitude)* 2. _____

3. Marina's __?__ in economics led to her election to a vice-presidency. *(astute)* 3. _____

4. Scott __?__ steered the motorboat between the jagged rocks. *(adept)* 4. _____

5. Some colleges have special programs for children whose __?__ makes grade school unchallenging for them. *(precocious)* 5. _____

6. A __?__ who attends one of these programs can learn a great deal and still be with children of the same age. *(prodigy)* 6. _____

7. Franz Liszt's __?__ at the piano led him to be called the greatest pianist of his time. *(virtuoso)* 7. _____

8. The entertainer __?__ juggled a small hoop, a cap, and an apple. *(dexterity)* 8. _____

Name _____ Date _____

9. The hikers' calmness and ___?___ saved them when they strayed from the Imperial Trail. *(resourceful)*

9. _____

10. *The Fifty Courtesies of the Table,* published in 1480, taught people how to eat with ___?___ . *(finesse)*

10. _____

Reading Comprehension

Each numbered sentence in the following passage contains an italicized vocabulary word. After you read the passage, you will complete an exercise.

Wolfgang Amadeus Mozart (1756–1791)

(1) Wolfgang Amadeus Mozart, a musical *virtuoso,* is regarded as one of the greatest musical geniuses of all time. (2) His symphonies, concertos, chamber music, and operas have furnished *inspiration* to musicians and music lovers for centuries.
(3) Because Mozart was considered *precocious* from his earliest youth, his composer father took over his musical education. (4) At first, he was overshadowed by the musical *dexterity* of his older sister, Maria-Anna. (5) Soon, however, he proved himself a musical *prodigy,* composing his first piece at six. (6) His *astute* father toured Europe with his children. (7) Their musical *aptitude* was applauded at many of the courts of Europe. (8) Although Maria-Anna was an *adept* musician, it was Wolfgang Amadeus who astounded the audiences. (9) He showed great *finesse* on the harpsichord, organ, and violin. In London he was known as the wonder of the age.
(10) Although his musical ability was unexcelled, he was not *resourceful* in financial matters. Almost always in debt and having no rich patron, he tried to pay off his debts by playing as many concerts as possible. Sick and debt-ridden, he died at the early age of thirty-five.

Reading Comprehension Exercise

Each of the following statements corresponds to a numbered sentence in the passage. Each statement contains a blank and is followed by four answer choices. Decide which choice fits best in the blank. The word or phrase that you choose must express roughly the same meaning as the italicized word in the passage. Write the letter of your choice on the answer line.

1. Wolfgang Amadeus Mozart was a ___?___ .
  a. talented performer   **c.** composer
  b. conductor   **d.** musical scholar

1. _____

Copyright © 1988 Houghton Mifflin Company. All rights reserved.

Ability   105

2. Musicians and music lovers have found his work to be ? .
   a. hard to understand   c. spiritually stimulating
   b. delightful   d. of limited range

3. Early in his life, Mozart was considered to be ? .
   a. spoiled   b. unhappy   c. unskilled   d. gifted

4. At first, the musical ? of Mozart's older sister overshadowed his own ability.
   a. style   b. skill   c. refinement   d. training

5. After he wrote his first composition at six, he was recognized as a(n) ? .
   a. natural musician   c. fine composer
   b. unusually gifted youth d. moderately talented performer

6. The father was ? and took his children on a tour of Europe.
   a. theatrical   b. musical   c. shrewd   d. ambitious

7. In Europe the children were applauded for their ? .
   a. manners   b. looks   c. delicacy   d. ability

8. Mozart's sister was a(n) ? musician.
   a. inferior   b. classical   c. skilled   d. intelligent

9. Wolfgang Amadeus showed his ? on the organ, the harpsichord, and the violin.
   a. musical excellence   c. musical talent
   b. refined skill   d. musical versatility

10. Although Mozart was a great musician, he was not ? in financial matters.
    a. capable   b. organized   c. forceful   d. trained

2. _____
3. _____
4. _____
5. _____
6. _____
7. _____
8. _____
9. _____
10. _____

Writing Assignment

Imagine that you are one of the ladies or gentlemen at the Hapsburg court in Austria in 1766. Write a letter to one of your relatives in England about the astounding performance of the ten-year-old Mozart you have just witnessed at the Belvedere Palace in Vienna. Use at least five of the words in the lesson and underline each one.

Vocabulary Enrichment

In the definition of *dexterity*, you have read that the word comes from the Latin *dexter*, which means "on the right" or "skillful." In ancient Rome, the right hand or the right side had positive connotations, while the left side, called *sinister* in Latin, had negative associations. This distinction has come down to us in the word *dexterity*, meaning "skill," and the word *sinister*, meaning "portending evil" or "threatening."

ACTIVITY Many common English words have been derived from words that originally indicated some kind of direction, such as *north* or *below*. Look up the following words in a dictionary and write the current meaning of the word as well as the directional indication from which it was initially derived.

1. gauche   2. haughty   3. Netherlands   4. orient

Lesson 17

Pride

In Greek mythology one of the greatest sins that people could commit against the gods was that of *hubris*, or excessive pride. Humans were expected to be respectful of the gods. If mortals dared to place themselves on the same level as the gods, the gods inevitably did something to remind the people of their limitations. Frequently, excessive pride led to someone's downfall.

Today *pride* has both positive and negative connotations. People deserve to have pride in their accomplishments and in themselves as individuals. On the other hand, conceited people can be difficult to deal with. The words in this lesson express both the positive and the negative aspects of pride.

WORD LIST
arrogant
diffident
egocentric
esteem
gloat
humility
modest
pompous
swagger
vaunt

DEFINITIONS

After you have studied the definitions and example for each vocabulary word, write the word on the line to the right.

1. **arrogant** (ăr′ə-gənt) *adjective*   Excessively and unpleasantly convinced of one's own importance; overbearingly proud; superior; vain. (From the Latin word *arrogare*, meaning "to make unjustified claims")

    RELATED WORDS   **arrogance** *noun*; **arrogantly** *adverb*

    EXAMPLE   The famous artist answered the reporter's questions in an *arrogant* tone of voice.

    1. _____
    USAGE NOTE *Humble* (see *humility*) is an antonym of *arrogant*.

2. **diffident** (dĭf′ĭ-dənt, dĭf′ĭ-dĕnt′) *adjective*   Hesitant through lack of self-confidence; timid. (From the Latin *dis-*, meaning "not," and *fidere*, meaning "to trust")

    RELATED WORDS   **diffidence** *noun*; **diffidently** *adverb*

    EXAMPLE   Max is a *diffident* boy who will benefit from taking part in the play.

    2. _____

3. **egocentric** (ē′gō-sĕn′trĭk, ĕg′ō-sĕn′trĭk) *adjective*   Limited in outlook or concern to one's own activities or needs; self-centered; selfish.

    RELATED WORD   **egocentricity** *noun*

    EXAMPLE   Young children tend to be *egocentric*, claiming others' toys as their own.

    3. _____
    MEMORY CUE Think *ego* + *center*.

Pride

4. **esteem** (ĭ-stēm′) *noun* Favorable regard; respect. *trans. verb* **a.** To regard with respect; admire; honor. **b.** To judge or consider to be. (From the Latin word *aestimare*, meaning "to estimate" or "to value")

   EXAMPLE   Katherine Hepburn is *esteemed* as one of America's finest actresses.

5. **gloat** (glōt) *intrans. verb* To feel or display triumphant, and often spiteful, satisfaction or delight.

   EXAMPLE   Jennifer *gloated* over her selection as soccer team captain.

6. **humility** (hyōō-mĭl′ĭ-tē) *noun* The quality of being humble; freedom from false pride. (From the Latin word *humus*, meaning "the ground")

   RELATED WORDS   **humiliate** *verb;* **humiliation** *noun*

   EXAMPLE   Lin Yan accepted the award for bravery with grace and *humility*.

7. **modest** (mŏd′ĭst) *adjective* **a.** Having or showing a moderate estimation of one's own talents, abilities, or accomplishments; lacking in vanity. **b.** Not elaborate or showy; unpretentious: *a modest house.* **c.** Moderate in size or amount: *a modest salary.* (From the Latin word *modus*, meaning "a proper measure")

   RELATED WORDS   **modestly** *adverb;* **modesty** *noun*

   EXAMPLE   For his college applications, Duncan wrote *modest* essays about his achievements in high school.

8. **pompous** (pŏm′pəs) *adjective* **a.** Characterized by an exaggerated show of dignity or self-importance. **b.** Excessively ornate: *pompous writing.* (From the Greek word *pompē*, meaning "procession")

   RELATED WORDS   **pomp** *noun;* **pompously** *adverb*

   EXAMPLE   Mr. Pumblechook, a character in Dickens's novel *Great Expectations*, is a *pompous* man who constantly offers ridiculous advice.

9. **swagger** (swăg′ər) *intrans. verb* To walk or conduct oneself in a conceited or boastful manner; strut.

   RELATED WORD   **swaggeringly** *adverb*

   EXAMPLE   The jockey *swaggered* out of the winner's circle, holding the silver trophy above her head.

10. **vaunt** (vônt, vŏnt) *trans. verb* To call attention to, often proudly or boastfully. *intrans. verb* To boast or brag. (From the Latin word *vanus*, meaning "empty" or "vain")

    EXAMPLE   The newspaper *vaunted* the success of the college wrestling team.

4. _____

5. _____

6. _____
USAGE NOTE *Humility* has positive connotations, but *humiliate*, "to lower the pride or dignity of" or "mortify," has negative ones. SEE also *modest*.

7. _____
USAGE NOTE Both *modest* and *humble* mean "unpretentious," but *humble* is humbler than *modest*.

8. _____

9. _____

10. _____
USAGE NOTE Do not confuse *vaunt* with *vault*, which means "to jump or leap over."

Name _____ Date _____

Exercise 1 Writing Correct Words

On the answer line, write the word from the vocabulary list that fits each definition.

1. Excessively convinced of one's own importance; vain   1. _____
2. Having a moderate estimation of one's own accomplishments   2. _____
3. Hesitant due to a lack of self-confidence; timid   3. _____
4. To call attention to boastfully   4. _____
5. Favorable regard; respect   5. _____
6. Characterized by an exaggerated show of dignity or self-importance   6. _____
7. To feel or display triumphant, spiteful satisfaction or delight   7. _____
8. The quality of being humble; freedom from false pride   8. _____
9. To walk or conduct oneself in a conceited or boastful manner; strut   9. _____
10. Limited in concern to one's own activities or needs; self-centered   10. _____

Exercise 2 Using Words Correctly

Decide whether the italicized vocabulary word has been used correctly in the sentence. On the answer line, write *Correct* for correct use and *Incorrect* for incorrect use.

1. A *diffident* person may not be comfortable when meeting strangers.   1. _____
2. He *vaunted* his success by apologizing for his shortcomings.   2. _____
3. The pirates *gloated* over the jewels stolen from the royal ship.   3. _____
4. The *egocentric* ballerina refused to talk about her enormous success.   4. _____
5. The *pompous* man said that he had been invited to the White House.   5. _____
6. Lily's *arrogant* attitude distressed both the teacher and other students.   6. _____
7. The assassin John Wilkes Booth held Abraham Lincoln in *esteem*.   7. _____
8. Cindy is a *modest* golfer who always brags about her scores.   8. _____
9. When Eric learned that he had not been chosen for the team, he
   swaggered out of school in a joyless mood.   9. _____
10. We received so many compliments on our concert that we needed a
    lesson in *humility* to balance the effects of the praise.   10. _____

Exercise 3 Choosing the Best Definition

For each italicized vocabulary word in the following sentences, write the letter of the best definition on the answer line.

1. Although Ansel Adams was admired throughout the world for his   1. _____
   ability as a photographer, he maintained a *modest* view of his success.
   a. moderate   b. superior   c. genuine   d. special

Copyright © 1988 Houghton Mifflin Company. All rights reserved.

Pride   109

2. The audience listened as *pompous* officials made dull speeches.
   a. boring   b. high-ranking   c. self-important   d. secretive

3. The *arrogant* clothing designer refused to attend the preview party.
   a. extremely anxious   c. talented
   b. overbearingly proud   d. aspiring

4. The *egocentric* King Louis XIV called himself the Sun King.
   a. spiteful   b. triumphant   c. humble   d. self-centered

5. The book was *esteemed* by the critics but ignored by the public.
   a. enjoyed   c. favorably regarded
   b. unfavorably reviewed   d. criticized

6. The owner of the prize-winning collie *swaggered* around the ring.
   a. boastfully walked   c. rudely sailed
   b. shyly ambled   d. happily skipped

7. "I must say that my director is mainly responsible for my success," the actor said with *humility*.
   a. good sense   c. gracefulness
   b. freedom from pride   d. a sense of style

8. The *diffident* salesperson worked in the store for a month before she had the courage to approach a customer.
   a. timid   b. reliable   c. orderly   d. confident

9. Sam *gloated* about his election victory.
   a. displayed anger   c. was ambitious
   b. was curious   d. displayed satisfaction

10. When Sam *vaunted* his success, his friends reminded him that he might not have won.
    a. predicted   c. bragged about
    b. explained   d. complained about

Exercise 4 Using Different Forms of Words

Decide which form of the vocabulary word in parentheses best completes the sentence. The form given may be correct. Write your answer on the answer line.

1. " ? is not becoming, particularly in one so young and inexperienced," stated the music teacher. *(arrogant)*

2. The Santiagos have furnished their summer house ? . *(modest)*

3. The Rockefellers are ? collectors of art. *(esteem)*

4. Howard's ? troubled his mother. *(egocentric)*

5. Carol hurt their feelings by ? about her new car. *(gloat)*

6. Richard sometimes forgets his audience and writes ? . *(pompous)*

7. ? the achievements of the seniors, the principal complimented their parents and teachers as well. *(vaunt)*

8. Our science team was ? at yesterday's practice for the quiz show. *(humility)*

9. Sheila outgrew her ? and became a poised speaker. *(diffident)*

10. ? to the door, Rocky turned and waved casually. *(swagger)*

110   Pride

Reading Comprehension

Each numbered sentence in the following passage contains an italicized vocabulary word or related form. After you read the passage, you will complete an exercise.

Mary, Queen of Scots (1542–1587)

Mary Stuart, Queen of Scots, was a beautiful and controversial woman whose life was filled with drama and adventure. **(1)** *Esteemed* initially by the Scots as a forceful ruler, she placed self-interest before her country's needs and lost her throne — and her head — as a result.

Mary Stuart became queen when she was only a week old, after her father, James V of Scotland, died suddenly. Her mother, Mary of Lorraine, was chosen as acting queen and sent her infant daughter to France. Living under the guardianship of her mother's powerful relatives, Mary Stuart grew into an intelligent and sophisticated young woman.

At the age of sixteen, she married the French crown prince, Francis. When he became King Francis II in 1559, Mary Stuart was Queen of France as well as Queen of Scotland. Their marriage was apparently a stormy one. **(2)** High-spirited and strong-willed, Mary could not get along with her sickly, *diffident* husband.

When Francis died in 1560, Mary Stuart was in a difficult position. **(3)** She was unwilling to stay in France and live under the domination of her *egocentric* mother-in-law, Catherine de Medici. She decided to return to Scotland and claim her throne.

(4) The first years of Mary's reign were marked by her *modesty*, good sense, and energy. In dealing with the tangled political and religious situation, she was both tolerant and firm. A Roman Catholic herself, she recognized the Reformed Protestant Church and won the respect of the Scottish nobility with her wise decisions. Unfortunately, this situation did not last long.

(5) In 1565 Mary seemed to put *humility* aside. **(6)** She *arrogantly* claimed that she, as a Roman Catholic, and not Elizabeth I, who was a Protestant, was the rightful Queen of England. Her desire to become Queen of England detracted from her chances of success as Queen of Scotland. **(7)** She spoke *pompously* of Scotland as her "small portion" with which she had to be content until a greater portion came her way. By claiming the English throne, Mary forced Elizabeth I to regard her as a dangerous enemy and to take every opportunity to diminish her power.

Mary's choice of a second husband was another major error. She married her cousin Henry Stuart, Lord Darnley, who had, in the eyes of the Roman Catholics, a claim to the English crown second only to Mary's own. **(8)** A Catholic marriage for their queen alarmed the Scots Protestants, who disliked the *swaggering* Lord Darnley. A group of powerful nobles led a rebellion, which Mary managed to suppress. **(9)** She *gloated* about her success, but her relationship with Elizabeth I and with the Protestants of Scotland was ruined.

In 1567 Mary added further to the chaotic situation in Scotland. After her husband died under mysterious circumstances, she married a third time. This marriage, to James Hepburn, Earl of Bothwell, was Mary's fatal mistake: Lord Bothwell was suspected of having murdered Lord Darnley, her second husband. Even Mary's closest supporters were horrified, and again the nobles banded together. **(10)** This time, however, Mary could not *vaunt* her loyal backing. She was captured, imprisoned, and forced to give up her throne.

Mary escaped from her prison in 1568 and raised a small army. When her forces were defeated, she fled to England for protection. Mary believed that Elizabeth would not dare to withhold support from a fellow monarch against rebels.

Elizabeth did allow her to stay in England. However, because of Mary's ambition, she was now too dangerous to be allowed freedom. For nineteen years she lived as a virtual prisoner until Elizabeth I could no longer ignore Mary's involvement in plots to overthrow the throne. Mary had placed her pride and personal desires ahead of political judgment; in 1587 she was beheaded.

Please turn to the next page.

Pride 111

Reading Comprehension Exercise

Each of the following statements corresponds to a numbered sentence in the passage. Each statement contains a blank and is followed by four answer choices. Decide which choice fits best in the blank. The word or phrase that you choose must express roughly the same meaning as the italicized word in the passage. Write the letter of your choice on the answer line.

1. Mary, Queen of Scots, was initially __?__ by the Scots.
   a. idolized   b. feared   c. respected   d. chosen

2. Mary was high-spirited and strong-willed and could not get along with her __?__ husband, Francis.
   a. timid   b. weak   c. superior   d. competitive

3. Mary Stuart was unwilling to remain in France under the domination of her __?__ mother-in-law.
   a. elegant   b. self-centered   c. adventurous   d. unkind

4. Mary's first years as Queen of Scotland were marked by her __?__ .
   a. responsiveness   c. freedom from vanity
   b. creativity   d. wisdom beyond her years

5. Mary put __?__ aside in 1565.
   a. freedom from greed   c. self-control
   b. self-interest   d. freedom from false pride

6. She claimed __?__ that she, not Elizabeth I, was the rightful Queen of England.
   a. overbearingly   c. truthfully
   b. insistently   d. with enthusiasm

7. She spoke __?__ of Scotland as her "small portion."
   a. with delight   c. hesitantly
   b. with exaggerated self-importance   d. angrily

8. The Scots Protestants disliked the __?__ Lord Darnley.
   a. soft-spoken   b. somewhat shy   c. formal   d. strutting

9. Mary __?__ about successfully stopping the rebellion.
   a. felt triumphant   b. felt sad   c. thought   d. dreamed

10. This time Mary could not __?__ her loyal backing.
    a. investigate   c. boast of
    b. keep silent about   d. remain logical about

1. _____
2. _____
3. _____
4. _____
5. _____
6. _____
7. _____
8. _____
9. _____
10. _____

Writing Assignment

Your teacher has asked you to provide a modern application of the following proverb: "Pride goeth before destruction and an haughty spirit before a fall." Write a brief story about a character whose excessive pride interferes in some way with his or her accomplishments. Use at least five of the vocabulary words from this lesson and underline each one.

Lesson 18

Truth and Value

In "The Squire's Tale," one of the famous *Canterbury Tales*, Geoffrey Chaucer wrote that "truth is the highest thing men can keep." Chaucer was placing considerable value on truth. Do you believe that truth is as important today as it was in fourteenth-century England? What do *you* value?

The words in this lesson are used to explain different aspects of truth or value. By studying the words, you will be better able to talk and write about these concepts.

WORD LIST
appraisal
base
candid
criterion
legitimate
mediocre
meritorious
subtle
truism
validate

DEFINITIONS

After you have studied the definitions and example for each vocabulary word, write the word on the line to the right.

1. **appraisal** (ə-prā′zəl) *noun* **a.** An evaluation or estimation of the nature, quality, or worth of something; a judgment. **b.** An expert or official valuation of something, as for taxation. (From the Latin *ad-*, meaning "to," and *pretium*, meaning "price")
   RELATED WORDS   **appraise** *verb;* **appraiser** *noun*
   EXAMPLE   The coach's *appraisal* of the competing hockey teams helped us to have an undefeated season.

   1. _____
   USAGE NOTE Do not confuse *appraise* with *apprise*, which means "to give notice to; inform."

2. **base** (bās) *adjective* **a.** Mean or contemptible; shameful. **b.** Inferior in quality; containing inferior substances: *base metals*. (From the Medieval Latin word *bassus*, meaning "low")
   RELATED WORDS   **basely** *adverb;* **baseness** *noun*
   EXAMPLE   Lying and cheating are *base* actions.

   2. _____

3. **candid** (kăn′dĭd) *adjective* **a.** Without pretense or reserve; straightforward; honest. **b.** Free of prejudice; impartial. **c.** Not posed or rehearsed: *a candid photograph*.   *noun* An unposed photograph. (From the Latin word *candidus*, meaning "bright white")
   RELATED WORDS   **candidly** *adverb;* **candor** *noun*
   EXAMPLE   Emily nervously anticipated her music teacher's *candid* assessment of her talent.

   3. _____

Copyright © Houghton Mifflin Company. All rights reserved.

Truth and Value   113

4. **criterion** (krī-tîr′ē-ən) *noun* A standard, rule, or test on which a judgment or decision can be based. (From the Greek word *kritēs*, meaning "a judge")

   EXAMPLE Many people consider the amount of profit a company makes to be the most important *criterion* of its success.

   4. _____
   USAGE NOTE *Criterion* is a singular noun that takes a singular verb. *Criteria* is the plural form and requires a plural verb.

5. **legitimate** (lə-jĭt′ə-mĭt) *adjective* **a.** Authentic; genuine; real. **b.** Being or acting in accordance with the law; lawful. **c.** In accordance with established or accepted patterns and standards. (From the Latin word *lex*, meaning "law")

   RELATED WORDS **legitimacy** *noun;* **legitimately** *adverb*

   EXAMPLE He proved that he was a *legitimate* opera star by showing us the reviews of his performances.

   5. _____

6. **mediocre** (mē′dē-ō′kər) *adjective* Of moderate to low quality; ordinary; average. (From the Latin word *medius*, meaning "middle")

   RELATED WORD **mediocrity** *noun*

   EXAMPLE Diane's speech was only *mediocre;* she certainly did not try as hard as she usually does.

   6. _____

7. **meritorious** (mĕr′ĭ-tôr′ē-əs) *adjective* Having superior value; deserving praise. (From the Latin word *meritorius*, meaning "earning money")

   RELATED WORDS **merit** *noun;* **meritoriously** *adverb*

   EXAMPLE Lenny's *meritorious* rescue of the drowning child resulted in an award for bravery.

   7. _____

8. **subtle** (sŭt′l) *adjective* **a.** Not immediately obvious; so slight as to be difficult to detect or analyze. **b.** Able to make precise distinctions; keen: *a subtle mind.* **c.** Characterized by slyness or deviousness: *subtle actions.* (From the Latin word *subtilis*, meaning "fine" or "delicate")

   RELATED WORDS **subtlety** *noun;* **subtly** *adverb*

   EXAMPLE The students studied the *subtle* differences in the styles of several authors.

   8. _____

9. **truism** (trōō′ĭz′əm) *noun* A statement of an obvious or self-evident truth.

   EXAMPLE Mr. O'Brien's favorite *truism* is "two heads are better than one."

   9. _____

10. **validate** (văl′ĭ-dāt′) *trans. verb* To confirm or support on a sound basis or authority; verify; substantiate. (From the Latin word *valere*, meaning "to be strong")

    RELATED WORDS **valid** *adjective;* **validation** *noun;* **validity** *noun*

    EXAMPLE Observations made by scientists *validated* William Harvey's theory that blood circulates in the body.

    10. _____

Name _____ Date _____

Exercise 1 Completing Definitions

On the answer line, write the word from the vocabulary list that best completes each definition.

1. Something that is authentic or lawful is __?__ .   1. _____
2. A judgment or evaluation of the worth of something is a(n) __?__ .   2. _____
3. A standard of judgment is a(n) __?__ .   3. _____
4. Something that is shameful or of inferior quality is __?__ .   4. _____
5. Something that is ordinary or undistinguished is __?__ .   5. _____
6. To be straightforward, honest, or impartial is to be __?__ .   6. _____
7. To confirm or verify something is to __?__ it.   7. _____
8. If something is not immediately obvious, it may be __?__ .   8. _____
9. A statement of an obvious truth is a(n) __?__ .   9. _____
10. An action that has superior value or is deserving of praise is __?__ .   10. _____

Exercise 2 Using Words Correctly

Decide whether the italicized vocabulary word has been used correctly in the sentence. On the answer line, write *Correct* for correct use and *Incorrect* for incorrect use.

1. The audience showed its favorable *appraisal* of the singer by giving her a standing ovation.   1. _____
2. "Get your ticket *validated* at the store, and I'll give you a discount on parking," said the lot attendant.   2. _____
3. The book was entirely fresh, full of new thoughts and *truisms*.   3. _____
4. Acts of charity are *base*.   4. _____
5. The show dogs were judged mainly on the *criterion* of obedience.   5. _____
6. Manuel was *candid* about his project, refusing to show it to anyone.   6. _____
7. Guy's grades were so *mediocre* that he was first in his class.   7. _____
8. I read the poem twice before I understood its *subtle* message of hope.   8. _____
9. The mayor was removed from office because of his *meritorious* service.   9. _____
10. "Your complaints are *legitimate*," said Mrs. Rambeaux, "and I will consider doing what you have suggested."   10. _____

Exercise 3 Choosing the Best Definition

For each italicized vocabulary word in the following sentences, write the letter of the best definition on the answer line.

1. The British poet Canning wrote, "But of all plagues, good Heaven,   1. _____
   thy wrath can send,/Save me, oh, save me, from the *candid* friend."
   a. spiteful   **b.** completely honest   **c.** gossiping   **d.** loyal

Copyright © 1988 Houghton Mifflin Company. All rights reserved.   Truth and Value

2. One *criterion* of happiness is the friendship of others.
   a. rule c. standard of judgment
   b. requirement d. standard of success

   2. _____

3. The lawyer tried to *validate* the defendant's story.
   a. confirm b. disprove c. improve d. reinforce

   3. _____

4. The candidate uttered several *truisms* about government but did not give her position on any issue.
   a. quotations b. obvious truths c. half-truths d. stories

   4. _____

5. The critics had nothing positive to say about the *mediocre* play.
   a. terrible b. excellent c. low-quality d. silly

   5. _____

6. Marianna reached several *subtle* conclusions about Greek mythology that the rest of the students had missed.
   a. fragile b. valuable c. ancient d. keen

   6. _____

7. Many of the tenants in the apartment building had *legitimate* grievances against the landlord.
   a. continuing b. legislated c. formal d. genuine

   7. _____

8. The mechanic spent two hours making a complete *appraisal* of the car.
   a. judgment b. description c. adjustment d. overhaul

   8. _____

9. "*Base* behavior toward others will not be tolerated in this camp," stated the camp director.
   a. Dull b. Destructive c. Shameful d. Joking

   9. _____

10. Dwight was proud of his *meritorious* academic success.
    a. praiseworthy b. talented c. trained d. ordinary

    10. _____

Exercise 4 Using Different Forms of Words

Decide which form of the vocabulary word in parentheses best completes the sentence. The form given may be correct. Write your answer on the answer line.

1. The antique dealer __?__ the furniture before the auction. *(appraisal)*

   1. _____

2. The __?__ of Copernicus's theory that the planets circle the sun did not occur until after the astronomer's death. *(validate)*

   2. _____

3. Caught cheating on a test, Leo behaved __?__, denying his guilt. *(base)*

   3. _____

4. Some people think that the only __?__ for judging success are how much money one has and how many friends one makes. *(criterion)*

   4. _____

5. The __?__ of garden mazes fascinates the British. *(subtle)*

   5. _____

6. Many wars in Europe have been fought over the __?__ of a monarch's claim to a throne. *(legitimate)*

   6. _____

7. Eleanor lives by the __?__ that first impressions are the most lasting. *(truism)*

   7. _____

8. In the 1972 Olympics, Mark Spitz swam __?__ and won seven gold medals. *(meritorious)*

   8. _____

9. The team's last-place standing illustrated its __?__. *(mediocre)*

   9. _____

10. Gossip about others should never be considered to be the same as __?__. *(candid)*

    10. _____

Truth and Value

Reading Comprehension

Each numbered sentence in the following passage contains an italicized vocabulary word or related form. After you read the passage, you will complete an exercise.

Pete Gray: One-Armed Major Leaguer

(1) Competition in professional baseball is so vigorous that players must have unusually *meritorious* skill in order to make the team. **(2)** Pete Wyshner Gray, an outfielder for the St. Louis Browns, illustrates this *truism* about competition and skill in baseball. With stubborn single-mindedness, this one-armed man made a name for himself, not as a curiosity but as a talented baseball player.

Born in Nanticoke, Pennsylvania, in 1917, Pete Gray had a youngster's interest in baseball. At the age of six, however, when he lost his right arm, his dream of playing ball professionally seemed doomed. Pete was determined, though, not to allow his disability to interfere with what he wanted to do. For long hours, he practiced throwing a ball up in the air and then hitting it with a bat held in the same hand. In fielding a ball, he let the ball hit his glove, tossed the ball upward, placed the glove under the stub of his arm, plucked the ball from the air—and threw it.

Pete's dedication paid off. **(3)** Although he was only a *mediocre* hitter and fielder in elementary school, he improved dramatically. **(4)** By the time he entered high school, he was the most skillful player in Nanticoke based on the three *criteria* of expert hitting, running, and fielding.

(5) After high school, Pete attained a *legitimate* status as a career player by making two semiprofessional teams. He wanted to play in the major leagues, however. **(6)** He went to several training camps for an *appraisal* by the team owners, managers, and coaches. Their verdict was that a one-armed player could never play professional baseball. **(7)** Pete felt that their judgments were unfair and even *base*. He refused to allow discrimination to interfere with his goal.

In 1943 Pete's high batting average — a league-leading .381 — won him a place with the Memphis Chicks, a minor-league team in the Southern Association. He proved to be an invaluable player and helped the team win the pennant. **(8)** His title of Most Valuable Player in the Southern Association *validated* Pete's superb athletic ability.

By 1945 Pete realized his dream — he became outfielder for the St. Louis Browns, a major-league team in those days. During the first part of the season, Pete played left field regularly and hit well.

Unfortunately, Pete played less often during the second half of the season. **(9)** He *candidly* admitted to difficulty in handling sizzling grounders and balls hit to his right. **(10)** He also confessed that some major-league pitchers had learned *subtle* ways to make him miss the ball. At the end of the 1945 baseball season, Pete decided to return to the minor leagues for the remainder of his career. Nevertheless, he had proven that disabled people could reach the top of the competitive sport of baseball.

Reading Comprehension Exercise

Each of the following statements corresponds to a numbered sentence in the passage. Each statement contains a blank and is followed by four answer choices. Decide which choice fits best in the blank. The word or phrase that you choose must express roughly the same meaning as the italicized word in the passage. Write the letter of your choice on the answer line.

1. Players must have __?__ skill in order to make a professional team.
   a. competitive   b. praiseworthy   c. acquired   d. perfected

1. _____

Copyright © 1988 Houghton Mifflin Company. All rights reserved.

Truth and Value   **117**

2. Pete Gray illustrates this __?__ about skill and competition in baseball.
   a. obvious truth   b. short story   c. proverb   d. generalization

3. Gray was only a(n) __?__ hitter and fielder in elementary school.
   a. poor   b. dedicated   c. average   d. minor

4. Pete was the most skillful player based on the three __?__ of expert hitting, running, and fielding.
   a. types   b. standards   c. reviews   d. achievements

5. Pete attained a(n) __?__ status as a career player after high school.
   a. admirable   b. public   c. complete   d. genuine

6. He went to several training camps for a(n) __?__ by team coaches.
   a. evaluation   b. agreement   c. tryout   d. decision

7. Pete felt that their judgments were unfair and even __?__ .
   a. wrong   b. ridiculous   c. shameful   d. honest

8. Being named Most Valuable Player in the Southern Association __?__ Pete's superb athletic ability.
   a. ruined   b. helped   c. returned   d. confirmed

9. Pete __?__ admitted to difficulty in handling balls hit to his right.
   a. honestly   b. soon   c. sorrowfully   d. indirectly

10. He also confessed that some major-league pitchers had learned __?__ ways to make him miss the ball.
    a. not carefully controlled   c. major
    b. not immediately obvious   d. unfair

Writing Assignment

Lloyd's of London is an unusual insurance company because it values and insures such things as the voice of an opera star or the hands of a surgeon. Choose something that you would like to insure, such as a special friend or a favorite location, and write a letter to Lloyd's, explaining why you value your choice. Use at least five vocabulary words from this lesson in your letter and underline each one.

Vocabulary Enrichment

Candid comes from the Latin word *candidus*, meaning "bright white." When a Roman citizen declared that he would run for a high office, he dressed in a white toga, or robe. He made the natural whiteness of the fabric even brighter by rubbing chalk into the robe. This shining whiteness, symbolizing honesty, purity, and morality, assured others that the character of the citizen was as unstained as the white robe that he wore. In time the color *candidus* came to stand for the person who wore the robe. This is the origin of the word *candidate*, one who runs for office.

ACTIVITY Using your dictionary, look up the following words and write their meanings and derivations. Then write a brief explanation for each, connecting the etymology with the current definition.

1. adroit   2. aquiline   3. dilapidated   4. coward   5. supercilious

Name _____ Date _____

Reading Skills

Context Clues: Substitution

Context clues are the words surrounding an unfamiliar word that can help you understand the word's meaning. In some sentences you can arrive at an accurate definition of an unknown word simply by substituting another word or words. To use substitution as a context clue, follow this three-step procedure.

PROCEDURE

1. *Read the entire sentence, omitting the difficult word and substituting the word* blank *for it*. Suppose you don't know the italicized word in the following sentence.

    The aspirin was *efficacious* in relieving my headache, and I soon felt better.

    You would say to yourself, "The aspirin was *blank* in relieving my headache, and I soon felt better."

2. *Reread the sentence, substituting a word you know that would make sense in the sentence*. You may have to try several words, but the one that makes the most sense will probably be a synonym of the unfamiliar word. In the sentence above, you might say, "The aspirin was *effective* in relieving my headache, and I soon felt better."

3. *Check the meaning of the word in the dictionary*. Although context clues are helpful, they usually provide approximate definitions only. The dictionary definition of *efficacious* is "capable of producing a desired effect."

Exercise Getting Meaning from Context by Using Substitution

Step 1: Using substitution context clues, write your own definition of the italicized word in each of the sentences in this exercise. *Step 2:* Write the appropriate dictionary definition of the word. *Step 3:* Write a sentence of your own in which you use the word according to the dictionary definition.

1. In her *eulogy* before the state senate, the governor spoke of Senator Rivera's distinguished career.

    YOUR DEFINITION _____

    DICTIONARY DEFINITION _____

    SENTENCE _____

Please turn to the next page.

Copyright © 1988 Houghton Mifflin Company. All rights reserved.   Context Clues: Substitution   119

2. Bonnie loved horses and *eschewed* the company of anyone who didn't share her love for them.

   YOUR DEFINITION _____
   DICTIONARY DEFINITION _____
   SENTENCE _____

3. After many complaints from the public, the county supervisors *rescinded* the unfair and burdensome law.

   YOUR DEFINITION _____
   DICTIONARY DEFINITION _____
   SENTENCE _____

4. If we can *allay* your fears about the dangers involved, will you join us in the search for the sunken ship?

   YOUR DEFINITION _____
   DICTIONARY DEFINITION _____
   SENTENCE _____

5. "The Constitution of the United States was made not merely for the generation that then existed, but for *posterity*—unlimited, undefined, endless, perpetual posterity." *(Henry Clay)*

   YOUR DEFINITION _____
   DICTIONARY DEFINITION _____
   SENTENCE _____

6. "Familiarity with danger makes a brave man braver, but less daring. Thus with seamen: he who goes the oftenest round Cape Horn goes the most *circumspectly*." *(Herman Melville)*

   YOUR DEFINITION _____
   DICTIONARY DEFINITION _____
   SENTENCE _____

7. Unfortunately, the meeting between the two quarreling groups only *exacerbated* their differences.

   YOUR DEFINITION _____
   DICTIONARY DEFINITION _____
   SENTENCE _____

8. To establish *hegemony* over its neighbors, the aggressive country threatened to ruin their economies.

   YOUR DEFINITION _____
   DICTIONARY DEFINITION _____
   SENTENCE _____

Context Clues: Substitution

Lesson 19

Communication

Which of the following situations involve communication?

Parents respond to a crying baby.
A track official waves a checkered flag, and drivers stop their race cars.
One computer can be connected with several others to form a network for the exchange of information.

If you accept the idea that communication is the process of sharing meaning, you will probably agree that all of the situations involve some aspect of the communication process.

Since words are necessary for communicating all but the simplest messages, this lesson focuses on verbal communication. These vocabulary words will help you to understand and describe the many ways in which people discuss ideas with others.

WORD LIST
circumlocution
discourse
euphemism
falter
literate
prattle
raconteur
reiterate
utterance
verbose

DEFINITIONS

After you have studied the definitions and example for each vocabulary word, write the word on the line to the right.

1. **circumlocution** (sûr′kəm-lō-kyōō′shən) *noun* **a.** The use of roundabout expressions or wordy and indirect language. **b.** Speech or writing that is wordy or evasive. (From the Latin *circum-*, meaning "around," and *loqui*, meaning "to speak")

   EXAMPLE The lecturer's *circumlocutions* convinced the audience that he was not familiar with the Great Barrier Reef.

2. **discourse** (dĭs′kôrs′) *noun* **a.** Verbal expression in the form of speech or writing. **b.** The formal and lengthy discussion of a subject, either written or spoken.   *intrans. verb* (dĭ-skôrs′) **a.** To speak or write formally and at length. **b.** To engage in conversation or discussion. (From the Latin word *discurrere*, meaning "to speak at length")

   EXAMPLE Rochelle enjoys the essays of Michel de Montaigne, which are *discourses* on various subjects.

   USAGE NOTE *Discourse* can mean "to discuss," but it implies formal and lengthy discussion. *Discourse* is often used with the word *on*.

3. **euphemism** (yōō′fə-mĭz′əm) *noun* The act or an example of the substitution of an inoffensive term for one that is considered offensive, unpleasant, or too direct. (From the Greek *eu-*, meaning "good," and *phēmē*, meaning "speech")

   RELATED WORDS **euphemistic** *adjective;* **euphemistically** *adverb*

   EXAMPLE The coach used the *euphemism* "high-spirited" rather than call her students "rowdy."

Communication   121

4. **falter** (fôl′tər) *intrans. verb* **a.** To speak hesitatingly; stammer. **b.** To waver in confidence. **c.** To move unsteadily; stumble. *noun* An unsteadiness in speech or action. (From the Middle English word *falteren*, meaning "to stagger")

   RELATED WORD **falteringly** *adverb*

   EXAMPLE Although Justin *faltered* as he began his speech, his voice became stronger as he grew more confident.

5. **literate** (lĭt′ər-ĭt) *adjective* **a.** Able to read and write; knowledgeable; educated. **b.** Well-written; polished. *noun* **a.** Someone who can read and write. **b.** A well-informed, educated person. (From the Latin word *littera*, meaning "letter")

   RELATED WORDS **literacy** *noun;* **literately** *adverb*

   EXAMPLE Charlemagne, a great emperor in the Middle Ages, did not become *literate* until he was an adult.

6. **prattle** (prăt′l) *intrans. verb* To talk idly or meaninglessly; babble. *trans. verb* To utter in a childish or silly way. *noun* Childish or meaningless sounds; babble.

   EXAMPLE Rosella *prattled* on endlessly about how wonderful her vacation had been.

7. **raconteur** (răk′ŏn-tûr′) *noun* A person who tells stories and anecdotes with skill and wit. (From the Old French word *raconter*, meaning "to tell")

   EXAMPLE Abraham Lincoln was a natural *raconteur* who used stories to communicate political messages.

8. **reiterate** (rē-ĭt′ə-rāt′) *trans. verb* To say over again; repeat. (From the Latin *re-*, meaning "again," and *iterare*, meaning "to repeat")

   RELATED WORD **reiteration** *noun*

   EXAMPLE Wendy *reiterated* the word *no* several times to her dog, which was intent upon chasing a neighbor's cat.

   USAGE NOTE *Iterate* and *reiterate* mean the same thing, but *reiterate* seems stronger and is used more often.

9. **utterance** (ŭt′ər-əns) *noun* **a.** The act of expressing vocally. **b.** Something that is expressed.

   RELATED WORD **utter** *verb*

   EXAMPLE When he learned that he had won the contest, he made an *utterance* of delight.

10. **verbose** (vər-bōs′) *adjective* Using or containing an excessive number of words. (From the Latin word *verbum*, meaning "word")

    RELATED WORDS **verbosely** *adverb;* **verbosity** *noun*

    EXAMPLE Because writing styles have changed, the long descriptions in eighteenth-century literature may seem *verbose* to the modern reader.

Name _____ Date _____

Exercise 1   Writing Correct Words

On the answer line, write the word from the vocabulary list that fits each definition.

1. To speak hesitatingly; stammer
2. To say over again
3. Using or containing an excessive number of words
4. Substitution of an inoffensive term for an offensive or unpleasant one
5. To talk idly or meaninglessly; babble
6. The act of expressing audibly; something said aloud
7. Able to read and write; knowledgeable; educated
8. A roundabout expression; the use of wordy, indirect language
9. Verbal expression in speech or writing
10. A skillful and witty storyteller

1. _____
2. _____
3. _____
4. _____
5. _____
6. _____
7. _____
8. _____
9. _____
10. _____

Exercise 2   Using Words Correctly

Each of the following statements contains an italicized vocabulary word. Decide whether the sentence is true or false, and write *True* or *False* on the answer line.

1. If a person uses *circumlocutions* in answering questions, he or she responds directly.
2. A person who *falters* has too many faults.
3. Parents are delighted when their children first begin to *prattle*.
4. A *verbose* acceptance speech would be clear and concise.
5. A *raconteur* pays careful attention to elegant penmanship.
6. An art historian might deliver a *discourse* on a particular painter or sculptor.
7. The cat's *utterance* might be a loud purr of contentment.
8. A *literate* person is a published writer.
9. When a teacher *reiterates* the directions for a test, he or she reads them only once.
10. A "memorial park" for animals may be a *euphemism* for a graveyard.

1. _____
2. _____
3. _____
4. _____
5. _____
6. _____
7. _____
8. _____
9. _____
10. _____

Exercise 3   Choosing the Best Word

Decide which vocabulary word or related form best completes the sentence, and write the letter of your choice on the answer line.

1. Some of the greatest __?__ are Native Americans, who tell intriguing stories handed down from the past.
   a. discourses   **b.** circumlocutions   **c.** raconteurs   **d.** falters

1. _____

Copyright © 1988 Houghton Mifflin Company. All rights reserved.   Communication

2. A person must be __?__ in order to understand food labels, signs, and newspapers.
   a. literate   b. faltering   c. verbose   d. euphemistic

3. Kelly did not __?__ in her determination to learn Chinese.
   a. prattle   b. discourse   c. reiterate   d. falter

4. The __?__ article in the medical journal was so filled with jargon that Bob found it difficult to understand.
   a. prattling   b. reiterating   c. euphemistic   d. verbose

5. In his eloquent __?__, Frederick Douglass, an abolitionist and journalist, argued for the freeing of slaves.
   a. raconteurs   b. discourses   c. prattles   d. euphemisms

6. Dr. Grodin thought that Ann's sigh of relief was actually a(n) __?__ of pain.
   a. utterance   b. discourse   c. euphemism   d. prattle

7. The unceasing __?__ of the students in the back of the room was annoying to the rest of the class.
   a. raconteur   b. euphemism   c. prattle   d. circumlocution

8. Experienced journalists can often break through the __?__ of politicians who prefer evasive statements.
   a. raconteurs   b. circumlocutions   c. literacy   d. reiterations

9. The train conductor __?__ his announcement that passengers should board the train.
   a. prattled   b. discoursed   c. faltered   d. reiterated

10. Margaret walked past the door __?__ marked "comfort station" when she was searching for a bathroom.
    a. verbosely   b. literately   c. falteringly   d. euphemistically

Exercise 4 Using Different Forms of Words

Decide which form of the vocabulary word in parentheses best completes the sentence. The form given may be correct. Write your answer on the answer line.

1. Many people agree that Mark Twain was one of the greatest __?__ in American literature. *(raconteur)*

2. Henry was uncertain about the meaning of the poet's __?__ of the words *smoke* and *fire* in each stanza. *(reiterate)*

3. When __?__ on the talent of Peter Carl Fabergé, Professor Forbes lost all track of time. *(discourse)*

4. __?__ detracts from clear and effective communication. *(verbose)*

5. The gymnast executed the back flip __?__ and lost several points. *(falter)*

6. Computer __?__ is becoming increasingly important in this technological age. *(literate)*

7. __?__ a shriek as the cat jumped onto her head, Danelle dropped the plate. *(utterance)*

8. Andrew, who could not organize his thoughts effectively, was criticized by members of the debate team for __?__. *(prattle)*

124   Communication

Name _____ Date _____

9. The brochure __?__ described the barren parcel of land as a corner of the Garden of Eden. *(euphemism)*

9. _____

10. The panelist's __?__ were annoying to the other members of the panel, who wanted to discuss the topic openly. *(circumlocution)*

10. _____

Reading Comprehension

Each numbered sentence in the following passage contains an italicized vocabulary word or related form. After you read the passage, you will complete an exercise.

The Art of Pausology

(1) Nearly everyone who has given a speech or has responded **falteringly** to questions in a classroom has been criticized for filling pauses in speech with useless words. (2) The **reiteration** of such phrases as "You know" and words or sounds such as *um, un, er,* and *well* contribute nothing to what is being said. (3) These speech fillers become mere **prattle,** reducing the impact of what is communicated. (4) A **raconteur** who punctuates his or her narrative with verbal fillers is not particularly entertaining. (5) In fact, an audience may actually be annoyed by **circumlocutions** of this kind.

(6) Effective, **literate** speakers must use silence as much as sound in order to communicate. (7) Good speakers pause to punctuate, to emphasize meaning, to arouse attention, or to allow themselves time to think of their next **utterance.** Not afflicted with the habit of vocalized pausing, they have poise as well as control over their timing.

An interesting outgrowth of these principles of good speaking was a study done by a British psychologist. His work represents an evolving area of the study of human speech. (8) Known somewhat **euphemistically** as *pausology,* it is the study of the ways in which people use their speech pauses. The scientist, in studying the impact that politicians and world leaders made during press conferences, noted that some were more effective than others. (9) One of the criteria he used for evaluating **discourse** was the number of times a speaker was interrupted. Ineffective speakers paused too long or too frequently. (10) Some would begin **verbose,** incoherent answers that were not thought out, only to stop abruptly. Interviewers often assumed that these pauses meant that the speakers had completed their answers. Therefore, the interviewers interrupted them with additional questions.

Effective speakers, on the other hand, gave certain signals that they were pausing to think. For example, one politician would respond to interviewers' questions by saying, "That is an interesting question" or "I'm glad you have raised that issue." This type of statement allowed a moment of additional time for the politician to frame an answer. Although the scientist did not advocate useless filler words or phrases, he did conclude that effective speakers develop some comfortable method of showing that they still want audience attention.

Whether you speak publicly or simply talk with others around you, it makes sense to be aware of how your use of pauses affects both the listener and the quality of the communication. Your ability to speak is every bit as important as the content of your speech or message.

Please turn to the next page.

Copyright © 1988 Houghton Mifflin Company. All rights reserved.

Communication 125

Reading Comprehension Exercise

Each of the following statements corresponds to a numbered sentence in the passage. Each statement contains a blank and is followed by four answer choices. Decide which choice fits best in the blank. The word or phrase that you choose must express roughly the same meaning as the italicized word in the passage. Write the letter of your choice on the answer line.

1. Nearly everyone who has responded __?__ to questions in a classroom has filled pauses in speech with useless words.
   a. quickly   b. appropriately   c. hesitatingly   d. humorously

2. The __?__ of such expressions as "You know" contributes nothing to what is said.
   a. repetition   b. lack   c. quality   d. nonsense

3. Such speech fillers as *uh* are __?__ .
   a. questions   c. interruptions
   b. excellent placeholders d. meaningless sounds

4. A __?__ who punctuates a narrative with verbal fillers is not especially entertaining.
   a. comedian   b. storyteller   c. performer   d. writer

5. An audience may become annoyed by such __?__ .
   a. roundabout expressions   c. confusion
   b. mistakes   d. ridiculous commentaries

6. __?__ speakers use silence as much as sound in communication.
   a. Nervous   b. Enjoyable   c. Useful   d. Knowledgeable

7. Effective speakers pause to allow themselves time to think about their next __?__ .
   a. quotation   b. gesture   c. words   d. speech

8. The study of the ways in which people use their speech pauses is known somewhat __?__ as *pausology*.
   a. negatively   b. inoffensively   c. humorously   d. randomly

9. One of the criteria used for evaluating __?__ was the number of times a speaker was interrupted.
   a. speech   b. debates   c. press conferences   d. questions

10. Some speakers began __?__ answers that they had not thought about.
    a. simple   b. literary   c. wordy   d. incorrect

1. _____
2. _____
3. _____
4. _____
5. _____
6. _____
7. _____
8. _____
9. _____
10. _____

Practice with Analogies

DIRECTIONS On the answer line, write the vocabulary word that completes each analogy.

See page 79 for some strategies to use with analogies.

1. LEGITIMATE : ILLEGITIMATE : : __?__ : illiterate
2. SPEECH : ORATOR : : story : __?__
3. ANNOUNCE : PROCLAIM : : chatter : __?__
4. CONCISE : SUCCINCT : : __?__ : wordy
5. DO : REPEAT : : say : __?__

1. _____
2. _____
3. _____
4. _____
5. _____

126   Communication

Lesson 20

The Roots -scribe- and -script-

The Latin roots -scribe- and -script- serve as the basis of many of our English words. In Latin the word *scribere* means "to write." Today the *script* of a play is the writing that actors memorize. A *manuscript* is a written document or book. In the Middle Ages, a *scribe* copied books by carefully writing each word. In this lesson you will learn other words that come from the Latin roots -scribe- and -script- and that are connected, in some way, with writing.

WORD LIST
ascribe
circumscribe
inscribe
nondescript
prescribe
proscribe
scripture
subscribe
subscript
transcribe

DEFINITIONS

After you have studied the definitions and example for each vocabulary word, write the word on the line to the right.

1. **ascribe** (ə-skrīb′) *trans. verb* To regard as caused by; assign; attribute. (From the Latin *ad-*, meaning "to," and *scribere*, meaning "to write")

   EXAMPLE The committee *ascribed* poor attendance at the lecture to the lack of advertising.

2. **circumscribe** (sûr′kəm-skrīb′) *trans. verb* **a.** To draw a line around; encircle. **b.** To confine within or as if within bounds; limit or restrict. **c.** To construct or be constructed around a geometrical figure so as to touch as many points as possible: *a circle circumscribing a triangle.* (From the Latin *circum-*, meaning "around," and *scribere*)

   EXAMPLE The outdoor running track *circumscribed* an area of grass and weeds.

3. **inscribe** (ĭn-skrīb′) *trans. verb* **a.** To write, print, carve, or engrave words or letters on a surface. **b.** To sign or write a brief message in or on a book or picture when giving it as a gift; dedicate to someone. **c.** To enter a name on a list or in a register; enroll. **d.** To draw within a figure so as to touch in as many places as possible: *inscribe a star within a pentagon.* (From the Latin *in-*, meaning "in," and *scribere*)

   RELATED WORD **inscription** *noun*

   EXAMPLE The sculptors *inscribed* their names on the base of the monument.

The Roots -scribe- and -script-

4. **nondescript** (nŏn′dĭ-skrĭpt′) *adjective* Lacking in distinctive or interesting qualities and therefore difficult to describe; dull; drab.

   EXAMPLE   The lost dog was a *nondescript* color and breed.

5. **prescribe** (prĭ-skrīb′) *trans. verb* **a.** To order or recommend the use of a remedy or treatment. **b.** To set down as a rule or guide; dictate. **c.** To state or indicate specifically; specify. (From the Latin *prae-*, meaning "before," and *scribere*)

   RELATED WORDS   **prescription** *noun;* **prescriptive** *adjective*

   EXAMPLE   The coach *prescribed* ice packs for Joe's bruised ankle.

6. **proscribe** (prō-skrīb′) *trans. verb* **a.** To prohibit; forbid as harmful or unlawful. **b.** To denounce or condemn. (From the Latin *pro-*, meaning "in front," and *scribere*)

   RELATED WORD   **proscription** *noun*

   EXAMPLE   A notice posted on the lifeguard's stand at the beach *proscribed* surfing.

7. **scripture** (skrĭp′chər) *noun* **a.** A sacred writing or book. **b.** A statement regarded as authoritative. (From the Latin word *scribere*)

   RELATED WORD   **scriptural** *adjective*

   EXAMPLE   The ancient *scripture* had been carefully preserved.

8. **subscribe** (səb-skrīb′) *intrans. verb* **a.** To contract to receive and pay in advance for something, such as a magazine, concert tickets, etc. **b.** To agree or approve: *subscribe to a belief*. (From the Latin *sub-*, meaning "under," and *scribere*)

   RELATED WORDS   **subscriber** *noun;* **subscription** *noun*

   EXAMPLE   George *subscribes* to a monthly book club.

9. **subscript** (sŭb′skrĭpt′) *noun*   A distinguishing symbol, such as a letter or numeral, written below and to the right of a letter or number, as in a mathematical expression or chemical formula. (From the Latin *sub-*, meaning "under," and *scriptus*, meaning "written")

   EXAMPLE   Monica's equations were incorrect because she had forgotten to include the necessary *subscripts*.

10. **transcribe** (trăn-skrīb′) *trans. verb* **a.** To make a written or typewritten copy of, as from notes. **b.** To adapt or arrange a musical composition for a voice or instrument other than the original. (From the Latin *trans-*, meaning "across," and *scribere*)

    RELATED WORDS   **transcript** *noun;* **transcription** *noun*

    EXAMPLE   Russ *transcribed* the minutes of the club meeting.

4. _____

5. _____

6. _____
MEMORY CUE   *Proscribe* means "prohibit."

7. _____

8. _____

9. _____
USAGE NOTE   In contrast to a subscript, a *super*script is written *above* and to the right of a letter or number.

10. _____

The Roots *-scribe-* and *-script*

Name _____ Date _____

Exercise 1 Writing Correct Words

On the answer line, write the word from the vocabulary list that fits each definition.

1. To prohibit or forbid as harmful or unlawful   1. _____
2. A symbol written below and to the right of a letter or number   2. _____
3. To regard as caused by; attribute   3. _____
4. To make a written or typewritten copy of something   4. _____
5. To surround by a line or boundary; limit or restrict   5. _____
6. To write, carve, or engrave words or letters on a surface; dedicate   6. _____
7. Without distinguishing characteristics; drab   7. _____
8. To advise the use of a remedy or treatment; set down as a guide   8. _____
9. To contract to receive and pay in advance for something   9. _____
10. A body of writing considered to be authoritative or sacred   10. _____

Exercise 2 Using Words Correctly

Each of the following statements contains an italicized vocabulary word. Decide whether the sentence is true or false, and write *True* or *False* on the answer line.

1. A *subscript* 2 is written beneath and to the right of the *H* to show that there are two atoms of hydrogen in one molecule of water.   1. _____
2. A clown whose appearance is *nondescript* might have flaming red hair and a nose like a doorknob.   2. _____
3. A secretary might *transcribe* the proceedings of the meeting.   3. _____
4. People save money when they *prescribe* to magazines.   4. _____
5. An author might *inscribe* a message on the flyleaf of a book.   5. _____
6. Many religions have *scriptures* that preserve their laws and beliefs.   6. _____
7. When experts *ascribe* a painting to a particular artist, they sell the painting for that artist.   7. _____
8. If people *subscribe* to a certain belief, they oppose it.   8. _____
9. A highway might be said to *circumscribe* a major metropolitan area.   9. _____
10. Dentists *proscribe* frequent brushing and flossing of the teeth.   10. _____

Exercise 3 Choosing the Best Word

Decide which vocabulary word or related form best completes the sentence, and write the letter of your choice on the answer line.

1. Because of Bonnie's beautiful penmanship, she was selected to __?__ her classmates' names on their high school diplomas.   1. _____
   a. prescribe   b. circumscribe   c. proscribe   d. inscribe

Copyright © 1988 Houghton Mifflin Company. All rights reserved.   The Roots *-scribe-* and *-script-*   129

2. Many people ___?___ to this magazine because they enjoy its photographs.
   a. subscribe   b. subscript   c. proscribe   d. circumscribe

3. Doctors ___?___ rest and fluids for the common cold.
   a. prescribe   b. subscribe   c. proscribe   d. ascribe

4. Pat's family reads a few verses of ___?___ every evening.
   a. subscription   b. prescription   c. scripture   d. transcription

5. Until the Nineteenth Amendment was passed, voting by women in the United States was in effect ___?___ .
   a. prescribed   b. proscribed   c. ascribed   d. inscribed

6. Leah was unable to read her class notes well enough to ___?___ them.
   a. subscribe   b. ascribe   c. inscribe   d. transcribe

7. In mathematics a ___?___ following a number usually indicates the numeric base that is being used.
   a. scripture   b. prescription   c. nondescript   d. subscript

8. In order to draw attention to the vivid colors of the flowers, the artist ___?___ the entire floral arrangement with a black border.
   a. prescribed   b. inscribed   c. circumscribed   d. proscribed

9. The soup consisted of a watery broth and a few ___?___ vegetables.
   a. subscribed   b. ascribed   c. nondescript   d. inscribed

10. The hundred-year-old man ___?___ his longevity to his habit of walking two miles every day.
    a. subscribed   b. ascribed   c. prescribed   d. proscribed

Exercise 4   Using Different Forms of Words

Decide which form of the vocabulary word in parentheses best completes the sentence. The form given may be correct. Write your answer on the answer line.

1. The pharmacist could not fill Maxine's ___?___ . *(prescribe)*

2. Scott spent many hours looking up ___?___ references. *(scripture)*

3. The veterinarian told the Gordons to ___?___ the activity of their cat until its stitches healed. *(circumscribe)*

4. The reversal of the two ___?___ in the chemical equation caused the scientist's experiment to fail. *(subscript)*

5. ___?___ her theatrical success to the support of her family, Annette accepted the award for her performance. *(ascribe)*

6. A ___?___ of the program can be ordered from the television station. *(transcribe)*

7. The ___?___ on the old tombstone was almost entirely worn away. *(inscribe)*

8. Erroll's parents ___?___ his dating until he was eighteen. *(proscribe)*

9. The detective wore a ___?___ khaki raincoat and a plaid hat. *(nondescript)*

10. Emily realized that her magazine ___?___ had expired. *(subscribe)*

Reading Comprehension

Each numbered sentence in the following passage contains an italicized vocabulary word or related form. After you read the passage, you will complete an exercise.

Egyptian Sands

(1) As the copper-colored sun slipped behind the pyramids, the archaeologists finished **circumscribing** the area where they would begin tomorrow's excavation. (2) Packing their tools, they spoke excitedly about their discovery of a fragile papyrus **scripture** at the entrance to an ancient tomb. (3) Tentatively **ascribing** it to the Sixth Dynasty of the Egyptian pharaohs, they were sure that they had found an important source of historical information.

In the fading light, Dr. Philip Arnold, one of the archaeologists, examined the document, now protected by a plastic envelope.

"Look at these hieroglyphics," Dr. Arnold said to his colleagues. (4) "Never before in my experience have I encountered Egyptian pictorial symbols accompanied by **subscripts**. (5) I can hardly wait to compare these with the **inscriptions** that are undoubtedly on the walls of the tomb."

(6) "I'll **transcribe** the symbols onto our code sheets before tomorrow's dig," said Dr. Arita Youssef, another member of the team. (7) As she prepared to leave the site, she spoke excitedly about how famous they would be when they published their findings in the archaeological journal to which all members of their profession **subscribed**.

None of the group responded to Dr. Youssef's comment, but as they walked back to camp, all mused happily about their good fortune. Striding ahead of the others, Dr. Arnold suddenly decided to remove his heavy socks and boots to relax his tired feet. (8) Forgetting the **proscription** against walking barefoot, he began to enjoy the warmth of the rough sand. He almost ignored the slight pinch on his ankle as he envisioned newspaper headlines. (9) Looking down, however, he watched with horror as a **nondescript** but very poisonous scorpion crawled back into the sand.

"Help!" he shouted to his colleagues. "I've been bitten! (10) Get me the serum that the university physician **prescribed**."

Dr. Youssef raced back to the tent, quickly returning to attend to the wound and administer the serum. Shaking her head at Dr. Arnold's foolish behavior, Dr. Youssef said gently, "Dr. Arnold, you ought to be more cautious about the Egyptian sands. They hold more than history, you know."

Reading Comprehension Exercise

Each of the following statements corresponds to a numbered sentence in the passage. Each statement contains a blank and is followed by four answer choices. Decide which choice fits best in the blank. The word or phrase that you choose must express roughly the same meaning as the italicized word in the passage. Write the letter of your choice on the answer line.

1. The archaeologists ___?___ the area for tomorrow's excavation.
   a. studied   b. encircled   c. closed   d. coded

2. The archaeologists had discovered a(n) ___?___ made of papyrus.
   a. scroll   b. magazine   c. ancient painting   d. sacred writing

3. They tentatively ___?___ the document to the Sixth Dynasty.
   a. presented   b. identified   c. located   d. assigned

4. Dr. Arnold had never before encountered pictorial symbols with __?__ .
   a. symbols placed below   c. footnotes
   b. the artist's signature   d. ancient marks

5. Dr. Arnold looked forward to comparing the document with __?__ that would be on the tomb walls.
   a. signs   b. rocks   c. engravings   d. details

6. Dr. Youssef planned to __?__ the symbols.
   a. copy   b. compare   c. research   d. underline

7. Dr. Youssef thought the team would be famous when they published their findings in a journal that archaeologists __?__ .
   a. know   b. order and pay for   c. make important   d. analyze

8. Dr. Arnold forgot the __?__ walking barefoot.
   a. advice about   c. signs regarding
   b. problems of   d. prohibition against

9. He saw the __?__ but poisonous scorpion.
   a. ugly   c. undistinguished-looking
   b. crawling   d. fierce-looking

10. Dr. Arnold shouted for the serum that the university physician had __?__ .
    a. ordered   b. asked for   c. consulted   d. treated

4. _____
5. _____
6. _____
7. _____
8. _____
9. _____
10. _____

Writing Assignment

Choose a period of history or a group of people, and do some library research about the history of writing. For example, you might investigate the ideographs of the Chinese or the Native Americans, or the hieroglyphics of the Egyptians. Write a brief report about the development of a specific form of writing; in the report use at least five of the vocabulary words from this lesson. Underline each of the words that you use.

Vocabulary Enrichment

As you have learned in this lesson, the word *proscribe* means both "to prohibit as harmful or unlawful" and "to denounce or condemn." In ancient Rome, however, the Latin word that *proscribe* comes from had only one meaning. To *proscribe* meant "to declare someone an outlaw," and a *proscription* was a public notice with the names of Roman citizens who had broken a law. Proscribed individuals were captured and executed by soldiers, and their property was confiscated by the government.

ACTIVITY Using a dictionary, look up the following words and write their Latin roots and their definitions. Then write a brief explanation of the connection between each root and definition.

1. dictator   2. magistrate   3. confiscate   4. clemency   5. innocent
6. fugitive

Lesson 21

Words from Spanish

At one time the Spanish empire covered more than half of South America, all of Central America and Mexico, and much of what is now the western United States. The Spanish empire in the Americas ended in the 1800s. Soon the population of the United States contained many Hispanic people, whose culture became part of the larger culture. In time, Spanish-speaking people from Puerto Rico, Cuba, and other parts of the Americas immigrated to the United States mainland. These groups, too, introduced Spanish words that were adopted into the English language. Geography, ranching, architecture, and food are a few of the areas from which these borrowed words came.

For example, the word *savanna* is an English adaptation of the Spanish *zavana*, meaning a treeless plain, while *sierra* refers to a chain of hills or mountains. The Hispanic experience in cattle ranching is reflected in such words as *corral*, *gaucho*, *lariat*, *lasso*, *ranch*, and *rodeo*. Architects include Spanish terms such as *patio* and *plaza* in their building plans. Spanish food such as paella, tortilla, and tuna became part of the American diet.

The words in this lesson are additional examples of Spanish terms that have became part of American English.

WORD LIST
aficionado
bonanza
bravado
embargo
flotilla
hacienda
junta
peccadillo
peon
renegade

DEFINITIONS

After you have studied the definitions and example for each vocabulary word, write the word on the line to the right.

1. **aficionado** (ə-fĭsh′ē-ə-nä′dō, ə-fĭs′ē-ə-nä′dō) *noun* A fan; an enthusiastic admirer.
   EXAMPLE Melanie is an *aficionado* of the sport of water polo and enjoys cheering for her favorite team.

   1. _____

2. **bonanza** (bə-năn′zə) *noun* **a.** A source of wealth or luck. **b.** A rich mine.
   EXAMPLE The hit play was a box-office *bonanza* that made its author and producers rich.

   2. _____

3. **bravado** (brə-vä′dō) *noun* False bravery; swaggering courage.
   EXAMPLE Simeon was merely displaying *bravado* in challenging the champion to a game.

   3. _____

4. **embargo** (ĕm-bär′gō) *noun* **a.** A government order preventing or prohibiting trade with a given nation. **b.** A prohibition. *verb* To impose an embargo upon. (From the Spanish word *embargar*, meaning "to impede")

   EXAMPLE The American *embargo* against importing Cuban sugar is long-standing.

   4. _____

5. **flotilla** (flō-tĭl′ə) *noun* **a.** A small fleet: *a flotilla of ships.* **b.** A small group resembling a small fleet of ships: *a flotilla of taxicabs.* (From the Spanish word *flotilla*, meaning "small fleet")

   EXAMPLE The *flotilla* of Christopher Columbus included the *Niña*, *Pinta*, and *Santa María*.

   5. _____

6. **hacienda** (hä′sē-ĕn′də) *noun* **a.** A large estate, ranch, or plantation. **b.** The main house of such an estate.

   EXAMPLE The Gutierrezes are very wealthy and easily maintain a large *hacienda* near Cuernavaca.

   6. _____

7. **junta** (ho͞on′tə, jŭn′tə) *noun* A group of rulers, particularly one seizing power after the overthrow of a government. (From the Spanish word *junta*, meaning "conference")

   EXAMPLE After years of careful planning, the *junta* seized power and ruled for many years.

   7. _____

8. **peccadillo** (pĕk′ə-dĭl′ō) *noun* A small fault or transgression. (From the Spanish word *pecadillo*, meaning "small sin")

   EXAMPLE "I don't criticize his *peccadillos* because my own faults are enormous," Larry admitted.

   8. _____

9. **peon** (pē′ŏn′, pē′ən) *noun* An unskilled laborer; a farm worker.
   RELATED WORD **peonage** *noun*

   EXAMPLE For very little money, *peons* were expected to work long hours in the hot sun.

   9. _____

10. **renegade** (rĕn′ĭ-gād′) *noun* A traitor or outlaw; a rebel.

    EXAMPLE The Whigs considered Lord Cavendish a *renegade* for voting with the Tories.

    10. _____

134   Words from Spanish

Name _____ Date _____

Exercise 1 Writing Correct Words

On the answer line, write the word from the vocabulary list that fits each definition.

1. A minor fault
2. A small group of ships
3. A government order prohibiting trade
4. A fan or enthusiastic admirer
5. A rebel or traitor
6. A group of rulers
7. A large estate or plantation
8. A show of false courage
9. A source of wealth or luck
10. An unskilled laborer

1. _____
2. _____
3. _____
4. _____
5. _____
6. _____
7. _____
8. _____
9. _____
10. _____

Exercise 2 Using Words Correctly

Each of the following statements contains an italicized vocabulary word. Decide whether the sentence is true or false, and write *True* or *False* on the answer line.

1. A film that is a box-office *bonanza* earns very little money.
2. *Haciendas* are usually found in the heart of the city.
3. A football *aficionado* might attend every home game.
4. One's *bravado* might collapse in the face of real danger.
5. A *peon* usually earns as much as the president of a corporation.
6. A *renegade* does not follow the crowd.
7. An *embargo* increases the exchange of goods between nations.
8. Many *juntas* have gained power by overthrowing governments.
9. There is usually a *flotilla* of taxicabs at an airport.
10. Respect for parents is a *peccadillo*.

1. _____
2. _____
3. _____
4. _____
5. _____
6. _____
7. _____
8. _____
9. _____
10. _____

Exercise 3 Choosing the Best Definition

For each italicized vocabulary word in the following sentences, write the letter of the best definition on the answer line.

1. During World War II, an epic retreat from Dunkirk in France was carried out by a *flotilla* of military and civilian craft.
   a. score   b. fleet   c. army   d. commander

2. In 1985 Congress voted for an *embargo* against Nicaragua.
   a. blockade   c. order preventing trade
   b. declaration   d. shipping license

1. _____

2. _____

Copyright © 1988 Houghton Mifflin Company. All rights reserved.   **Words from Spanish**   135

3. Phil, a baseball *aficionado*, has been to every major-league park.
   a. expert   b. trainer   c. fan   d. owner

   3. _____

4. The small South American country was ruled by a military *junta*.
   a. group of rulers   c. band
   b. group of volunteers   d. commander

   4. _____

5. Lenore's *bravado* gave way to panic when the tests were distributed.
   a. false courage   b. cowardice   c. happiness   d. bravery

   5. _____

6. The winter's record snowfall was a *bonanza* to ski-slope owners.
   a. source of worry   c. source of wealth
   b. source of joy   d. source of humor

   6. _____

7. In Fielding's novel *Tom Jones*, Sophia forgives Tom his *peccadillos*.
   a. happy wanderings   c. merry escapades
   b. small faults   d. petty lies

   7. _____

8. In old Mexico the *peons* had to work long hours in the fields.
   a. farm workers   b. artisans   c. volunteers   d. ranchers

   8. _____

9. The *hacienda* has been in the Montalvo family for eight generations.
   a. factory   b. countryside   c. estate   d. hut

   9. _____

10. The *renegades* from the infantry were court-martialed.
    a. officers   b. heroes   c. lost soldiers   d. rebels

    10. _____

Exercise 4   Choosing the Best Word

Decide which vocabulary word or related form best expresses the meaning of the italicized word or phrase in the sentence. On the answer line, write the letter of that word.

1. Estelle, who is an *enthusiastic admirer* of Italian food, has a dozen Italian cookbooks.
   a. embargo   b. peon   c. aficionado   d. renegade

   1. _____

2. A *group of ships* met the *Queen Mary* as it sailed into the harbor.
   a. flotilla   b. junta   c. peccadillo   d. bonanza

   2. _____

3. The civilian *group of rulers* was overthrown by the military.
   a. aficionado   b. junta   c. peon   d. renegade

   3. _____

4. The boys shouted at each other with *false bravery* but did not fight.
   a. aficionado   b. peccadillo   c. bravado   d. bonanza

   4. _____

5. Many years ago in Argentina, a young man learned a trade that freed him from his *condition of being an unskilled laborer*.
   a. hacienda   b. peccadillo   c. bonanza   d. peonage

   5. _____

6. A *rebel*, Will spent a lot of time in the vice principal's office.
   a. embargo   b. renegade   c. bravado   d. peon

   6. _____

7. After the shearing, all hands feasted at the *main house on the estate*.
   a. aficionado   b. bonanza   c. hacienda   d. junta

   7. _____

8. The candidate had a few *small faults* but nothing very damaging.
   a. peccadillos   b. peons   c. bravados   d. juntas

   8. _____

9. No ships went in or out of Gdynia during the *trade prohibition*.
   a. aficionado   b. renegade   c. embargo   d. bonanza

   9. _____

10. Sponsoring the Olympic Games was a *source of wealth* for the city.
    a. bonanza   b. peccadillo   c. flotilla   d. bravado

    10. _____

Words from Spanish

Reading Comprehension

Each numbered sentence in the following passage contains an italicized vocabulary word. After you read the passage, you will complete an exercise.

La Ranchera

The history of the United States is filled with stories of immigrants who came to the country with nothing and built successful lives for themselves and their posterity. Doña Mercedes in this story is not a real person, but she exemplifies exceptional women in every group.

(1) Mercedes Albuquerque de Irigoyen oversees the enormous *Hacienda* del Norte, with its ten thousand head of cattle, two thousand sheep, fields planted with three crops, and natural gas deposits. Doña Mercedes (as she is often called) was born seventy-six years ago in a small Latin American country. **(2)** When *renegades* took over the government, the Albuquerques along with other families decided to seek their freedom in the United States. **(3)** The *junta,* however, did not allow anyone to leave. **(4)** For this reason the families had to set off secretly at night in a *flotilla* of fishing boats.

When they arrived in the United States, the Albuquerques sought work in the fields of west Texas. **(5)** The working conditions were only slightly better than those of *peons,* but after several years the Albuquerques, along with another immigrant family, the Irigoyens, bought a small parcel of land that they could farm themselves. **(6)** Many of their friends thought this was just an act of *bravado,* but within ten years the Hacienda del Norte was one of the largest ranches in the area. When Mercedes married Pascual Irigoyen Ruiz, the son of the co-owners of the ranch, everyone knew that the Hacienda del Norte would continue to thrive.

(7) Both Mercedes and Pascual were *aficionados* of every new advance in ranching methods. By employing them judiciously, the ranch continued to grow, as did the Irigoyen family. Mercedes and Pascual had four children, all of whom stayed on the ranch with their families. After Pascual died, all of them helped to run the place, but Mercedes was clearly the final authority.

(8) The discovery of natural gas on the property in the late 1960s proved to be a *bonanza,* and the Irigoyens did a fine job of exploiting this new resource. **(9)** With the Middle East oil *embargo* in the 1970s, domestic sources of oil and gas were in great demand.

The success of Doña Mercedes and her family has been a great benefit to many people. The Irigoyens built two local schools, and over the years many newcomers to this country started a new life by working at the Hacienda del Norte.

To this day, Doña Mercedes remains actively involved in running the ranch, and she is a source of joy and pride to all who know her. **(10)** Of course, she has her *peccadillos,* such as riding her favorite palomino at breakneck speed across the open plains; but her life has been one of purpose and achievement, and those values are carried on by her children and grandchildren.

Please turn to the next page.

Copyright © 1988 Houghton Mifflin Company. All rights reserved.

Words from Spanish

Reading Comprehension Exercise

Each of the following statements corresponds to a numbered sentence in the passage. Each statement contains a blank and is followed by four answer choices. Decide which choice fits best in the blank. The word or phrase that you choose must express roughly the same meaning as the italicized word in the passage. Write the letter of your choice on the answer line.

1. Mercedes Albuquerque de Irigoyen oversees the __?__.
   a. ranch   b. work   c. bills   d. land

2. __?__ took over the government in Mercedes's native land.
   a. Military officers   b. Outlaws   c. Tyrants   d. A group

3. The __?__ allowed no one to leave.
   a. government   c. group of rulers
   b. council   d. revolutionaries

4. The families escaped in a __?__ of boats.
   a. pair   b. navy   c. large fleet   d. small group

5. When they arrived, the working conditions of the Albuquerques and Irigoyens was only slightly better than that of __?__.
   a. farmers   b. unskilled laborers   c. artisans   d. ranchers

6. Friends thought that the purchase of land was an act of __?__.
   a. false courage   b. false hope   c. bravery   d. distinction

7. The Irigoyens were __?__ of modern ranching techniques.
   a. afraid   b. wary   c. admirers   d. defenders

8. The discovery of natural gas was a __?__.
   a. source of happiness   c. source of wealth
   b. source of trouble   d. source of fuel

9. In the 1970s there was a __?__ oil from the Middle East.
   a. trade restriction on   c. domestic source of
   b. glut of   d. scarcity of

10. Mercedes has some __?__.
    a. major talents   c. arguments
    b. minor faults   d. fine qualities

1. _____
2. _____
3. _____
4. _____
5. _____
6. _____
7. _____
8. _____
9. _____
10. _____

Writing Assignment

You are a young Spaniard traveling with the conquistadors in South America in the sixteenth century, and you are responsible for keeping a detailed diary to be published when you return to Spain in two years. Write a sample day's entry, using at least four of the words in this lesson and underlining each one. Consult an encyclopedia or other reference book as needed.

Reading Skills

The Prefixes *ex-* and *e-*

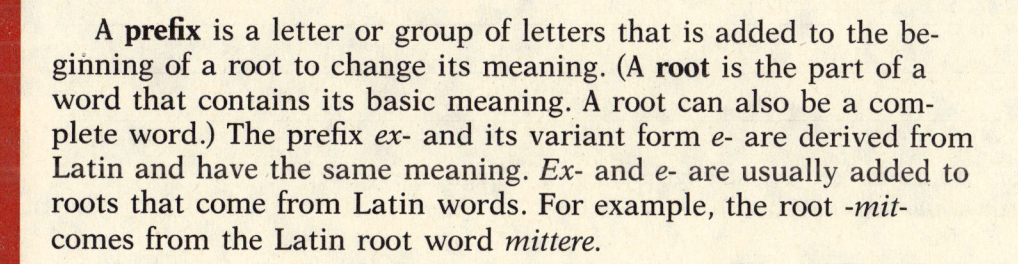

A **prefix** is a letter or group of letters that is added to the beginning of a root to change its meaning. (A **root** is the part of a word that contains its basic meaning. A root can also be a complete word.) The prefix *ex-* and its variant form *e-* are derived from Latin and have the same meaning. *Ex-* and *e-* are usually added to roots that come from Latin words. For example, the root *-mit-* comes from the Latin root word *mittere*.

PREFIX MEANING	ROOT WORD	WORD	WORD DEFINITION
out, out from	*mittere*, "to send"	emit	to send out
	cavare, "to hollow"	excavate	to hollow out

When the prefix *ex-* is added with a hyphen to a whole word, as in *ex-president*, it has the special meaning of "former."

The more prefixes and roots you know, the more often you will be able to analyze unfamiliar words. Use the following procedure to determine the meaning of words that begin with a prefix.

PROCEDURE

1. *Substitute the prefix and root definitions for the prefix and root.* The word *erupt* is formed from the prefix *e-* and the Latin root *-rupt-* from the root word *rumpere* (also the root of such words as *disrupt* and *interrupt*). The prefix means "out" or "out from," and the root means "to break."

2. *Think of possible definitions of the entire word.* Combining the prefix and root definitions given above results in "to break out from."

3. *Check your definition of the word in the dictionary.* Word analysis will give you only an approximate definition. A dictionary definition of *erupt* is "to emerge violently from restraint or limits; explode."

Exercise Using the Prefixes *ex-* and *e-*

Each sentence on the next page contains an italicized word beginning with the prefix *ex-* or *e-*. The sentence is followed by the appropriate Latin root word and its meaning. *Step 1:* Write your own definition of the word. *Step 2:* Write the dictionary definition of the word. Choose the definition that best fits the way the word is used in the sentence. *Step 3:* Write a sentence of your own in which you use the word correctly.

Please turn to the next page.

1. Carlos *exerts* as much effort in math as he does in history. (Root word: *serere,* "to bring forth")

   YOUR DEFINITION _____
   DICTIONARY DEFINITION _____
   SENTENCE _____

2. The exercise club's *exorbitant* fees discouraged many people from joining. (Root word: *orbita,* "path")

   YOUR DEFINITION _____
   DICTIONARY DEFINITION _____
   SENTENCE _____

3. Mrs. Weigand helped Lisa to *enumerate* her strengths for her college applications. (Root word: *numerus,* "number")

   YOUR DEFINITION _____
   DICTIONARY DEFINITION _____
   SENTENCE _____

4. Mr. Henshaw was in such an *expansive* mood that he extended the deadline for our term projects. (Root word: *pandere,* "to spread")

   YOUR DEFINITION _____
   DICTIONARY DEFINITION _____
   SENTENCE _____

5. Riana always manages to *evade* washing the dishes. (Root word: *vadere,* "to go")

   YOUR DEFINITION _____
   DICTIONARY DEFINITION _____
   SENTENCE _____

6. The rumor *emanated* from one of the government agencies. (Root word: *manare,* "to flow")

   YOUR DEFINITION _____
   DICTIONARY DEFINITION _____
   SENTENCE _____

7. The new supervisor issued strict *edicts* concerning office procedures. (Root word: *dicere,* "to speak")

   YOUR DEFINITION _____
   DICTIONARY DEFINITION _____
   SENTENCE _____

Lesson 22

Boldness

People are held in high regard after they achieve great feats. The first mountain climber to reach the top of Mount Everest, the first astronaut to walk on the moon, and the first aviator to break the sound barrier have gained international attention and praise for their daring accomplishments. Courage, perseverance, and the willingness to take risks are qualities that all bold individuals seem to share. In this lesson you will learn words about boldness.

WORD LIST
assert
dauntless
ferocity
flout
headstrong
incisive
outspoken
temerity
vehement
vibrant

DEFINITIONS

After you have studied the definitions and example for each vocabulary word, write the word on the line to the right.

1. **assert** (ə-sûrt′) *trans. verb* To state or express positively, forcefully, or boldly; affirm. (From the Latin word *assertus*, meaning "claimed")
   RELATED WORDS **assertion** *noun;* **assertive** *adjective*
   EXAMPLE The defendants in the burglary trial repeatedly *assert* that they are innocent.

2. **dauntless** (dônt′lĭs, dŏnt′lĭs) *adjective* Not able to be discouraged or threatened; bold; audacious. (From the Latin word *domitare*, meaning "to subdue")
   RELATED WORDS **daunt** *verb;* **dauntlessly** *adverb*
   EXAMPLE The *dauntless* Sir Percival slew the dragon that had terrorized the fair damsel.

3. **ferocity** (fə-rŏs′ĭ-tē) *noun* Savagery; fierceness; barbarity. (From the Latin word *ferus*, meaning "untamed")
   RELATED WORD **ferocious** *adjective*
   EXAMPLE The *ferocity* of the lion's growl frightened the children at the zoo.

4. **flout** (flout) *trans. verb* To show scorn or contempt for; show defiance.
   EXAMPLE The sailor *flouted* the instructions of her captain and was confined to quarters.

1. _____

2. _____

3. _____

4. _____
USAGE NOTE *Flout* and *flaunt* are often confused. *Flout* means "to defy openly." *Flaunt* means "to show off."

Boldness   141

5. **headstrong** (hĕd′strông′, hĕd′strŏng′) *adjective*   Determined to have one's own way and to do as one pleases; obstinate.
   EXAMPLE   Ezekiel is a *headstrong* child who plays only games of his own choosing.

6. **incisive** (ĭn-sī′sĭv) *adjective*   **a.** Sharp; keen; perceptive: *an incisive comment.*   **b.** Able to analyze in depth. (From the Latin *in-*, meaning "into," and *caedere*, meaning "to cut")
   RELATED WORDS   **incisively** *adverb;* **incisiveness** *noun*
   EXAMPLE   Joseph Frank has made some *incisive* remarks on *Crime and Punishment*.

7. **outspoken** (out-spō′kən) *adjective*   Spoken without reserve; frank; unrestrained in speech; forthright.
   RELATED WORD   **outspokenness** *noun*
   EXAMPLE   Alice Roosevelt Longworth was an *outspoken* member of Washington society for many years.

8. **temerity** (tə-mĕr′ĭ-tē) *noun*   Foolish or heedless disregard of danger; rash boldness; impudence. (From the Latin word *temeritas*, meaning "rashness")
   EXAMPLE   Prudence had the *temerity* to criticize the paintings at the Livingstones' when she spent the weekend in their home.

9. **vehement** (vē′ə-mənt) *adjective*   Showing intense emotion or passion; forceful. (From the Latin word *vehementer*, meaning "eagerly" or "violently")
   RELATED WORD   **vehemently** *adverb*
   EXAMPLE   The conservationist offered a *vehement* appeal for the park to be saved.

10. **vibrant** (vī′brənt) *adjective*   Pulsing with energy; vigorous; lively. (From the Latin word *vibrans*, meaning "vibrating")
    RELATED WORDS   **vibrancy** *noun;* **vibrantly** *adverb*
    EXAMPLE   The audience loudly applauded Williamson's *vibrant* performance in *Hamlet*.

5. _____

6. _____
USAGE NOTE Compare with *decisive* (literally, "cutting off"), which means "conclusive," "resolute," or "unmistakable."

7. _____

8. _____
USAGE NOTE The adjective formed from the same Latin root is *temerarious*.

9. _____

10. _____

Boldness

Name _____ Date _____ Boldness

Exercise 1 Matching Words and Definitions

Match the definition in Column B with the word in Column A. Write the letter of the correct definition on the answer line.

Column A   *Column B*
1. incisive   a. to declare positively; affirm
2. vibrant   b. showing intense emotion; forceful
3. ferocity   c. fearless; incapable of being discouraged
4. outspoken   d. keen, sharp, perceptive; able to analyze in depth
5. flout   e. stubborn; obstinate; determined
6. vehement   f. pulsating with energy
7. assert   g. savagery; barbarity
8. temerity   h. frank, forthright; unrestrained in speech
9. dauntless   i. to show defiance or scorn
10. headstrong   j. reckless boldness without concern for danger

1. _____
2. _____
3. _____
4. _____
5. _____
6. _____
7. _____
8. _____
9. _____
10. _____

Exercise 2 Using Words Correctly

Decide whether the italicized vocabulary word has been used correctly in the sentence. On the answer line, write *Correct* for correct use and *Incorrect* for incorrect use.

1. The *ferocity* of the tiger frightened the explorer.
2. The soldiers had such *temerity* that whenever the enemy attacked, they retreated.
3. Erica was a *dauntless* mountain climber and kept climbing even after her fall.
4. Lavinia is a *headstrong* girl and will do what she wishes.
5. The artist used black, brown, gray, and other *vibrant* colors in his painting.
6. People who lack confidence frequently *assert* their opinions.
7. The Town Council voiced *vehement* disapproval of the decision to tear down Whipple House.
8. Andy *flouted* his talent by describing himself as a versatile actor.
9. Mr. Mumford-Spears was an *outspoken* coach who would always tell the members of the team what he thought of their skills or attitude.
10. Rupert's *incisive* remarks on the history of American industry were neither clear nor accurate.

1. _____
2. _____
3. _____
4. _____
5. _____
6. _____
7. _____
8. _____
9. _____
10. _____

Exercise 3 Identifying Antonyms

Decide which word has the meaning that is opposite to that of the capitalized vocabulary word. Write the letter of your choice on the answer line.

1. FLOUT:
   a. dictate   b. scorn   c. insist   d. obey

1. _____

Copyright © 1988 Houghton Mifflin Company. All rights reserved.

2. **TEMERITY:**
   a. stupidity   b. cautiousness   c. cleverness   d. anger

   2. _____

3. **DAUNTLESS:**
   a. timid   b. scornful   c. keen   d. insistent

   3. _____

4. **INCISIVE:**
   a. fearless   b. energetic   c. vague   d. stubborn

   4. _____

5. **VIBRANT:**
   a. enthusiastic   b. dull   c. reckless   d. courageous

   5. _____

6. **FEROCITY:**
   a. stubbornness   b. fierceness   c. ignorance   d. meekness

   6. _____

7. **VEHEMENT:**
   a. uninterested   b. fearful   c. understanding   d. lucky

   7. _____

8. **HEADSTRONG:**
   a. scholarly   b. uncertain   c. obstinate   d. muscular

   8. _____

9. **ASSERT:**
   a. research   b. declare   c. understand   d. hesitate

   9. _____

10. **OUTSPOKEN:**
    a. unrestrained   b. fortunate   c. shy   d. sociable

    10. _____

Exercise 4   Using Different Forms of Words

Decide which form of the vocabulary word in parentheses best completes the sentence. The form given may be correct. Write your answer on the answer line.

1. Helen __?__ crossed the suspension bridge. *(dauntless)*

   1. _____

2. All of the committee members were too __?__ to agree on anything. *(headstrong)*

   2. _____

3. The __?__ personality of the gymnast was noted by the sports reporter. *(vibrant)*

   3. _____

4. The teacher was impressed with the __?__ of the student's essay. *(incisive)*

   4. _____

5. The dog's deep growl made him sound very __?__ . *(ferocity)*

   5. _____

6. During the trial the defense lawyer argued __?__ with the prosecuting attorney. *(vehement)*

   6. _____

7. "Be more __?__ !" the career counselor advised his client. *(assert)*

   7. _____

8. Bob, the quarterback, had the __?__ to insult all of the defensive players of the opposing team. *(temerity)*

   8. _____

9. "You are deliberately __?__ my orders!" the baby sitter warned. *(flout)*

   9. _____

10. The politician was well known for his rash __?__ . *(outspoken)*

    10. _____

144   Boldness

Reading Comprehension

Each numbered sentence in the following passage contains an italicized vocabulary word or related form. After you read the passage, you will complete an exercise.

Sacajawea: "A Tireless, Resourceful Woman"

(1) When picturing the famed Lewis and Clark expedition of 1804–1806, one might imagine the two *dauntless* explorers blazing a trail alone through the wilderness. **(2)** In reality, Lewis and Clark would never have had the *temerity* to travel by themselves from Missouri to the Pacific Northwest. Many other people were involved. One person in particular, a young Native American woman called Sacajawea, contributed greatly to the expedition's success.

Sacajawea (1786–1812) belonged to the Lemhi band of Shoshone, or Snake, Indians who lived in what is now called Idaho. **(3)** Her group attempted to move eastward in 1800, only to encounter the *ferocity* of a war party of the Hidatsa band of Indians. Sacajawea was kidnapped and eventually sold as a slave to Toussaint Charbonneau, a French Canadian, who lived with the Hidatsas in the region now called North Dakota.

In 1804 North Dakota also became the winter stopping-place for weary members of the Lewis and Clark expedition. At this time Lewis and Clark met Charbonneau and asked him to serve as the interpreter when they resumed the expedition. Charbonneau agreed to join them if he was allowed to bring Sacajawea, now his wife, and their newborn baby.

It was Sacajawea more than her husband who proved to be of great value to the expedition. From previous experience, Lewis and Clark knew that the success of their venture would depend largely upon how well they got along with the Indians along the way. **(4)** Scouts and pioneers before them had sometimes acted in a *headstrong* manner, refusing to make any accommodations with the Indians who already inhabited the land. **(5)** These early trailblazers had openly *flouted* the rights of the native inhabitants and often lost their lives because of it.

(6) Therefore, the decision to include Sacajawea and her baby was an *incisive* one on the part of Lewis and Clark. The Indian mother and baby's presence would show the Indians that the explorers were on a peaceful mission. In addition, Sacajawea's knowledge of the Mandan and Shoshone languages would make it possible for the explorers to communicate with bands of Indians along the way.

Nowhere was this better demonstrated than when the exploration party encountered a group of Shoshones who were, in fact, the very Indians with whom Sacajawea had grown up. **(7)** When Sacajawea first recognized the Shoshones, she was filled with *vibrant* joy and, according to Lewis and Clark, danced to show that these were her people. **(8)** At first, some of the Shoshones were *vehemently* opposed to helping the exploration party cross the Continental Divide, but they dropped their objections once Sacajawea identified herself. Her reunion became even more joyful after Sacajawea discovered that her brother had become chief of the band.

Lewis and Clark thought very highly of Sacajawea, and there were numerous references to her dedicated service to the expedition in the explorers' journals. In addition to helping communicate with the Indians of the Pacific Northwest, Sacajawea looked for and prepared edible wild foods. She even saved valuable instruments and records from being lost during a storm on a river. **(9)** Lewis *asserted* that Sacajawea's unselfish attitude inspired all the members of the expedition.

(10) As the years went by, such others as Susan B. Anthony, an early women's rights leader, were *outspoken* in their praise of the young Indian woman. On the occasion of the unveiling of a bronze statue of Sacajawea in Oregon, Anthony said, "This is a fitting recognition of a tireless, resourceful woman who, as Lewis and Clark reported, 'inspired us all.'"

Please turn to the next page.

Reading Comprehension Exercise

Each of the following statements corresponds to a numbered sentence in the passage. Each statement contains a blank and is followed by four answer choices. Decide which choice fits best in the blank. The word or phrase that you choose must express roughly the same meaning as the italicized word in the passage. Write the letter of your choice on the answer line.

1. When imagining the Lewis and Clark expedition, one pictures __?__ explorers.
   a. strong   b. bold   c. powerful   d. timid

2. Lewis and Clark did not have the __?__ to travel alone.
   a. courage   b. good sense   c. incentive   d. rash boldness

3. In 1800 Sacajawea and her people encountered the __?__ of a war party.
   a. savagery   b. confusion   c. kindness   d. attack

4. Lewis and Clark did not want to duplicate the __?__ manner of other scouts and pioneers.
   a. conceited   b. daring   c. obstinate   d. foolhardy

5. Some of these early trailblazers had openly __?__ the rights of the Indians.
   a. agreed with   c. argued for
   b. talked against   d. shown contempt for

6. Lewis and Clark's decision to include Sacajawea on the expedition was a __?__ one.
   a. perceptive   b. difficult   c. spontaneous   d. critical

7. When she saw other Shoshones, Sacajawea was filled with __?__ joy.
   a. graceful   b. timid   c. sudden   d. intense

8. Some of the Shoshones were __?__ opposed to helping the explorers.
   a. barely   b. strongly   c. indifferently   d. weakly

9. Lewis __?__ that Sacajawea was the inspiration of the trip.
   a. questioned   b. explained   c. affirmed   d. argued

10. Others were __?__ in their praise of the young Indian woman.
    a. unrestrained   b. low-key   c. dramatic   d. insincere

1. _____
2. _____
3. _____
4. _____
5. _____
6. _____
7. _____
8. _____
9. _____
10. _____

Practice with Analogies

See page 79 for some strategies to use with analogies.

DIRECTIONS   On the answer line, write the vocabulary word that completes each analogy.

1. FLEXIBLE : EASYGOING : : stubborn : __?__
2. ENERGETIC : LACKLUSTER : : __?__ : listless
3. CALM : IMPASSIVE : : __?__ : emotional
4. DENY : DISCLAIM : : affirm : __?__
5. MALICIOUS : VILLAIN : : __?__ : hero

1. _____
2. _____
3. _____
4. _____
5. _____

146   Boldness

Lesson 23

Accident and Purpose

You probably know many people who believe in luck or fate. These people may look for a four-leaf clover, carry a rabbit's foot, or wish on a star. They may practice a variety of such superstitions, hoping for good fortune. On the other hand, you probably know an equal number of people who believe that they are in charge of their lives. These people assume responsibility for their successes and failures.

Regardless of which viewpoint you adopt and practice, you will encounter many accidents as well as many purposeful situations. Not all accidents are negative, and not all plans turn out as you expect. The vocabulary words in this lesson will help you to express your ideas about the accidental and purposeful circumstances that you experience.

WORD LIST
arbitrary
coincidental
contrive
deliberation
fortuitous
haphazard
intent
premeditated
spontaneous
unwitting

DEFINITIONS

After you have studied the definitions and example for each vocabulary word, write the word on the line to the right.

1. **arbitrary** (är′bĭ-trĕr′ē) *adjective* **a.** Based on whim or impulse rather than on reason or law. **b.** Subject to individual judgment. (From the Latin word *arbiter*, meaning "judge")

   RELATED WORDS **arbitrarily** *adverb;* **arbitrariness** *noun*

   EXAMPLE Mrs. Lemoine was upset about her daughter's *arbitrary* invitation to fifteen friends to join the family for dinner.

   1. _____
   SEE *spontaneous.*

2. **coincidental** (kō-ĭn′sĭ-dĕn′təl) *adjective* **a.** Occurring as a combination of circumstances that, although accidental, is so remarkable that it seems to have been planned or arranged. **b.** Resulting from the condition of occupying the same point in space or time. (From the Latin *co-*, meaning "together," *in-*, meaning "upon," and *cadere*, meaning "to fall")

   RELATED WORDS **coincide** *verb;* **coincidence** *noun;* **coincidentally** *adverb*

   EXAMPLE It was entirely *coincidental* that Jane and I were visiting Washington, D.C., the same week.

   2. _____

3. **contrive** (kən-trīv′) *trans. verb* **a.** To plan cleverly; invent, especially without preparation. **b.** To plot or scheme with evil intent.   *intrans. verb* To plot or scheme.

   RELATED WORD **contrivance** *noun*

   EXAMPLE Mother *contrived* a costume from old draperies.

   3. _____

Copyright © 1988 Houghton Mifflin Company. All rights reserved.

Accident and Purpose **147**

4. **deliberation** (dĭ-lĭb′ə-rā′shən) *noun* **a.** Careful thought in decision-making or action. **b.** Slowness of motion or manner. (From the Latin word *deliberare*, meaning "to consider")

   RELATED WORDS **deliberate** *verb;* **deliberate** *adjective;* **deliberately** *adverb;* **deliberateness** *noun*

   EXAMPLE After several weeks of *deliberation,* Phoebe returned to college to complete her degree.

5. **fortuitous** (fôr-tōō′ĭ-təs, fôr-tyōō′ĭ-təs) *adjective* **a.** Occurring unexpectedly or without any known cause; happening by accident or chance; unplanned. **b.** Lucky. (From the Latin word *fortuitous,* meaning "by chance")

   RELATED WORD **fortuitously** *adverb*

   EXAMPLE We had not been told about the change in flight time; our early arrival at the airport was simply *fortuitous.*

6. **haphazard** (hăp-hăz′ərd) *adjective* **a.** Lacking any definite plan or order; random. **b.** Dependent upon chance.

   RELATED WORDS **haphazardly** *adverb;* **haphazardness** *noun*

   EXAMPLE The *haphazard* arrangement of the artist's work did not show his paintings to their best advantage.

7. **intent** (ĭn-tĕnt′) *noun* **a.** An aim or purpose. **b.** The state of mind at the time of an action. **c.** Meaning or connotation: *the intent of a poem.*   *adjective* Firmly fixed; determined; intense. (From the Latin word *intendere,* meaning "to intend")

   RELATED WORDS **intend** *verb;* **intently** *adverb*

   EXAMPLE During the first class, the teacher stated his *intent* to improve our public speaking.

8. **premeditated** (prē-mĕd′ĭ-tā′tĭd) *adjective* Planned, arranged, or plotted in advance. (From the Latin *prae-,* meaning "before," and *meditari,* meaning "to consider")

   RELATED WORDS **premeditate** *verb;* **premeditation** *noun*

   EXAMPLE The detective said that the crime was *premeditated.*

9. **spontaneous** (spŏn-tā′nē-əs) *adjective* **a.** Happening without external cause; self-generated. **b.** Impulsive. (From the Latin word *sponte,* meaning "voluntarily")

   RELATED WORDS **spontaneity** *noun;* **spontaneously** *adverb*

   EXAMPLE Caitlin was so happy to have reached the ocean that she did a *spontaneous* dance for the seagulls.

10. **unwitting** (ŭn-wĭt′ĭng) *adjective* Not knowing; unaware. (From the Old English *un-,* meaning "not," and *witan,* meaning "to know")

    RELATED WORD **unwittingly** *adverb*

    EXAMPLE Since the sign was not visible on the property, the hikers became *unwitting* trespassers.

---

4. _____

5. _____
   SEE *haphazard.*

6. _____
   USAGE NOTE *Haphazard* and *fortuitous* refer to unplanned events. *Fortuitous* has the added connotation of luck.

7. _____

8. _____

9. _____
   USAGE NOTE *Spontaneous* behavior occurs naturally and without thought. An *arbitrary* action may involve some thought.

10. _____

Name _____ Date _____

Exercise 1 Writing Correct Words

On the answer line, write the word from the vocabulary list that fits each definition.

1. Occurring unexpectedly or without any known cause; lucky   1. _____
2. Happening without external cause; impulsive   2. _____
3. Not planned; dependent upon chance   3. _____
4. Not knowing; unaware   4. _____
5. Careful thought in decision-making or action   5. _____
6. Accidentally occurring at the same time but seeming planned or arranged 6. _____
7. An aim or purpose   7. _____
8. Based on impulse rather than reason   8. _____
9. To plan with cleverness; plot or scheme   9. _____
10. Planned in advance   10. _____

Exercise 2 Using Words Correctly

Decide whether the italicized vocabulary word has been used correctly in the sentence. On the answer line, write *Correct* for correct use and *Incorrect* for incorrect use.

1. For two weeks before their arrival, Connie looked forward to her grandparents' *fortuitous* visit.   1. _____
2. The students *contrived* to have the flowers on the teacher's desk before she arrived.   2. _____
3. The golfer's lengthy *deliberation* over which club to use made his partner impatient.   3. _____
4. After considering all the possibilities, Petra made a *spontaneous* decision.   4. _____
5. The similarity between the two poems was too obvious to be *coincidental*.   5. _____
6. Just as the train pulled into the station, Leander acted according to a *premeditated* plan.   6. _____
7. The *haphazard* arrangement of books in a library makes any book easy to locate.   7. _____
8. Since they did not know the judges' standards, the contestants believed that the selection of the winner had been *arbitrary*.   8. _____
9. When Paul Revere rode out of Boston on April 18, 1775, his *intent* was to warn the colonists that the British were coming.   9. _____
10. After paying his money and signing the sales agreement, Blake became the *unwitting* owner of a new car.   10. _____

Copyright © 1988 Houghton Mifflin Company. All rights reserved.   Accident and Purpose

Exercise 3 Choosing the Best Definition

For each italicized vocabulary word in the following sentences, write the letter of the best definition on the answer line.

1. We tried to persuade the Rogerses that the arrival of ten people on their doorstep at six o'clock was *coincidental*.
   a. accidentally occurring at the same time
   b. gradually acknowledged
   c. purposefully planned
   d. surprisingly accurate

2. Kim's decision to go to the beach on Saturday was an *arbitrary* one.
   a. based on careful thought   c. based on impulse
   b. based on the weather   d. based on deduction

3. Neil continues to be an *unwitting* victim of his brother's teasing.
   a. unstable   b. unaware   c. unreasonable   d. unofficial

4. With *deliberation* Leslie located a reliable toehold on the cliff.
   a. effectiveness   b. great care   c. energy   d. measuring

5. The *haphazard* directions had been scribbled on an envelope.
   a. clearly explained   c. lacking neatness
   b. competently written   d. lacking a definite plan

6. The comedian's jokes produced *spontaneous* laughter.
   a. noisy   b. excessive   c. natural   d. unexpected

7. Lyle *contrived* a way for us to attend the opening of the play.
   a. cleverly planned   c. accidentally found
   b. foolishly planned   d. knew of

8. Denise's *fortuitous* introduction to Norman Rockwell changed her ideas about magazine illustration.
   a. long-awaited   b. unplanned   c. satisfying   d. memorable

9. The robbery was obviously *premeditated* because the thieves knew exactly where to find the jewelry and silver.
   a. successful   b. created   c. committed   d. planned

10. It was my *intent* to finish my book before starting the dishes.
    a. hope   b. wish   c. assignment   d. aim

Exercise 4 Using Different Forms of Words

Decide which form of the vocabulary word in parentheses best completes the sentence. The form given may be correct. Write your answer on the answer line.

1. The phone call came __?__, as we walked in the door. *(fortuitous)*

2. By __?__ both climbing parties reached the mountain's summit on the same day. *(coincidental)*

3. The __?__ of the applause pleased the performers. *(spontaneous)*

4. In 1796 Edward Jenner, an English physician, __?__ inoculated an eight-year-old boy against smallpox. *(deliberation)*

5. Jenner __?__ to show that the vaccine he had given the boy two months earlier would protect him from smallpox. *(intent)*

150   Accident and Purpose

Name _____ Date _____

6. The game-show judges ___?___ chose the college professor as a contestant. *(unwitting)*

6. _____

7. Since the families could not agree on a date for the wedding, the future bride and groom ___?___ chose June 28. *(arbitrary)*

7. _____

8. Susanne had placed her sweaters so ___?___ that they fell off the shelf. *(haphazard)*

8. _____

9. The jury decided that the purchase of the insurance policy indicated ___?___ . *(premeditated)*

9. _____

10. Judy ___?___ to keep her car running until she could reach a gas station. *(contrive)*

10. _____

Reading Comprehension

Each numbered sentence in the following passage contains an italicized vocabulary word or related form. After you read the passage, you will complete an exercise.

Gold Fever

Throughout history, gold has been one of the most sought-after possessions on earth. Because of its value and appeal, battles have been fought and kingdoms have risen and fallen. People have left their homes in search of riches that could be obtained simply by digging the precious metal out of the ground.

Although gold was first discovered in the United States in North Carolina in 1799, the age of dramatic gold rushes did not begin until 1848. **(1)** On January 24, 1848, James Marshall *fortuitously* came upon something shining in the water next to Captain John Sutter's mill in California. **(2)** Fishing the pebble out of the water with *deliberation*, Marshall took it to Captain Smith, who tested its properties. The pebble was gold! **(3)** News of the discovery spread rapidly, and by spring, much of the population of California had *spontaneously* swarmed to Sutter's Mill. By August and September, gold fever had swept through the United States and Europe. **(4)** Eighty thousand people of every conceivable occupation and social and economic level *contrived* ways of traveling to California to seek quick riches.

Whether they traveled by boat or by wagon train, many forty-niners, as the gold hunters were called, organized themselves into companies before they left home. **(5)** Their *premeditation* failed in most cases, however. Virtually all of these groups broke up when they reached the gold fields.

(6) Because the first miners had neither money nor technical knowledge, prospecting was an individual and *haphazard* pursuit. **(7)** Each forty-niner would *arbitrarily* choose an area of a stream. Standing in the icy waters, the prospector panned for gold by scooping up sand or gravel and water in a bowl or pan. When the pan was tilted to let the water drain and carry off the sand, any gold dust would show up as a streak of gold. If a prospector "had a lucky strike" or "hit pay dirt," he staked a claim at his spot and continued the panning process. **(8)** Once he panned off the easily available gold, he sold his claim to an *unwitting* newcomer and began the process over again.

Although the California gold fields produced two hundred million dollars' worth of gold between 1848 and 1853, the Gold Rush brought more disappointment than success. **(9)** *Intent* on getting rich, most forty-niners failed. The average daily earnings of those who prospected for gold in 1849 were estimated at about sixteen dollars per person. **(10)** Finding several hundred dollars' worth of gold in a day seemed more *coincidental* than certain. As more prospectors arrived to stake claims, there was less gold for everyone.

Please turn to the next page.

Reading Comprehension Exercise

Each of the following statements corresponds to a numbered sentence in the passage. Each statement contains a blank and is followed by four answer choices. Decide which choice fits best in the blank. The word or phrase that you choose must express roughly the same meaning as the italicized word in the passage. Write the letter of your choice on the answer line.

1. James Marshall __?__ came upon something shining in the water at Sutter's Mill.
   a. almost   b. unexpectedly   c. victoriously   d. fearfully

2. Marshall fished the shiny pebble out of the water with __?__.
   a. careful slowness   b. haste   c. shaking hands   d. excitement

3. By spring large numbers of people had __?__ swarmed to Sutter's Mill.
   a. uncompromisingly   c. ultimately
   b. considerately   d. impulsively

4. Eighty thousand people __?__ ways of traveling to California.
   a. sought   b. planned   c. offered   d. found

5. Their __?__ failed in most cases.
   a. dreams   b. choices   c. arrangements   d. attempts

6. Prospecting was an individual and __?__ pursuit.
   a. chancy   b. lonely   c. challenging   d. trivial

7. Each forty-niner __?__ chose an area of a stream.
   a. carefully   b. on impulse   c. by sight   d. primarily

8. A successful prospector would sell his claim to a(n) __?__ newcomer.
   a. frightened   b. enthusiastic   c. sophisticated   d. unaware

9. Most forty-niners were __?__ to get rich.
   a. determined   b. trying   c. prepared   d. clever enough

10. Finding hundreds of dollars' worth of gold was more __?__ than certain.
    a. expected   b. dramatic   c. special   d. accidental

1. _____
2. _____
3. _____
4. _____
5. _____
6. _____
7. _____
8. _____
9. _____
10. _____

Writing Assignment

Write a brief story about a character who purposefully plans each aspect of his or her life. In your story show how something totally unexpected changes or influences the character's life. For example, you might write a story about a person who plans a vacation, only to get lost and end up miles from his or her destination. This character's unhappiness might turn to pleasure when he or she discovers a beautiful, isolated beach or some other unexpected place. Use at least five of the words from this lesson in your story and underline each one.

Lesson 24

Words from the Latin *Facere*

Facere in Latin means "to make" or "to do." Hundreds of English words contain roots derived from *facere,* and the forms of these roots vary greatly. For example, *-fect* in *perfect,* *-fici-* in *official,* and *fact-* in *factual* all come from *facere.* In this lesson you will learn ten words that can in part be traced to this basic Latin word.

> **WORD LIST**
> affectation
> beneficiary
> defect
> efficacy
> faction
> factor
> officiate
> officious
> prolific
> suffice

DEFINITIONS

After you have studied the definitions and example for each vocabulary word, write the word on the line to the right.

1. **affectation** (ăf′ĕk-tā′shən) *noun* Artificial behavior adopted to impress others; pretense; a pose. (From the Latin word *affectare,* meaning "to aspire to")

   RELATED WORD **affect** *verb*

   EXAMPLE Since Jerry has lived only in Ohio, his English accent is an *affectation.*

2. **beneficiary** (běn′ə-fĭsh′ē-ĕr′ē, běn′ə-fĭsh′ə-rē) *noun* **a.** A person who receives funds from an insurance policy or will upon another's death. **b.** Anyone who receives help or advantage from something. (From the Latin phrase *bene facere,* meaning "to do well")

   RELATED WORDS **beneficial** *adjective;* **benefit** *noun;* **benefit** *verb*

   EXAMPLE At the reading of the will, Ernie discovered that he was his uncle's sole *beneficiary.*

3. **defect** (dē′fĕkt′, dĭ-fĕkt′) *noun* **a.** A flaw or imperfection. **b.** A deficiency. *intrans. verb* (dĭ-fĕkt′) To desert one's country or party in order to adopt or join another.

   RELATED WORDS **defection** *noun;* **defective** *adjective;* **defectiveness** *noun;* **defector** *noun*

   EXAMPLE Merchandise labeled "irregular" usually has some sort of *defect.*

Words from the Latin Word *Facere* 153

4. **efficacy** (ĕf′ĭ-kə-sē) *noun* The power or capacity to produce the desired effect; effectiveness. (From the Latin word *efficere*, meaning "to accomplish")

   RELATED WORD **efficacious** *adjective*

   EXAMPLE A drastic reduction in cases of smallpox demonstrated the *efficacy* of Jenner's vaccine.

5. **faction** (făk′shən) *noun* A group of persons forming a united but sometimes discontented and troublesome minority within a larger group.

   RELATED WORD **factional** *adjective*

   EXAMPLE Instead of voting to play tapes at the dance, one *faction* in the Student Council demanded a live band.

6. **factor** (făk′tər) *noun* **a.** Something that helps bring about a certain result; an ingredient. **b.** One of two or more numbers or expressions that have a given product: *Two and three are factors of six.* *trans. verb* To find the factors of (a number of expression). (From the Latin word *factor*, meaning "maker")

   EXAMPLE Skin sensitivity is an important *factor* to consider when buying suntan lotion.

7. **officiate** (ə-fĭsh′ē-āt′) *intrans. verb* **a.** To serve in a position of authority; to preside. **b.** To serve as a referee or an umpire in sports. (From the Latin words *ops*, meaning "help," and *facere*, meaning "to do")

   RELATED WORDS **official** *adjective;* **official** *noun*

   EXAMPLE Mayor Bridges will *officiate* at the Memorial Day festivities.

8. **officious** (ə-fĭsh′əs) *adjective* Excessively forward in offering one's services or advice to others; meddlesome.

   RELATED WORD **officiousness** *noun*

   EXAMPLE After Joan moved to a new apartment, she found the neighbors to be *officious* and annoying.

9. **prolific** (prə-lĭf′ĭk) *adjective* **a.** Causing or maintaining abundant growth. **b.** Producing numerous works: *a prolific writer.* (From the Latin words *proles*, meaning "children," and *facere*)

   RELATED WORDS **proliferate** *verb;* **proliferation** *noun*

   EXAMPLE Rain-forest plants are *prolific*.

10. **suffice** (sə-fīs′) *intrans. verb* To meet present needs; be adequate.

    RELATED WORDS **sufficiency** *noun;* **sufficient** *adjective*

    EXAMPLE "On the days that I eat a large lunch, a small dinner will *suffice*," Alfred told Melanie.

Name _____ Date _____

Exercise 1   Completing Definitions

On the answer line, write the word from the vocabulary list that best completes each definition.

1. To serve in a position of authority is to __?__ .
2. Offering unwanted assistance means acting __?__ .
3. The capacity to produce a desired effect is __?__ .
4. Artificial behavior used to impress others is __?__ .
5. A small, often discontented, group within a larger group is a(n) __?__ .
6. To desert one's country is to __?__ .
7. To be adequate is to __?__ .
8. Maintaining or causing abundant growth is a sign of being __?__ .
9. An ingredient that helps bring about a certain result is a(n) __?__ .
10. A person who receives funds from a will or benefits directly from something is a __?__ .

1. _____
2. _____
3. _____
4. _____
5. _____
6. _____
7. _____
8. _____
9. _____
10. _____

Exercise 2   Using Words Correctly

Each of the following questions contains an italicized vocabulary word. Decide the answer to the question, and write *Yes* or *No* on the answer line.

1. Is price usually a *factor* when a consumer chooses a car?
2. Is someone who ignores others likely to be an *officious* person?
3. Does a referee *officiate* at a football game?
4. Is *affectation* the love of a parent for a child?
5. Is a novelist with writer's block creating at a *prolific* rate?
6. If you wanted a new bike, would buying roller skates *suffice*?
7. If you inherited money, would you be called a *beneficiary*?
8. Is the *efficacy* of a medicine important to you when you are ill?
9. Is a hole in the bottom of a bucket a *defect*?
10. Do members of a *faction* usually agree with one another?

1. _____
2. _____
3. _____
4. _____
5. _____
6. _____
7. _____
8. _____
9. _____
10. _____

Exercise 3   Choosing the Best Word

Decide which vocabulary word or related form best expresses the meaning of the italicized word or phrase in the sentence. On the answer line, write the letter of the correct choice.

1. Rabbits are well known for *producing numerous offspring*.
   a. being officious   c. being defective
   b. being prolific   d. being beneficial

1. _____

Words from the Latin Word *Facere*

2. The *meddlesome* salespeople would not leave Paul alone.
   a. officious   b. prolific   c. official   d. officiating

3. Cost was a *consideration* in our decision not to take a vacation this year.
   a. affectation   b. factor   c. faction   d. defect

4. Both teachers and students were *persons receiving benefit* of the donation of new computers.
   a. affectations   b. factions   c. factors   d. beneficiaries

5. The people who *perform official duties* at soccer matches know every rule of the game.
   a. defect   b. officiate   c. are officious   d. suffice

6. Only a *small group* within the audience disliked the play.
   a. faction   b. efficacy   c. beneficiary   d. affectation

7. One turkey *was not adequate* to feed the hungry dinner guests.
   a. was too officious   c. could not suffice
   b. was too defective   d. was not prolific enough

8. Arkady Shevchenko *deserted his country* and now lives in New York.
   a. officiated   b. sufficed   c. affected   d. defected

9. After starring in the school play, Calvin developed *a pose* of offering his autograph to everyone.
   a. an affectation   c. the proliferation
   b. the officiousness   d. an efficacy

10. When Lucy was having her tooth pulled, she was impressed by the *effectiveness* of the anesthetic.
    a. beneficiary   b. efficacy   c. affectation   d. defect

Exercise 4 Using Different Forms of Words

Each sentence contains an italicized vocabulary word in a form that does not fit the sentence. On the answer line, write the form of the word that does fit the sentence.

1. Jessica *affectation* the look of a debutante when she goes to parties.
2. Are four instruments *suffice* for playing a quartet?
3. The college *officiate* presided at the commencement activities.
4. The encore was for the audience's *beneficiary*.
5. The peonies began to *prolific* after the summer rains.
6. A wagon with only three wheels is considered *defect*.
7. The State Department granted asylum to the *defect*.
8. Buck and Tracy are tired of Harold's *officious* and wish that he would leave them alone.
9. The ice pack was *efficacy*, and the swelling has stopped.
10. The possibility of *faction* behavior is always present in governmental systems.

Reading Comprehension

Each numbered sentence in the following passage contains an italicized vocabulary word. After you read the passage, you will complete an exercise.

Margaret Bourke-White: Photojournalist

(1) Margaret Bourke-White (1906–71) was one of America's greatest and most ***prolific*** news photographers. For approximately twenty-five years (1930 to the mid fifties), Bourke-White's photographs captured the drama of world events. **(2)** Today we are all the **beneficiaries** of her rich visual legacy.

Bourke-White's interest in photography began while she was in college. **(3)** Critics still consider many of the pictures she took during this time to be extraordinarily fine and without **defects** of any kind.

After Bourke-White completed college, she became a professional photographer. At this time she decided to adopt the surname Bourke-White, a combination of her middle and last names. **(4)** While some may have thought that this was an **affectation** on her part, others found that the change made the photographer's name more distinctive and professional-sounding.

(5) A big break in Bourke-White's career came in 1929 when Henry Luce, the editor in chief of *Time* magazine, saw her work and knew that not only would it **suffice** for his new business magazine, *Fortune*, but would make the publication even more appealing. Bourke-White then divided her working time, spending six months a year on *Fortune* and taking pictures for advertising agencies during the remaining six months.

Bourke-White's work for *Fortune* was and still is praised by critics. **(6)** Her photo stories on meatpacking, on the **efficacy** of German industrial development before World War II, and on the depression-era droughts in the United States created quite a stir.

Always looking for new challenges, Bourke-White visited the Soviet Union in the thirties, a time when this country was off-limits to most Americans. **(7)** A strong interest in the photographic possibilities of the rapid industrialization of the Soviet Union was the principal **factor** in Bourke-White's decision to visit this country. **(8) Officious** acquaintances warned her about the difficulties of travel in the Soviet Union.

(9) However, Bourke-White managed very well and took a variety of photographs — of everything from huge Russian dams to a bishop **officiating** at a religious ceremony. These photographs gave Americans a rare look at the early years of Soviet development.

During the last twenty years of her life, Bourke-White suffered from Parkinson's disease. She struggled against it valiantly and continued to take photographs for as long as her illness would allow her to.

Photography is now a recognized art form, with many photographers displaying their work in art galleries. **(10)** Within the world of art critics and collectors and the artists themselves, there are **factions** with conflicting opinions. However, the pictures of Margaret Bourke-White were, and still are, widely respected by both amateur and professional photographers.

Please turn to the next page.

Copyright © 1988 Houghton Mifflin Company. All rights reserved.

Words from the Latin Word *Facere*

Reading Comprehension Exercise

Each of the following statements corresponds to a numbered sentence in the passage. Each statement contains a blank and is followed by four answer choices. Decide which choice fits best in the blank. The word or phrase that you choose must express roughly the same meaning as the italicized word in the passage. Write the letter of your choice on the answer line.

1. Margaret Bourke-White was a ___?___ photographer.
    a. productive   b. talented   c. natural   d. vivid

2. We are the ___?___ of her visual legacy.
    a. inheritors   b. students   c. witnesses   d. friends

3. Many of the pictures that Bourke-White took while she was in college are without ___?___ .
    a. color   b. frames   c. distinction   d. flaws

4. Some may have thought her hyphenated last name a(n) ___?___ .
    a. mistake   b. error   c. conceited gesture   d. curiosity

5. Luce knew that Bourke-White's work would not only ___?___ but would also enhance his new magazine.
    a. decorate   b. illustrate   c. be useful   d. be adequate

6. Bourke-White's photographs showed the ___?___ of German industrial development.
    a. instructiveness   c. disruptiveness
    b. effectiveness   d. repressiveness

7. The industrialization of the Soviet Union was the principal ___?___ in her decision to go there.
    a. ingredient   b. problem   c. hindrance   d. development

8. ___?___ acquaintances gave advice.
    a. Meddlesome   b. Official   c. Important   d. Numerous

9. One of Bourke-White's Russian photographs showed a Soviet bishop ___?___ at a religious service.
    a. praying   b. reading   c. presiding   d. singing

10. There are ___?___ within the art world.
    a. large teams   c. problems
    b. small rival groups   d. components

1. _____
2. _____
3. _____
4. _____
5. _____
6. _____
7. _____
8. _____
9. _____
10. _____

Practice with Analogies

See page 79 for some strategies to use with analogies.

DIRECTIONS On the answer line, write the vocabulary word that completes each analogy.

1. MEET : FULFILL : : ___?___ : satisfy
2. PUSHY : PRESUMPTUOUS : : meddlesome : ___?___
3. INGREDIENT : RECIPE : : ___?___ : equation
4. CHIP : VASE : : ___?___ : merchandise
5. BARREN : FERTILE : : unproductive : ___?___

1. _____
2. _____
3. _____
4. _____
5. _____

158 Words from the Latin Word *Facere*   Copyright © Houghton Mifflin Company. All rights reserved.

Name _____ Date _____

Reading Skills

The Prefixes *ab-*, *a-*, and *abs-*

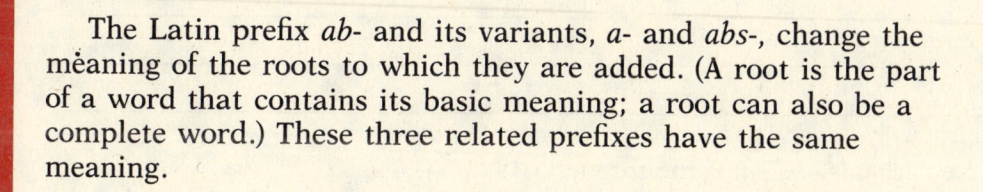

The Latin prefix *ab-* and its variants, *a-* and *abs-*, change the meaning of the roots to which they are added. (A root is the part of a word that contains its basic meaning; a root can also be a complete word.) These three related prefixes have the same meaning.

PREFIX MEANING	ROOT WORD	WORD	WORD DEFINITION
away, away from	*ducere*, "to lead"	abduct	to carry away by force
	vertere, "to turn"	avert	to turn away, prevent
	esse, "to be"	absent	not present

To determine the meaning of words with the prefix *ab-* or its variants, use the following procedure. Remember that the more prefixes and roots you know, the more often you will be able to analyze unfamiliar words.

PROCEDURE

1. *Substitute the prefix and the root definitions for the prefix and root.*
2. *Think of possible definitions of the entire word.*
3. *Check your definition of the word in the dictionary.*

Exercise   Using the Prefixes *ab-*, *a-*, and *abs-*

Each sentence in this exercise contains an italicized word beginning with the prefix *ab-* or one of its variants. The sentence is followed by the appropriate Latin root word and its meaning. *Step 1:* Write your own definition of the word. *Step 2:* Write the dictionary definition of the word. Choose the definition that best fits the way the word is used in the sentence. *Step 3:* Write a sentence of your own in which you use the word correctly.

1. Antonio was *averse* to being in elevators and in the presence of large dogs. (Root word: *vertere*, "to turn")

   YOUR DEFINITION _____
   DICTIONARY DEFINITION _____
   SENTENCE _____

Please turn to the next page.

Copyright © 1988 Houghton Mifflin Company. All rights reserved.   The Prefixes *ab-*, *a-*, and *abs-*   **159**

2. The nurse washed the patient's *abrasion* with antiseptic. (Root word: *radere*, "to scrape")

   YOUR DEFINITION _____
   DICTIONARY DEFINITION _____
   SENTENCE _____

3. We were surprised by the *abrupt* ending of the song. (Root word: *rumpere*, "to break")

   YOUR DEFINITION _____
   DICTIONARY DEFINITION _____
   SENTENCE _____

4. Queen Wilhelmina of the Netherlands *abdicated* the throne in 1948. (Root word: *dicare*, "to proclaim")

   YOUR DEFINITION _____
   DICTIONARY DEFINITION _____
   SENTENCE _____

5. The audience *abhorred* the ending of the movie. (Root word: *horrere*, "to shudder")

   YOUR DEFINITION _____
   DICTIONARY DEFINITION _____
   SENTENCE _____

6. The *abnormal* results of his experiments puzzled Dr. Scott. (Root word: *norma*, "rule")

   YOUR DEFINITION _____
   DICTIONARY DEFINITION _____
   SENTENCE _____

7. Mr. Brighton's leadership rescued the membership drive from *abject* failure. (Root word: *jacere*, "to throw")

   YOUR DEFINITION _____
   DICTIONARY DEFINITION _____
   SENTENCE _____

8. Although Ms. Jordan's profession is law, her *avocation* is painting. (Root word: *vocare*, "to call")

   YOUR DEFINITION _____
   DICTIONARY DEFINITION _____
   SENTENCE _____

The Prefixes *ab-*, *a-*, and *abs-*

Lesson 25

Praise and Criticism

It is opening night. You have just seen a terrible performance by your best friend. When you meet her backstage, you say, "You've never been better," but you are thinking, "Of course, you've never been worse either." Your friend isn't much of an actress.

Praise and criticism are tricky. Praise is not always good (think of flattery, which is insincere praise), nor is criticism always bad (constructive criticism may help your friend to improve her acting). In this lesson you will learn words of praise and criticism.

WORD LIST
accolade
adulation
anathema
commend
eulogy
extol
homage
laudable
reproach
reverence

DEFINITIONS

After you have studied the definitions and example for each vocabulary word, write the word on the line to the right.

1. **accolade** (ăk′ə-lād′, ăk′ə-läd′) *noun* An expression of strong approval or praise. (From the Provençal word *acolar*, meaning "to embrace")

    EXAMPLE The firefighters received *accolades* from the town council for their bravery in fighting the Peshtigo Forest blaze.

   1. _____

2. **adulation** (ăj′ə-lā′shən) *noun* Enthusiastic or even excessive praise; fawning admiration. (From the Latin word *adulare*, meaning "to flatter")

    EXAMPLE Some celebrities enjoy the *adulation* of their fans; others dislike it.

   2. _____

3. **anathema** (ə-năth′ə-mə) *noun* **a.** A strong denunciation. **b.** A formal religious condemnation. **c.** Anything or anyone so condemned. (From the Greek word *anathēma*, meaning "an accursed thing")

    EXAMPLE I know that if I play rock music I will be *anathema* in my father's house.

   3. _____

4. **commend** (kə-měnd′) *trans. verb* To mention approvingly; praise. (From the Latin word *commendare*, meaning "to entrust" or "to recommend")

    RELATED WORDS **commendable** *adjective*; **commendation** *noun*

    EXAMPLE Both you and I *commend* Laura for her championship skiing.

   4. _____
   SEE *extol*.

Copyright © Houghton Mifflin Company. All rights reserved.

Praise and Criticism 161

5. **eulogy** (yōō′lə-jē) *noun* A speech or written tribute of praise, most often one delivered at a memorial service in honor of the deceased. (From the Greek *eu-*, meaning "good," and *logos*, meaning "speech")

   RELATED WORD **eulogize** *verb*

   EXAMPLE Mark Antony's *eulogy* of Caesar is one of the best-known passages in Shakespeare.

6. **extol** (ĭk-stōl′) *trans. verb* To praise highly. (From the Latin words *ex*, meaning "off," and *tollere*, meaning "to lift")

   EXAMPLE Miguel grew embarrassed as the principal continued to *extol* him for a full five minutes during the awards program.

   USAGE NOTE *Commend* means "to praise," but *extol* means "to praise *highly*."

7. **homage** (hŏm′ĭj, ŏm′ĭj) *noun* Particular respect or honor shown publicly.

   EXAMPLE At his inauguration the new mayor paid *homage* to the former mayor for her achievements in office.

8. **laudable** (lô′də-bəl) *adjective* Worthy of praise. (From the Latin word *laus*, meaning "praise")

   RELATED WORD **laud** *verb*

   EXAMPLE Sparky took a first in the steeplechase because of his *laudable* jumps over the water hazards.

9. **reproach** (rĭ-prōch′) *trans. verb* To blame or criticize for something. *noun* Blame; discredit; an act of criticism: *to be above reproach*.

   RELATED WORD **reproachful** *adjective*

   EXAMPLE Why does Alice *reproach* me for doing what I am asked to do?

10. **reverence** (rĕv′ər-əns) *noun* **a.** A feeling of great respect, even of awe or love; veneration. **b.** An act showing respect, such as a bow or curtsy. *trans. verb* To venerate; show respect toward. (From the Latin word *reverentia*, meaning "respect" or "fear")

    RELATED WORDS **revere** *verb*; **reverend** *adjective, noun*; **reverent** *adjective*

    EXAMPLE Elizabeth shows great *reverence* for her grandfather.

162 Praise and Criticism

Name _____   Date _____

Exercise 1 Matching Words and Definitions

Match the definition in Column B with the word in Column A. Write the letter of the correct definition on the answer line.

Column A	Column B
1. reproach	a. an expression of great praise
2. reverence	b. excessive praise or admiration
3. accolade	c. a condemnation
4. laudable	d. a speech or written tribute of praise
5. commend	e. to praise highly
6. homage	f. to blame or criticize
7. adulation	g. worthy of praise
8. anathema	h. to mention approvingly
9. eulogy	i. a feeling of great respect
10. extol	j. respect shown publicly

1. _____
2. _____
3. _____
4. _____
5. _____
6. _____
7. _____
8. _____
9. _____
10. _____

Exercise 2 Using Words Correctly

Decide whether the italicized vocabulary word has been used correctly in the sentence. On the answer line, write *Correct* for correct use and *Incorrect* for incorrect use.

1. The townspeople showed great *reverence* for the outlaw by driving him out of their town.
2. The Nobel Prize is an *accolade* for extraordinary achievement.
3. Parents usually *reproach* their children for good grades.
4. The prosecutor *extolled* the criminal record of the defendant.
5. Michelle is studying *eulogy* at college.
6. The reviewer *commended* the new book by saying that the writing is meaningless.
7. The young teacher was delighted by his students' *adulation*.
8. Arthur gave Hester an *anathema* for her birthday.
9. The subjects showed their *homage* to the king by swearing to defend him and his realm.
10. For his *laudable* actions during the war, Samuel Graves was invited to the White House.

1. _____
2. _____
3. _____
4. _____
5. _____
6. _____
7. _____
8. _____
9. _____
10. _____

Exercise 3 Identifying Antonyms

Decide which word has the meaning that is opposite to that of the capitalized vocabulary word. Write the letter of your choice on the answer line.

1. ANATHEMA:
   a. hymn   b. commendation   c. criticism   d. condemnation

1. _____

Praise and Criticism

2. **LAUDABLE:**
   a. commendable   b. blameworthy   c. debatable   d. good

3. **EXTOL:**
   a. praise   b. charge   c. applaud   d. condemn

4. **HOMAGE:**
   a. reverence   b. disrespect   c. praise   d. criticism

5. **REPROACH:**
   a. contempt   b. praiseworthy   c. praise   d. worth

6. **EULOGY:**
   a. funeral   b. poem   c. anathema   d. obituary

7. **ADULATION:**
   a. condemnation   b. comparison   c. eulogy   d. worry

8. **ACCOLADE:**
   a. praise   b. surprise   c. honor   d. censure

9. **REVERENCE:**
   a. respect   b. disrespect   c. honor   d. glory

10. **COMMEND:**
    a. blame   b. recommend   c. tolerate   d. exult

Exercise 4   Using Different Forms of Words

Decide which form of the vocabulary word in parentheses best completes the sentence. The form given may be correct. Write your answer on the answer line.

1. I cannot stand Tricia's __?__ glances. (*reproach*)
2. Yesterday they were __?__ us as if we were saints. (*extol*)
3. My friend Marta received a letter of __?__ for her efforts on behalf of the homeless. (*commend*)
4. King Kamehameha acknowledged the __?__ of the crowds. (*adulation*)
5. The movie *Black Orpheus* won __?__ around the world when it was first released. (*accolade*)
6. Is __?__ behavior expected when visiting a cathedral? (*reverence*)
7. Pay __?__ where homage is due. (*homage*)
8. Steven is __?__ to us since he broke the window. (*anathema*)
9. Whom shall we ask to __?__ Dolores? (*eulogy*)
10. Your decision to become a missionary is __?__. (*laudable*)

164   Praise and Criticism

Reading Comprehension

Each numbered sentence in the following passage contains an italicized vocabulary word. After you read the passage, you will complete an exercise.

Charles Lindbergh: Aviation Pioneer

(1) In 1927 a twenty-five-year-old aviator named Charles Lindbergh won the *adulation* of all Americans. **(2)** In fact, he received *accolades* from around the world, for he had become the first person to make a solo flight across the Atlantic.

After two years of college, Lindbergh took flying lessons. Soon he bought a World War I plane with which he made stunt-flying tours. **(3)** He then became an airmail pilot flying the mail from St. Louis to Chicago, and during this time he developed a *reverence* for flying and for aircraft that was to last for the rest of his life.

In 1919 a New York hotel owner offered a prize of $25,000 to the first person to fly across the Atlantic. For years no one attempted the feat. On the morning of May 20, 1927, however, Charles Lindbergh took off from New York and landed thirty-three and a half hours later in France. **(4)** This *laudable* achievement made him an international hero. **(5)** A crowd estimated at one hundred thousand people turned out to pay *homage* to the courageous young pilot. **(6)** He was *extolled* in the press and by heads of state for his bravery.

Returning to the United States, he received many honors. He subsequently became a valued consultant for the aircraft industry and the military. He continued to be honored and decorated by many nations. **(7)** One of these was Germany, a country that many nations *reproached* for its actions during the 1930s. **(8)** Critics found little to *commend* in Lindbergh's decision to accept an award from Germany. **(9)** Later these critics would hurl *anathemas* against him for his opposition to American involvement in World War II. Many critics thought him a traitor, although he flew combat missions in the war and continued to advise the United States government on aviation.

After the war ended, Lindbergh retired to a quieter life in Connecticut and Hawaii with his wife, the distinguished writer Anne Morrow Lindbergh. **(10)** On his death in 1974, many political, military, and business leaders throughout the world gave *eulogies* of this hero.

Reading Comprehension Exercise

Each of the following statements corresponds to a numbered sentence in the passage. Each statement contains a blank and is followed by four answer choices. Decide which choice fits best in the blank. The word or phrase that you choose must express roughly the same meaning as the italicized word in the passage. Write the letter of your choice on the answer line.

1. The young Lindbergh received ___?___ from all Americans.
   a. unfair criticism   c. respectful tributes
   b. love   d. great admiration

   1. _____

2. ___?___ poured in from around the world.
   a. Reporters   c. Expressions of approval
   b. Gifts of money   d. Job offers

   2. _____

3. Lindbergh had ___?___ for flying and aircraft.
   a. talent   b. respect   c. time   d. nerve

   3. _____

Copyright © 1988 Houghton Mifflin Company. All rights reserved.   Praise and Criticism 165

4. His __?__ achievement made him a hero.
   a. praising   **b.** unique   **c.** blameworthy   **d.** praiseworthy

4. _____

5. A huge crowd turned out to __?__ to the pilot.
   a. give money   **c.** sing praises
   b. send greetings   **d.** show respect

5. _____

6. Chiefs of state and publications __?__ his bravery.
   a. praised   **b.** criticized   **c.** questioned   **d.** cheered

6. _____

7. Many nations __?__ Germany for its harmful actions in the 1930s.
   a. blamed   **b.** praised   **c.** fought   **d.** attacked

7. _____

8. Critics did not __?__ Lindbergh's decision to accept an award from Germany.
   a. mention approvingly   **c.** deal harshly with
   b. comment on   **d.** tolerate

8. _____

9. They hurled __?__ at him.
   a. remarks   **b.** stones   **c.** denunciations   **d.** criticisms

9. _____

10. Many gave __?__ upon his death.
    a. poems   **b.** their lives   **c.** tributes   **d.** flowers

10. _____

Writing Assignment

The birthdays of both George Washington and Abraham Lincoln are commemorated on the third Monday in February. Suppose your school is planning a program to honor the memory of these two Presidents. Using at least five vocabulary words from this lesson and underlining each one, write a fitting tribute to one of these men for a public presentation to be made at your school.

Vocabulary Enrichment

The word *homage* dates from the French Middle Ages. When the groups of men known as vassals sought the protection of strong leaders, known as lords, the latter would require of the vassals a formal, public declaration of loyalty. This declaration was known as *homage*, from the French word *homme*, meaning "man," for the vassal thus declared himself to be the lord's man. Thereafter, the vassal was obliged to serve the lord, and the lord was obliged to protect the vassal.

Such feudal political arrangements no longer exist, but the word *homage* is still in use with the more general meaning of "any public display or declaration of honor and respect."

ACTIVITY The culture of the Middle Ages in Europe has contributed a number of words to modern English. Consulting a dictionary, write the etymology for each of the following words. The etymology will probably give you some sense of what the word meant or how it was used in the Middle Ages. Then, using the definition of the word given in your dictionary, write a sentence in which the word appears.

1. chivalry   2. fealty   3. feudal   4. mortgage   5. serf

Lesson 26

Ignoring and Paying Attention

According to Charles Dickens, "The one serviceable, safe, certain, remunerative, attainable quality in every study and every pursuit is the quality of attention." Even though Dickens made his observation in the nineteenth century, you probably experience daily the real-life applications of his statement. For example, when you ignore distractions and concentrate on what you are studying, you undoubtedly understand and remember more information. On the other hand, when you overlook certain key phrases in a set of directions, you may get lost or confused. The words in this lesson will help you to understand and apply the value of attention.

WORD LIST
assess
disregard
enthrall
heedless
indifferent
oblivious
preoccupy
receptive
scrutinize
vigilant

DEFINITIONS

After you have studied the definitions and example for each vocabulary word, write the word on the line to the right.

1. **assess** (ə-sĕs′) *trans. verb* **a.** To determine the significance or importance of; evaluate; appraise. **b.** To estimate the value of property for taxation; set the amount of a tax, fine, or other payment. (From the Latin word *assidere*, meaning "to sit by in council")

   RELATED WORDS **assessment** *noun;* **assessor** *noun*

   EXAMPLE The personnel director *assessed* the skills of each applicant for the job.

2. **disregard** (dĭs′rĭ-gärd′) *trans. verb* **a.** To pay little or no attention to; ignore or neglect. **b.** To treat as unworthy of notice. *noun* Lack of thoughtful attention or proper respect.

   EXAMPLE Realizing that Pat was in a bad mood, Jared *disregarded* her apparent rudeness.

3. **enthrall** (ĕn-thrôl′) *trans. verb* To captivate; hold spellbound; charm. (From the English *en-*, meaning "in," and the Old Norse word *thraell*, meaning "slave")

   RELATED WORD **enthrallment** *noun*

   EXAMPLE Luciano Pavarotti's voice *enthralls* opera lovers throughout the world.

Ignoring and Paying Attention 167

4. **heedless** (hēd′lĭs) *adjective* **a.** Unmindful; inattentive; unobservant. **b.** Careless.
   RELATED WORDS   **heed** *noun;* **heed** *verb;* **heedful** *adjective;* **heedlessly** *adverb;* **heedlessness** *noun*
   EXAMPLE   Karen, *heedless* of the weather report, did not take a raincoat or umbrella.

4. _____
USAGE NOTE The noun *heed* is usually used with *give* and *to* or with *pay* and *to*: "*Pay* heed *to* my warning."

5. **indifferent** (ĭn-dĭf′ər-ənt, ĭn-dĭf′rənt) *adjective* **a.** Marked by a lack of interest in or concern about something; uninvolved. **b.** Showing no preference; impartial; unbiased. **c.** Neither good nor bad; mediocre.
   RELATED WORDS   **indifference** *noun;* **indifferently** *adverb*
   EXAMPLE   The nonvoters were *indifferent* to the outcome of the election.

5. _____

6. **oblivious** (ə-blĭv′ē-əs) *adjective* **a.** Lacking conscious awareness. **b.** Forgetful. (From the Latin word *oblivisci*, meaning "to forget")
   RELATED WORDS   **oblivion** *noun;* **obliviously** *adverb;* **obliviousness** *noun*
   EXAMPLE   When Zoe is reading a book, she is *oblivious* to almost anything happening around her.

6. _____

7. **preoccupy** (prē-ŏk′yə-pī′) *trans. verb* To hold the attention or interest of; engross.
   RELATED WORDS   **preoccupation** *noun;* **preoccupied** *adjective*
   EXAMPLE   The technical details of database development often *preoccupy* Alan.

7. _____

8. **receptive** (rĭ-sĕp′tĭv) *adjective* Ready or willing to receive something favorably. (From the Latin word *recipere*, meaning "to receive")
   RELATED WORDS   **receptively** *adverb;* **receptivity** *noun*
   EXAMPLE   The director of the play appreciated the *receptive* attitude of the cast.

8. _____

9. **scrutinize** (skro͞ot′n-īz′) *trans. verb* To pay close attention to minute detail; examine something carefully, critically, or searchingly. (From the Latin word *scrutari*, meaning "to search" or "to examine")
   RELATED WORD   **scrutiny** *noun*
   EXAMPLE   The structural engineer *scrutinized* the damage to the apartment building.

9. _____

10. **vigilant** (vĭj′ə-lənt) *adjective* Watchful; on the alert; wary. (From the Latin word *vigilare*, meaning "to be watchful")
    RELATED WORDS   **vigil** *noun;* **vigilance** *noun;* **vigilantly** *adverb*
    EXAMPLE   Without the efforts of the *vigilant* forest ranger, many acres of trees might have been destroyed by the fire.

10. _____

Name _____ Date _____

Exercise 1 Completing Definitions

On the answer line, write the word from the vocabulary list that best completes each definition.

1. If you examine something carefully, you __?__ it.
2. People who lack conscious awareness are __?__ .
3. To captivate or charm is to __?__ .
4. To evaluate something is to __?__ it.
5. One who is watchful or on the alert is __?__ .
6. To pay little attention to or to neglect is to __?__ .
7. If something holds your attention, it __?__ you.
8. One who is inattentive or careless is __?__ .
9. If someone has little concern about something, that person is __?__ .
10. A person who is willing to receive something favorably is __?__ .

1. _____
2. _____
3. _____
4. _____
5. _____
6. _____
7. _____
8. _____
9. _____
10. _____

Exercise 2 Using Words Correctly

Each of the following statements contains an italicized vocabulary word. Decide whether the sentence is true or false, and write *True* or *False* on the answer line.

1. Banks *assess* the value of houses before giving mortgages.
2. A good zoo keeper is *oblivious* to the basic needs of the animals.
3. A *heedless* mountain climber is one who closely follows the leader's directions.
4. A *vigilant* security guard would notice an open window.
5. Skimming an article means *scrutinizing* the information in it.
6. A *receptive* person may be willing to try a variety of new activities.
7. People who *disregard* a fire alarm might leave the building quickly through the emergency exit.
8. A student could be so *preoccupied* with an English test that she would not notice the class period was over.
9. The hockey game *enthralled* the spectators, many of whom left at the half.
10. Most parents are *indifferent* about their children's future.

1. _____
2. _____
3. _____
4. _____
5. _____
6. _____
7. _____
8. _____
9. _____
10. _____

Exercise 3 Choosing the Best Word

Decide which vocabulary word or related form best completes the sentence, and write the letter of your choice on the answer line.

1. The __?__ dog growled at any stranger who approached the house.
   a. receptive   b. vigilant   c. indifferent   d. oblivious

1. _____

Copyright © 1988 Houghton Mifflin Company. All rights reserved.   **Ignoring and Paying Attention**   **169**

2. The sailor almost drowned during the storm because he was __?__ the severe weather warning.
   a. enthralled by   c. preoccupied with
   b. receptive to   d. heedless of

3. The experienced jeweler __?__ the value of Mrs. Phillips's antique pearl necklace.
   a. enthralled   b. preoccupied   c. assessed   d. disregarded

4. Lynn was __?__ fixing her bike, so she would not come to the beach with us.
   a. preoccupied with   c. heedless of
   b. assessed by   d. indifferent to

5. Maura __?__ the notice about crew practice because she played lacrosse.
   a. assessed   c. was enthralled by
   b. was preoccupied with   d. disregarded

6. After Mitch tried unsuccessfully to build a treehouse, he became more __?__ his father's suggestions.
   a. indifferent to   b. receptive to   c. oblivious to   d. heedless of

7. Because the candidate was __?__ the concerns of farmers in her state, she lost the election.
   a. enthralled by   c. oblivious to
   b. receptive to   d. scrutinized by

8. Mr. Garibaldi __?__ the painting to determine its authenticity.
   a. disregarded   b. preoccupied   c. scrutinized   d. enthralled

9. The blizzard __?__ Lani, who had never seen snow.
   a. assessed   b. scrutinized   c. disregarded   d. enthralled

10. We were disappointed by the violinist's __?__ performance.
    a. indifferent   b. enthralling   c. receptive   d. vigilant

Exercise 4 Using Different Forms of Words

Each sentence contains an italicized vocabulary word in a form that does not fit the sentence. On the answer line, write the form of the word that does fit the sentence.

1. Victor *heedless* ignored the sign that said "Keep Out."

2. Malvina listened *receptive* to her gymnastics coach.

3. Contest entries are subject to the *scrutinize* of the judges.

4. Zola's *oblivious* of the cold surprised the spectators, who never expected to see her run barefoot in the snow.

5. The insurance agent sent Mr. Cooney an *assess* of the damage done to his orchard during the winter freeze.

6. The mother hawk *vigilant* guarded the nest.

7. Sean *disregard* the instructions in the cookbook.

8. Kayla's *indifferent* upset her friends.

9. The children enjoyed the *enthrall* mime show.

10. Paul's *preoccupy* with computers annoys his friends.

Reading Comprehension

Each numbered sentence in the following passage contains an italicized vocabulary word or related form. After you read the passage, you will complete an exercise.

The Vanishing Animals

What do the fur seal, blue whale, and California condor have in common? These creatures are among the twelve hundred species of animals that are presently regarded as endangered. **(1)** According to the **assessment** of zoologists and biologists, many of these creatures are unlikely to survive unless special measures are taken for their protection. **(2)** While some species are killed off by natural causes, the greatest danger to wildlife survival comes from **heedless** human activity. As human beings occupy more land for their homes, highways, and industries, their influence spreads over larger areas, destroying the habitats of many species. **(3)** In clearing forests, plowing grasslands, and draining swamps, people have sometimes **disregarded** the protective cover and food sources vital to wildlife. For example, the lumber industry in China has affected the growth of bamboo, the primary food of pandas.

(4) Since pandas are not **receptive** to changes in their diet, they are condemned to starvation. Only one thousand pandas remain in the wild.

Industrial pollution and insecticides used in farming have threatened the survival of many species. For example, chemicals in the atmosphere cause peregrine falcons to produce fragile eggs that are easily crushed before the young are hatched. In addition, water pollution has destroyed fish and algae that birds eat. **(5)** Modern technology is **indifferent** to the severe pressures that it exerts on countless animals.

Excessive commercial hunting has also taken its toll on many species of animals. **(6)** Consumers' **enthrallment** with luxurious furs stimulated hunters to kill huge numbers of fur seals. Because fur seals produce only one pup every two years, the species has not been able to renew itself. Whales, too, have been utilized beyond their capacity to reproduce. **(7)** **Preoccupied** with the heavy demands for whale by-products used to make soap, pharmaceutical, and cosmetic products, some industries have placed commercial rewards above the quotas set to restrict whale killing.

(8) The changes made in the environment by humans **oblivious** to the need for protecting it have been disastrous for many organisms. **(9)** According to the scientists who **scrutinize** environmental changes, an increasing number of animal species will become extinct. By ignoring the need for conservation, we lose much that cannot be replaced. **(10)** Greater effort and **vigilance** are needed to protect today's endangered species and to prevent future threats to wildlife. Because every species plays a role in maintaining the balanced, living systems of the earth, a world no longer fit for wild creatures might also become unfit for people.

Reading Comprehension Exercise

Each of the following statements corresponds to a numbered sentence in the passage. Each statement contains a blank and is followed by four answer choices. Decide which choice fits best in the blank. The word or phrase that you choose must express roughly the same meaning as the italicized word in the passage. Write the letter of your choice on the answer line.

1. In the __?__ of scientists, many creatures are unlikely to survive without protective measures.
   a. judgment   **b.** philosophy   **c.** books   **d.** theories

1. _____

2. ___?___ human activity threatens wildlife survival.
   a. Uncaring   b. Increased   c. Creative   d. Certain

3. People sometimes ___?___ the protective cover and food sources of animals when they clear forests and drain swamps.
   a. value   b. improve   c. ignore   d. build

4. Pandas do not ___?___ changes in diet.
   a. make   b. look for   c. object to   d. react favorably to

5. Modern technology is ___?___ the pressures it exerts on animals.
   a. liable for   c. responsible for
   b. unconcerned about   d. aware of

6. People's ___?___ luxurious furs caused hunters to kill many fur seals.
   a. captivation with   c. interest in
   b. dismay about   d. disillusionment with

7. People are ___?___ the demands for whale by-products.
   a. happy with   c. excessively concerned with
   b. disgusted by   d. responsible for

8. ___?___ human beings have failed to protect the environment.
   a. Without hesitation   c. Without conscience
   b. Without conscious awareness d. Without expert advice

9. Certain scientists ___?___ these environmental changes.
   a. pay close attention to   c. pay lip service to
   b. neglect   d. wonder about

10. ___?___ is needed to protect today's endangered species.
    a. Interest   b. Prevention   c. Education   d. Watchfulness

Writing Assignment

Suppose that you are the writer of a newspaper column on advice to teen-agers. You have received a letter from a fifteen-year-old who has just entered a new school and feels ignored by other students. Write a response, suggesting some positive ways in which this person can get attention and make new friends. Use at least five of the words from this lesson in your letter and underline each one.

Vocabulary Enrichment

Vigilant comes from the Latin word *vigilare*, meaning "to watch." The English word *vigilante*, meaning "a person belonging to an unauthorized group organized to keep watch and punish crime," and the expression *to keep a vigil*, meaning "to keep watch," also come from *vigilare*.

Vigilant, *vigil*, and *vigilante* have a connection with Roman history. *Vigiles* were watchers who acted as guards, police officers, and firefighters. Thus, the word *vigiles* is related to our English words *vigilant*, *vigil*, and *vigilante* through the common idea of alert watchfulness.

ACTIVITY Using your dictionary, look up the following words, and write their meanings and the oldest form of their roots. Then write a brief explanation for each, connecting the root with the current definition.

1. doctor   2. custodian   3. accountant   4. carpenter   5. architect

Lesson 27

The Root -tract-

The root -tract- is derived from the Latin word *tractus*, meaning "a drawing" or "a pulling," and occurs in many English words. When a magnet *attracts* something metallic, it draws the object toward itself. *Subtraction* involves drawing one number out of another, and a *tractor* pulls other farm implements. In this lesson you will learn ten English words derived from the Latin *tractus* or from its French derivative *trait*.

WORD LIST
contract
detract
distraction
entreaty
extract
portray
protracted
retract
tract
trait

DEFINITIONS

After you have studied the definitions and example for each vocabulary word, write the word on the line to the right.

1. **contract** (kŏn'trăkt') *noun* **a.** A formal agreement between two or more parties, particularly one enforceable by law. **b.** The document containing such an agreement. *trans. verb* (kən-trăkt', kŏn'trăkt') To enter into a formal agreement. *intrans. verb* To grow smaller.
   RELATED WORDS **contraction** *noun;* **contractor** *noun;* **contractual** *adjective*
   EXAMPLE Some athletes have *contracts* worth millions of dollars.

2. **detract** (dĭ-trăkt') *intrans. verb* To take away something desirable; diminish the value of. (From the Latin word *detractus*, meaning "drawn away")
   EXAMPLE Their bad manners *detract* from their pleasant appearance.

3. **distraction** (dĭ-străk'shən) *noun* Something that draws the mind away from the original direction of attention or interest; a diversion of attention. (From the Latin word *distractus*, meaning "pulled apart")
   RELATED WORD **distract** *verb*
   EXAMPLE Loud music can be a *distraction* when one is reading.

4. **entreaty** (ĕn-trē′tē) *noun* An earnest request or plea.
   RELATED WORD **entreat** *verb*
   EXAMPLE The conservationist made an *entreaty* to all visitors to Big Bend National Park that they keep the footpaths and streams clean.

5. **extract** (ĭk-străkt′) *trans. verb* To pull or draw out forcibly. *noun* (ĕk′străkt′) **a.** A passage from a literary work; an excerpt. **b.** A concentrated substance, such as a food flavoring. (From the Latin word *extractus*, meaning "pulled out")
   RELATED WORD **extraction** *noun*
   EXAMPLE The dentist will *extract* your tooth this afternoon.

6. **portray** (pôr-trā′) *trans. verb* **a.** To make a likeness or representation of. **b.** To describe in words. **c.** To play the part of in a movie or play.
   RELATED WORDS **portrait** *noun;* **portrayal** *noun*
   EXAMPLE The paintings *portray* Washington in military uniforms.

7. **protracted** (prō-trăk′tĭd, prə-trăk′tĭd) *adjective* Drawn out or lengthened in time; prolonged.
   EXAMPLE A *protracted* illness is one that lasts for a long time.

8. **retract** (rĭ-trăkt′) *trans. verb* To draw back; withdraw. (From the Latin word *retractus*, meaning "drawn back")
   RELATED WORD **retraction** *noun*
   EXAMPLE I *retract* the statement that I made earlier.

9. **tract** (trăkt) *noun* **a.** A stretch of land. **b.** A system of related organs: *the digestive tract.* **c.** A leaflet or pamphlet, particularly one on a religious or political theme.
   EXAMPLE The peasants in Bosnia lived and worked on a small *tract* of farmland.

10. **trait** (trāt) *noun* A distinguishing quality or feature. (From the French word *trait*, meaning "a line" or "a stroke")
    EXAMPLE *Traits* to look for when buying a dog are friendliness and intelligence.

4. _____

5. _____

6. _____

7. _____

8. _____

9. _____

10. _____

Name _____ Date _____

Exercise 1 Matching Words and Definitions

Match the definition in Column B with the word in Column A. Write the letter of the correct definition on the answer line.

Column A

1. entreaty
2. trait
3. contract
4. protracted
5. distraction
6. tract
7. detract
8. portray
9. retract
10. extract

Column B

a. a disturbance of thought or attention
b. a stretch of land
c. a distinguishing feature
d. a formal agreement between two or more parties
e. to withdraw
f. an earnest plea
g. to take away something desirable
h. prolonged; lengthy
i. to pull out forcibly
j. to create a likeness of

1. _____
2. _____
3. _____
4. _____
5. _____
6. _____
7. _____
8. _____
9. _____
10. _____

Exercise 2 Using Words Correctly

Decide whether the italicized vocabulary word has been used correctly in the sentence. On the answer line, write *Correct* for correct use and *Incorrect* for incorrect use.

1. Molly *retracted* her statement by repeating it.
2. Irving found it very easy to study for the test because of the many *distractions* in the library.
3. One of the most notable *traits* of Abraham Lincoln was his honesty.
4. In *Alice in Wonderland*, the Queen of Hearts is *portrayed* as a mean and selfish woman.
5. The fullback signed a *contract* with the Seattle Seahawks for three years.
6. The Boardmans purchased a *tract* of land near Higgins Cove in Maine.
7. Aunt Rosa's *protracted* cold worried us.
8. The carefully trimmed lawn *detracted* from the appearance of the yard.
9. Mr. Sullivan *extracted* a nail from the board by forcefully hammering it into the wood.
10. The prisoner made an *entreaty* to the captain to free him.

1. _____
2. _____
3. _____
4. _____
5. _____
6. _____
7. _____
8. _____
9. _____
10. _____

Exercise 3 Choosing the Best Word

Decide which vocabulary word or related form best completes the sentence, and write the letter of your choice on the answer line.

1. The artist could not concentrate because of the __?__ of the children's noise.
   a. entreaty   b. retraction   c. distraction   d. extraction

1. _____

Copyright © 1988 Houghton Mifflin Company. All rights reserved.   The Root *-tract-*   175

2. As a result of the drought, the twelve-hundred-acre __?__ of land was no longer good for farming.
   a. tract   b. trait   c. portrayal   d. contract

3. The Blumenthals __?__ their offer for the house when they saw the termites.
   a. protracted   b. portrayed   c. distracted   d. retracted

4. Before building the submarines, the company signed a(n) __?__ with the Navy.
   a. entreaty   b. tract   c. contract   d. retraction

5. Two __?__ of the eagle are keen eyesight and sharp talons.
   a. distractions   b. traits   c. extractions   d. tracts

6. The peeling paint __?__ from the beauty of the historic house.
   a. detracted   b. entreated   c. protracted   d. extracted

7. Melba's __?__ that her brother be given a second chance fell on deaf ears.
   a. distraction   b. portrayal   c. contract   d. entreaty

8. Oliver and Nina had a __?__ ride to school because of the long detour on the Misquamicut Road.
   a. contract   b. protracted   c. retraction   d. distracted

9. Dr. Spencer-Churchill __?__ the splinter from Karen's foot.
   a. distracted   b. detracted   c. protracted   d. extracted

10. The writer __?__ the Alameda Forest as a place of adventure and exploration.
    a. tracts   b. entreated   c. portrayed   d. contracted

Exercise 4   Using Different Forms of Words

Decide which form of the vocabulary word in parentheses best completes the sentence. The form given may be correct. Write your answer on the answer line.

1. Yesterday the organizers repeatedly __?__ the audience to be quiet. *(entreaty)*

2. Mrs. Elias decided to make a __?__ of her statement to the press. *(retract)*

3. The __?__ agreement calls for two shows per night. *(contract)*

4. Marina knew that the __?__ would be easy because the tooth was very loose. *(extract)*

5. The audience was pleased by the actor's __?__ of Agamemnon. *(portray)*

6. Penny's bad sportsmanship __?__ from her effectiveness in the game of hockey. *(detract)*

7. Moira handed out political __?__ to the people in the street. *(tract)*

8. The snowfall is __?__ the children today. *(distraction)*

9. Which __?__ are important for bankers? *(trait)*

10. The __?__ debate went on for seven hours. *(protracted)*

Reading Comprehension

Each numbered sentence in the following passage contains an italicized vocabulary word or related form. After you read the passage, you will complete an exercise.

Mohandas Gandhi: "Great Soul"

As the spiritual and political leader of modern India, Mohandas Gandhi (1869–1948) led a life dedicated to his country. **(1)** Determined to **extract** a promise of independence from Britain, he received international attention. **(2)** Gandhi's **protracted** efforts to improve the living conditions of the Indian people also brought him respect from people in all parts of the world. **(3)** His unusual tactics for achieving social and economic reform did not **detract** from the idealism of his political beliefs.

Gandhi was born in western India and attended University College, Cambridge, where he became a lawyer. In 1893 he went to South Africa as a defense attorney. **(4)** However, he was soon **distracted** from his legal work when he began to work on behalf of the ill-treated Indian residents. **(5)** For more than twenty years, he campaigned against the unfair **contracts** under which the Indian peasants had to work. His methods, including that of deliberately breaking the law, eventually led to some reforms.

After World War I, Gandhi directed his attention toward his homeland. **(6)** He made an **entreaty** to the British government that India be granted independence. **(7)** Refusing to **retract** his demands, he continued the practice of nonviolent civil disobedience, which, nevertheless, stirred up riots against the British. Several times he went on hunger strikes to win political reforms, and he was imprisoned on many occasions for his political activities. Finally, in August, 1947, Gandhi's dream of a free India came true when the independent nations of India and Pakistan were created.

(8) Gandhi is **portrayed** by many writers as a wise and gentle man of very simple tastes. **(9)** Like the poorest Indian peasant living on the smallest **tract** of land, he wore simple clothing and ate meagerly. Often seen spinning thread with a primitive spinning wheel, he encouraged the development of simple Indian industries. **(10)** Some Indians held Gandhi's **traits** of goodness and devotion in such high regard that they bestowed upon him the title Mahatma, which means "great soul."

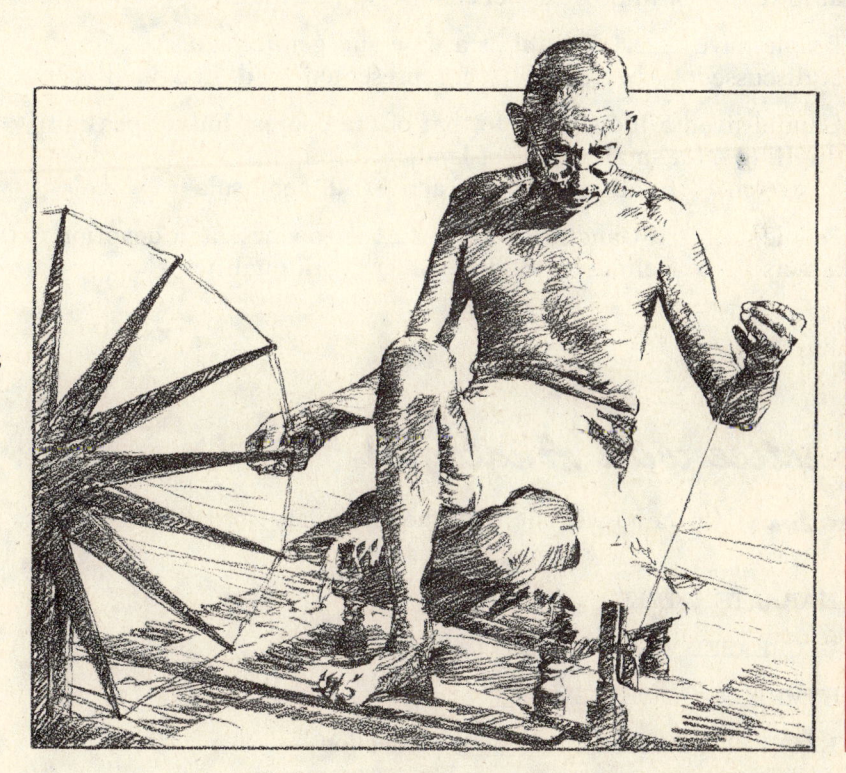

Please turn to the next page.

Reading Comprehension Exercise

Each of the following statements corresponds to a numbered sentence in the passage. Each statement contains a blank and is followed by four answer choices. Decide which choice fits best in the blank. The word or phrase that you choose must express roughly the same meaning as the italicized word in the passage. Write the letter of your choice on the answer line.

1. Gandhi had made up his mind to __?__ a promise from Britain.
   a. request   b. keep   c. obtain   d. ignore

2. His __?__ efforts to help the Indian people also won him respect.
   a. kindly   b. prolonged   c. courageous   d. dedicated

3. His tactics did not __?__ the idealism of his political beliefs.
   a. achieve   b. increase   c. diminish   d. match

4. He was soon __?__ his legal work because of the ill-treatment of Indians.
   a. diverted from   c. an expert in
   b. bored with   d. engrossed in

5. The Indian peasants had to work under unfair __?__ .
   a. conditions   b. masters   c. agreements   d. rules

6. After World War I, Gandhi issued a __?__ to the British for independence.
   a. demand   b. proclamation   c. statement   d. plea

7. Gandhi refused to __?__ his demands.
   a. lower   b. improve   c. change   d. withdraw

8. People have __?__ Gandhi as a wise and gentle man.
   a. discussed   b. treated   c. represented   d. imagined

9. Gandhi lived a life similar to that of the poorest Indian peasant dwelling on a small __?__ of land.
   a. stretch   b. allotment   c. acre   d. peninsula

10. People admired Gandhi for his __?__ of goodness and devotion.
    a. acts   b. feelings   c. personality   d. qualities

Practice with Analogies

See page 79 for some strategies to use with analogies.

DIRECTIONS On the answer line, write the vocabulary word that completes each analogy.

1. NARRATE : TELL : : depict : __?__
2. DECREASED : SHORTENED : : extended : __?__
3. SYMPTOM : DISEASE : : __?__ : personality
4. EXCERPT : PASSAGE : : __?__ : selection
5. TREATY : NATIONS : : __?__ : persons

178   The Root -tract-

Name _____ Date _____

Reading Skills

The Suffixes *-ful* and *-ous*

A **suffix** is a group of letters added to the end of a word or a root. A suffix changes the part of speech of the word or the root. Many words, such as *joyful, furious, beautiful,* and *gracious,* end with the suffix *-ful* or *-ous*. These suffixes usually change nouns into adjectives. For example, when *-ful* is added to *joy,* the adjective *joyful* is formed; when *-ous* is added to *fury,* the adjective *furious* is formed. (Sometimes, however, *-ful* is used as a noun suffix of measurement, as in *handful* or *cupful*.) Notice that when *-ful* or *-ous* is added to a word, it may undergo a spelling change. In *beautiful,* for example, the *y* of *beauty* becomes an *i;* and in *gracious* the *e* of *grace* is replaced with an *i*.

The common meanings of the suffixes *-ful* and *-ous* are as follows.

SUFFIX MEANING	WORD	DEFINITION
1. *-ful:* full of	hopeful	full of hope
-ful: causing	dreadful	causing dread
2. *-ous:* possessing; characterized by	hilarious	characterized by hilarity

To determine the meanings of words ending with these suffixes, use the same procedure that you use for analyzing words with prefixes. Remember, however, that word analysis gives you an approximate definition. To verify the meaning of an unfamiliar word, look the word up in the dictionary.

Exercise Using the Suffixes *-ful* and *-ous*

Each sentence in this exercise contains an italicized noun. *Step 1:* Form an adjective by adding *-ful* or *-ous* to the italicized word. Write the resulting word, making any necessary spelling changes. *Step 2:* Write your definition of the adjective. In your definition try not to repeat the original noun. *Step 3:* Check your definition and spelling of the word in the dictionary. Then write a sentence of your own in which you use the adjective correctly.

1. At the Kavanaugh wedding reception, there was much gaiety and *mirth*.

ADJECTIVE FORM _____

DEFINITION _____

SENTENCE _____

Please turn to the next page.

Copyright © 1988 Houghton Mifflin Company. All rights reserved. The Suffixes *-ful* and *-ous* 179

2. Franklin lay in the hammock all day, but considering what he had accomplished in the past month, his *languor* was understandable.

   ADJECTIVE FORM _____
   DEFINITION _____
   SENTENCE _____

3. Gloomy Mr. Binxley always has a tale of *woe*.

   ADJECTIVE FORM _____
   DEFINITION _____
   SENTENCE _____

4. Some people live by *caprice* and just let things happen.

   ADJECTIVE FORM _____
   DEFINITION _____
   SENTENCE _____

5. She had little *mercy* for those who broke training rules.

   ADJECTIVE FORM _____
   DEFINITION _____
   SENTENCE _____

6. Carter experienced a few *tremors* just before her cue to appear on stage.

   ADJECTIVE FORM _____
   DEFINITION _____
   SENTENCE _____

7. A strange noise in the attic gave us all a *fright*.

   ADJECTIVE FORM _____
   DEFINITION _____
   SENTENCE _____

8. Jean's *sagacity* explains why so many of her friends seek her advice.

   ADJECTIVE FORM _____
   DEFINITION _____
   SENTENCE _____

9. I have always had a great *respect* for the achievements of Mother Teresa.

   ADJECTIVE FORM _____
   DEFINITION _____
   SENTENCE _____

The Suffixes *-ful* and *-ous*

Lesson 28

Thinking and Believing

Each day you use your mind to analyze problems, make decisions, form ideas, answer questions, and comprehend information. The ability to process knowledge in a logical way and to make judgments based on data is a valuable skill for all aspects of your life. Whether you read a science textbook in school or determine the value of a savings plan at work, you mentally organize information. In this lesson you will study words that refer to a range of thought processes.

WORD LIST
dogmatic
pensive
philosophy
plausible
ponder
postulate
rational
reverie
skeptical
speculation

DEFINITIONS

After you have studied the definitions and example for each vocabulary word, write the word on the line to the right.

1. **dogmatic** (dôg-măt′ĭk, dŏg-măt′ĭk) *adjective* Expressing a belief or opinion as if it were fact; excessively positive or emphatic. (From the Greek word *dogma*, meaning "belief")

   RELATED WORDS **dogma** *noun;* **dogmatically** *adverb;* **dogmatism** *noun*

   EXAMPLE The actor's *dogmatic* statements about the meaning of the play mystified the producer and director.

   1. _____

2. **pensive** (pĕn′sĭv) *adjective* Dreamily, and often sadly, thoughtful. (From the Latin word *pendere*, meaning "to weigh")

   RELATED WORDS **pensively** *adverb;* **pensiveness** *noun*

   EXAMPLE Darryl becomes *pensive* when his friends refer to the injury that ended his athletic career.

   2. _____

3. **philosophy** (fĭ-lŏs′ə-fē) *noun* **a.** The study of reality based on logical reasoning rather than factual observation. **b.** A personal set of opinions and values by which one lives. **c.** A basic, practical rule or set of rules: *Vince Lombardi's philosophy of coaching.* (From the Greek words *philos*, meaning "loving," and *sophia*, meaning "wisdom")

   RELATED WORDS **philosopher** *noun;* **philosophical** *adjective;* **philosophically** *adverb;* **philosophize** *verb*

   EXAMPLE *Philosophy* is not a body of specialized knowledge; instead, it is an activity directed toward understanding the nature of the world and reality.

   3. _____

Copyright © 1988 Houghton Mifflin Company. All rights reserved.

Thinking and Believing

4. **plausible** (plô′zə-bəl) *adjective* **a.** Appearing true or reasonable. **b.** Giving a deceptive impression of truth, acceptability, or reliability. (From the Latin word *plausibilis*, meaning "deserving applause")

   RELATED WORDS   **plausibility** *noun*; **plausibly** *adverb*

   EXAMPLE   Rosemary had a *plausible* explanation for the popularity of the Art Deco style in architecture.

5. **ponder** (pŏn′dər) *trans. verb* To think about something carefully and at length; weigh an idea in the mind.   *intrans. verb* To consider seriously and deeply. (From the Latin word *ponderare*, meaning "to weigh" or "to consider")

   EXAMPLE   Elspeth *pondered* the meaning of her recurring dream.

6. **postulate** (pŏs′chə-lāt′) *trans. verb* To assume the truth of something without proof, especially as the basis for study or argument; take something for granted.   *noun* (pŏs′choo-lĭt, pŏs′choo-lāt′) A theory proposed as the basis of a chain of reasoning; a basic principle. (From the Latin word *postulare*, meaning "to request" or "to claim")

   EXAMPLE   In geometry, students *postulate* theorems and then work problems to prove them.

7. **rational** (răsh′ən-əl) *adjective* **a.** Consistent with or based on reason; logical. **b.** Of sound mind; sane. (From the Latin word *ratio*, meaning "calculation" or "reckoning")

   RELATED WORD   **rationally** *adverb*

   EXAMPLE   The senator gave a *rational* argument for the new economic plan.

8. **reverie** (rĕv′ər-ē) *noun* **a.** The condition of being lost in thought. **b.** A daydream. (From the Old French word *rever*, meaning "to dream")

   EXAMPLE   The telephone failed to penetrate Grace's *reverie*.

9. **skeptical** (skĕp′tĭ-kəl) *adjective* Doubting; questioning. (From the Greek word *skeptesthai*, meaning "to examine")

   RELATED WORDS   **skeptic** *noun*; **skeptically** *adverb*; **skepticism** *noun*

   EXAMPLE   We were *skeptical* about the plane's arriving on time.

10. **speculation** (spĕk′yə-lā′shən) *noun* **a.** An idea based on incomplete evidence; guessing. **b.** A conclusion, idea, or opinion reached through reasoning; a theory. **c.** Business dealings that involve risk but offer the chance for a quick profit. (From the Latin word *specere*, meaning "to look at")

    RELATED WORDS   **speculate** *verb*; **speculative** *adjective*; **speculator** *noun*

    EXAMPLE   There was much *speculation* about who would win the World Series.

Name _____ Date _____

Exercise 1 Writing Correct Words

On the answer line, write the word from the vocabulary list that fits each definition.

1. Doubting; questioning
2. Expressing a belief as if it were fact; excessively positive
3. To think about carefully and at length
4. Based on reason; logical
5. Appearing true or reasonable
6. Guessing; a conclusion reached through reasoning
7. To assume the truth of something without proof; take for granted
8. Dreamily thoughtful
9. The study of the nature of things based on logical reasoning rather than factual observation
10. The condition of being lost in thought; a daydream

1. _____
2. _____
3. _____
4. _____
5. _____
6. _____
7. _____
8. _____
9. _____
10. _____

Exercise 2 Using Words Correctly

Decide whether the italicized vocabulary word has been used correctly in each sentence. On the answer line, write *Correct* for correct use and *Incorrect* for incorrect use.

1. *Dogmatic* speakers appear to be unsure of themselves.
2. People are usually more *rational* when they are calm than when they are upset.
3. A *skeptical* person would probably research a topic thoroughly before accepting information as factual.
4. Carlos *pondered* the question by answering it quickly.
5. Libby was in a *pensive* mood as her senior year drew to a close.
6. *Plausible* excuses are generally believable.
7. Although he had never tried the experiment, Gary *postulated* that the liquid would change to a gas.
8. During her daily *reverie*, Margo wrote letters and made telephone calls.
9. A thoughtful person, Ling had always wanted to study *philosophy*.
10. The archaeologist's *speculation* about the cave location was tested that very afternoon.

1. _____
2. _____
3. _____
4. _____
5. _____
6. _____
7. _____
8. _____
9. _____
10. _____

Copyright © 1988 Houghton Mifflin Company. All rights reserved.   Thinking and Believing

Exercise 3 Choosing the Best Word

Decide which vocabulary word or related form best expresses the meaning of the italicized word or phrase in the sentence. On the answer line, write the letter of the correct choice.

1. While looking out his window at Mount Greylock, Herman Melville *carefully weighed ideas* for the plot of *Moby Dick*.
   a. philosophized   b. pondered   c. speculated   d. postulated

2. Mrs. Hurdle realized that Kristen probably had a *reasonable* explanation of why she was two hours late.
   a. dogmatic   b. skeptical   c. philosophical   d. plausible

3. The barking dog jarred Lucien out of his *dreamlike state*.
   a. reverie   b. philosophy   c. skepticism   d. dogmatism

4. Dr. Lisle's *excessively positive* presentation of weather theory angered the audience of meteorologists.
   a. skeptical   b. pensive   c. rational   d. dogmatic

5. In Da Vinci's portrait, Mona Lisa wears a *sadly thoughtful* smile.
   a. rational   b. dogmatic   c. pensive   d. postulate

6. Dictators follow the *personal set of values* of "Might makes right."
   a. philosophy   b. plausibility   c. speculation   d. reverie

7. Early peoples *assumed without proof* that Earth was flat.
   a. philosophized   b. postulated   c. speculated   d. pondered

8. When electricity was discovered, many were *doubtful* about its use.
   a. pensive   b. skeptical   c. rational   d. dogmatic

9. There was much *guessing* among the office workers about the rumored sale of the company.
   a. reverie   b. dogmatism   c. philosophy   d. speculation

10. The committee admired Alexander's *logical* approach to the problem.
    a. pensive   b. dogmatic   c. rational   d. skeptical

1. _____
2. _____
3. _____
4. _____
5. _____
6. _____
7. _____
8. _____
9. _____
10. _____

Exercise 4 Using Different Forms of Words

Decide which form of the vocabulary word in parentheses best completes the sentence. The form given may be correct. Write your answer on the answer line.

1. The jeweler stated __?__ that pearls were once more valuable than diamonds. *(dogmatic)*

2. Uncle Ben nearly lost his temper but managed to respond __?__ . *(rational)*

3. Mother's __?__ was understandable since we had promised twice before to clean the basement. *(skeptical)*

4. __?__ his answer to the essay question, Joshua took several minutes to outline his major points. *(ponder)*

5. Phil explained his lateness __?__ . *(plausible)*

6. Ms. Ayala does not allow even a moment of __?__ in class. *(reverie)*

7. Carl was at the beach, staring __?__ at the whitecaps. *(pensive)*

1. _____
2. _____
3. _____
4. _____
5. _____
6. _____
7. _____

Name _____ Date _____

8. "Neither a borrower nor a lender be," Nadine reminded us __?__ . *(philosophy)*

8. _____

9. One important __?__ of gardening is that watering should be done only in early morning or evening. *(postulate)*

9. _____

10. Gerard and his family have decided to invest in a __?__ stock. *(speculation)*

10. _____

Reading Comprehension

Each numbered sentence in the following passage contains an italicized vocabulary word or related form. After you read the passage, you will complete an exercise.

Galileo: Astronomer and Physicist

Galileo Galilei (1564–1642), an Italian scientist, inventor, and mathematician, is regarded as one of the founders of modern experimental science. In addition to perfecting the telescope and inventing the pendulum clock, Galileo made a tremendous impact on the history of ideas.

In 1581 Galileo entered the University of Pisa to study medicine. He soon realized, however, that he was far more interested in mathematics. **(1)** One day, in a **pensive** mood, he sat in the cathedral. **(2)** As he **pondered** his new field, he noticed that the chandeliers swung in wide arcs once their candles were lit. **(3)** Deep in his **reverie,** Galileo theorized that the more widely swinging chandeliers would require longer periods to complete their arcs. By timing several with his pulse beat, he was surprised to discover that they all took approximately the same amount of time to complete a circle. From this informal experiment, Galileo worked out the laws of motion that govern pendulums. He then applied his findings to inventing a pendulum clock. Galileo had discovered an important pattern. **(4)** His simple observations led to questions, **speculations,** and experiments. **(5)** These, in turn, led to new knowledge and **plausible** applications.

Abandoning medicine for mathematical research, Galileo continued his study of motion. **(6)** Physics had previously been treated as a branch of **philosophy** and not as an experimental science. **(7)** Aristotle and other philosophers had **postulated** that heavy objects fall at speeds proportional to their weights. **(8)** Galileo believed that he had a more **rational** approach. He reasoned that gravity pulls all objects to the earth with the same acceleration regardless of their weight. According to a story, Galileo dropped two objects of different weights from the top of the Leaning Tower of Pisa. A crowd of students and professors waited below as both objects struck the ground at the same time. Galileo had proven his theory of falling bodies. **(9)** However, many at the university held opposing views, which they expressed **dogmatically.** Galileo was forced to leave Pisa.

In addition to making contributions to physics, Galileo improved upon the design of the first telescope and made practical use of the instrument. He observed that the planet Jupiter had moons revolving around it and that Venus, like the moon, went through phases. Galileo's observations led him to uphold firmly the theory that Earth moves around the sun. Unfortunately, his theory once again involved him in disputes with those who held accepted religious beliefs. **(10)** Leaders of European thought were **skeptical** of anyone who dared to challenge the traditional idea that all the planets revolve around Earth. As a Catholic, Galileo had no desire to quarrel with his church, but he thought that traditional belief should yield to mathematical proof.

In 1633 Galileo was condemned to life imprisonment for his ideas. Although his sentence was modified to house arrest, Galileo was forced to deny his theories publicly, and his works were banned. Although he was unable to influence the opinions of other people of his time, his contributions initiated a scientific and technological revolution.

Please turn to the next page.

Reading Comprehension Exercise

Each of the following statements corresponds to a numbered sentence in the passage. Each statement contains a blank and is followed by four answer choices. Decide which choice fits best in the blank. The word or phrase that you choose must express roughly the same meaning as the italicized word in the passage. Write the letter of your choice on the answer line.

1. One day, in a __?__ mood, Galileo sat in the cathedral.
   a. hopeful   c. excessively ambitious
   b. happy   d. dreamily thoughtful

2. Galileo __?__ his new field as he sat in the cathedral.
   a. had doubts about   c. mentally weighed
   b. criticized   d. wrote about

3. Lost in his __?__, Galileo observed the swinging chandeliers.
   a. depression   b. inspiration   c. prayers   d. deep thought

4. Galileo's observations led to questions, __?__, and experiments.
   a. conflicts   b. theories   c. laughter   d. reading

5. His questions and experiments led to new knowledge and __?__ applications.
   a. scientific   b. easy   c. reasonable   d. fascinating

6. Physics had previously been treated as a branch of the study of __?__.
   a. reality   b. animals   c. nature   d. astronomy

7. Aristotle and other philosophers had __?__ that heavy objects fall at speeds proportional to their weights.
   a. doubts   c. argued
   b. observed carefully d. assumed without proof

8. Galileo believed that he had a more __?__ approach.
   a. possible   b. logical   c. exciting   d. complicated

9. Many people at the university held opposing views, which they expressed __?__.
   a. very emphatically   c. in a civilized manner
   b. publicly   d. hesitantly

10. Leaders of European thought were __?__ anyone who spoke against traditional beliefs.
    a. envious of   b. against   c. doubtful about   d. interested in

Writing Assignment

Do some library research on the life and work of a scientist, physician, mathematician, educator, or economist whose ideas have influenced the world in which we live. For example, you might investigate the contributions of Benjamin Franklin, Maria Montessori, Albert Einstein, or Marie Curie. Write a biographical sketch using at least five of the words from this lesson. Underline each word that you use.

Lesson 29

Argument and Debate

People getting into minor arguments is a familiar part of everyday life. For example:

PAUL: Let's go to the movies and see *Attack of the Ant People*.
SARAH: I don't want to see that. It's supposed to be bad.
PAUL: Why?
SARAH: I don't know. It just is. I don't want to go.
PAUL: You have to have a reason for saying that.

Obviously, Sarah's argument against seeing *Attack of the Ant People* could have been greatly strengthened by supplying some good reasons for her opinion. In that case Paul could have defended his position, and the argument might have become a debate. The words in this lesson will help you to understand the processes of reasoning and debating and will enable you to make your own arguments more effective.

WORD LIST
apologist
contend
dissuade
fallacy
hypothesis
indisputable
inference
red herring
refute
substantiate

DEFINITIONS

After you have studied the definitions and example for each vocabulary word, write the word on the line to the right.

1. **apologist** (ə-pŏl′ə-jĭst) *noun* A person who argues in defense or justification of an idea or cause: *an apologist for high tariffs*. (From the Greek word *apologia*, meaning "a speech in defense of someone or something")

   EXAMPLE   Henry Jacobs, an *apologist* for unregulated land development, was the guest speaker at the chamber of commerce meeting.

2. **contend** (kən-tĕnd′) *trans. verb* To maintain or assert; argue (for) a point of view.   *intrans. verb*   **a.** To strive or struggle in controversy or debate; dispute.   **b.** To strive, as in battle; fight.   **c.** To compete, as in a race. (From the Latin *com-*, meaning "with," and *tendere*, meaning "to strive")

   RELATED WORDS   **contender** *noun;* **contention** *noun*

   EXAMPLE   Some scientists *contend* that the legendary island of Atlantis actually existed.

3. **dissuade** (dĭ-swād′) *trans. verb* To discourage or keep (someone) from a purpose or course of action. (From the Latin *dis-*, meaning "not," and *suadere*, meaning "to advise")

   EXAMPLE   Experienced guides *dissuaded* Clint from making the dangerous climb.

Argument and Debate

4. **fallacy** (făl′ə-sē) *noun* **a.** An idea or opinion based on mistaken assumptions or logic; a false notion. **b.** False reasoning, belief, or argument. (From the Latin word *fallere*, meaning "to deceive")

   RELATED WORDS **fallacious** *adjective;* **fallaciously** *adverb*

   EXAMPLE The idea that every cloud has a silver lining is a *fallacy*.

5. **hypothesis** (hī-pŏth′ĭ-sĭs) *noun* **a.** A statement that accounts for a set of facts but cannot be proved by direct supporting evidence; a theory. **b.** Something that is assumed as a basis for action or discussion. (From the Greek word *hypotithenai*, meaning "to suppose")

   RELATED WORDS **hypothesize** *verb;* **hypothetical** *adjective*

   EXAMPLE The *hypothesis* that the solar system has at least nine planets was not confirmed until astronomers first saw Pluto.

6. **indisputable** (ĭn′dĭ-spyo͞o′tə-bəl) *adjective* Undeniable; true beyond all doubt.

   RELATED WORD **indisputably** *adverb*

   EXAMPLE As first-born son of the king, Maximilian had an *indisputable* right to the throne.

7. **inference** (ĭn′fər-əns) *noun* **a.** A conclusion based on evidence. **b.** The act or process of concluding something from evidence; a deduction. (From the Latin word *inferre*, meaning "to bring in" or "to deduce")

   RELATED WORD **infer** *verb*

   EXAMPLE After questioning the suspects, the detective drew an *inference* about the one who had committed the crime.

   USAGE NOTE Do not confuse *infer* with *imply*. *Imply* means "to hint at" or "to suggest."

8. **red herring** (rĕd hĕr′ĭng) *noun* Something that draws attention away from the matter or issue at hand.

   EXAMPLE The publicity agent's focus on personality was a *red herring* meant to disguise the political candidate's lack of experience.

   ETYMOLOGY NOTE Raw cured (red) herring used to be dragged across the trail of an animal to pull hunting dogs off the animal scent.

9. **refute** (rĭ-fyo͞ot′) *trans. verb* To prove a person or idea to be wrong: *refute their statements*. (From the Latin *re-*, meaning "back," and *-futare*, meaning "to beat")

   RELATED WORDS **refutable** *adjective;* **refutation** *noun*

   EXAMPLE For centuries scientists gathered evidence to *refute* the mistaken belief that the sun rotated around Earth.

10. **substantiate** (səb-stăn′shē-āt′) *trans. verb* To support with proof or evidence; verify. (From the Latin words *sub*, meaning "under," and *stare*, meaning "to stand")

    RELATED WORDS **substantial** *adjective;* **substantiation** *noun*

    EXAMPLE Mary *substantiated* her claim of ownership by producing a deed to the property.

188 Argument and Debate

Name _____ Date _____

Exercise 1 Writing Correct Words

On the answer line, write the word from the vocabulary list that fits each definition.

1. A conclusion based on evidence
2. A false idea or argument
3. To prove something is wrong
4. A theory that explains a set of known facts
5. To persuade a person not to do something
6. To verify or support with evidence
7. To argue a point of view; compete
8. One who argues in defense of an idea or a cause
9. True beyond all doubt
10. Something that draws attention away from the real issue

1. _____
2. _____
3. _____
4. _____
5. _____
6. _____
7. _____
8. _____
9. _____
10. _____

Exercise 2 Using Words Correctly

Each of the following questions contains an italicized vocabulary word. Decide the answer to the question, and write *Yes* or *No* on the answer line.

1. To *substantiate* an opinion, should you offer proof or evidence?
2. If you draw an *inference*, are you making a wild guess?
3. If something is *indisputable*, can it ever be proved wrong?
4. Can you usually *dissuade* stubborn people from doing what they want to do?
5. Would an opinionated person be likely to *contend* with someone who disagrees?
6. Is an *apologist* someone who is constantly saying "I'm sorry"?
7. Is an argument based on a *fallacy* a logical one?
8. When people state a *hypothesis*, are they citing a proven theory?
9. If I *refute* your theories, have I disproved them?
10. Could introducing a *red herring* into a discussion prove distracting?

1. _____
2. _____
3. _____
4. _____
5. _____
6. _____
7. _____
8. _____
9. _____
10. _____

Exercise 3 Choosing the Best Definition

For each italicized vocabulary word or phrase in the following sentences, write the letter of the best definition on the answer line.

1. At the age of four, Becky rejected the *fallacy* that the moon is made of green cheese.
   a. evidence   b. insinuation   c. proposal   d. false idea

1. _____

Copyright © 1988 Houghton Mifflin Company. All rights reserved.   Argument and Debate   **189**

2. Marlene is a loyal *apologist for* an organization that favors school years of eleven months.
   a. critic of   b. opponent of   c. defender of   d. worker for

3. No one has *substantiated* the existence of the Loch Ness monster.
   a. proved   b. photographed   c. denied   d. written about

4. "Don't drag in a *red herring* to confuse the issue; just explain why you are so late," Arthur demanded.
   a. distracting point   b. mystery   c. big problem   d. apology

5. Tad *contends* that he cannot concentrate without the radio on.
   a. promises   b. maintains   c. hopes   d. predicts

6. Even though Luke was unable to *refute* Selena's argument, he felt that her ideas were wrong.
   a. believe   b. follow   c. disprove   d. defend

7. Professor Hite introduced an exciting *hypothesis* about the effect of black holes on time travel.
   a. article   b. theory   c. diagram   d. conversation

8. "You will never *dissuade* me from taking my European vacation," Ralph said.
   a. distract   b. convince   c. discourage   d. detour

9. Claws is the *indisputable* winner of the cat show.
   a. fortunate   b. melancholy   c. overjoyed   d. undeniable

10. The microbiologist's *inference* was the result of two months of experiments.
    a. conclusion   b. report   c. advice   d. illusion

Exercise 4 Using Different Forms of Words

Decide which form of the vocabulary word in parentheses best completes the sentence. The form given may be correct. Write your answer on the answer line.

1. Is there no ? Ted from attempting that difficult dive? *(dissuade)*

2. The ? for higher income taxes explained their views to the newspaper reporter. *(apologist)*

3. "I hope that you don't try to use ? statements in your term paper," Janet cautioned. *(fallacy)*

4. This is ? the toughest golf course in the country. *(indisputable)*

5. As a music critic, Cleo spends a great deal of her time ? about the future of current music. *(hypothesis)*

6. Dr. Kim's ? of Paul's argument was brilliant. *(refute)*

7. "You may ? what you like; I can only tell you what I know," Martha explained. *(inference)*

8. Pat knows that the tax issue is a ? in this election. *(red herring)*

9. Mr. Culpepper won't accept your report without adequate ? . *(substantiate)*

10. Richard is still in ? for first place in the 400-meter dash. *(contend)*

Argument and Debate

Reading Comprehension

Each numbered sentence in the following passage contains an italicized vocabulary word. After you read the passage, you will complete an exercise.

Shirley Chisholm: "Unbought and Unbossed"

Shirley Chisholm (born 1924), the first black woman ever elected to the United States Congress, was a true candidate of the people. Not officially encouraged by Democratic party leaders, Chisholm first ran for public office in 1964 because the people of the Bedford-Stuyvesant section of Brooklyn asked her to represent them. With the voters of her community firmly behind her, Shirley Chisholm went from the New York State Assembly in 1964 to the House of Representatives in 1968 and, finally, to her campaign as a Democratic presidential candidate in 1972.

As a political champion of the people, Chisholm was a strong spokesperson for the rights of disadvantaged blacks, Puerto Ricans, women, and children. Better education and child care for minorities were key issues throughout Chisholm's long career. **(1)** She challenged the *apologists* for the inadequate system of caring for the city's children.

Growing up in the Bedford-Stuyvesant section of Brooklyn made Chisholm sensitive to the problems of the people living there. After graduating from a girls' high school in Brooklyn, Chisholm received a scholarship to Brooklyn College, where she majored in sociology. **(2)** Because of her *indisputable* talent for debating, Chisholm's professors urged her to consider a career in politics.

Later, Chisholm would take their advice, but first she taught nursery school and went on to direct a large child-care center in lower Manhattan. **(3)** Chisholm was a strong supporter of early schooling: her *hypothesis* was that the sooner students begin their education, the more they are capable of learning. **(4)** She argued against what she considered to be a *fallacy:* the idea that children should wait until the age of five or six to begin formal schooling. Chisholm herself learned to read when she was only three and a half years old. **(5)** As an educational consultant for New York City's Bureau of Child Welfare, Chisholm made many valuable *inferences* about standard day-care practices and worked hard to improve child-care conditions.

Chisholm was also very active in such community groups as the Democratic Women's Workshop. This involvement set the scene for future political campaigning and also established her reputation for trustworthiness within the black and Puerto Rican communities. It was this trust that motivated the people of Bedford-Stuyvesant to ask Chisholm to enter the political arena in 1964.

(6) Direct and honest, Chisholm never had to use *red herrings* in her election campaign. She described herself as "unbought and unbossed" and would later write a book with that title. In 1964 Chisholm became the first black woman from Brooklyn to serve in the state assembly in Albany. Characterized as knowing her own mind, she was quick to jump into a debate. **(7)** Chisholm was sometimes slow to form an opinion, but when she did, she could not be *dissuaded* from it.

In 1968 Chisholm ran against a Republican-Liberal opponent, James Farmer, for a seat in the House of Representatives. **(8)** Not immodestly, Chisholm *contended* that she would win. She pointed out that the people of Brooklyn knew her and her work and that she understood their problems. **(9)** This claim was *substantiated* when Chisholm defeated her opponent by a *margin* of two and a half to one.

Although Chisholm did not win the Democratic nomination for President in 1972, her determination to represent the people in the highest office was a landmark in her successful political career. **(10)** Chisholm's candidacy *refuted* for the first time the old-fashioned idea that a woman should not run for President.

Please turn to the next page.

Argument and Debate

Reading Comprehension Exercise

Each of the following statements corresponds to a numbered sentence in the passage. Each statement contains a blank and is followed by four answer choices. Decide which choice fits best in the blank. The word or phrase that you choose must express roughly the same meaning as the italicized word in the passage. Write the letter of your choice on the answer line.

1. Shirley Chisholm challenged the __?__ of city day-care practices.
   a. defenders   b. friends   c. critics   d. managers

2. Chisholm's talent for debate was __?__ .
   a. questionable   c. undeniable
   b. understandable   d. second-rate

3. Her experience as an educator led Chisholm to form a(n) __?__ .
   a. opinion   b. organization   c. argument   d. theory

4. She argued against a(n) __?__ .
   a. opinion   b. false notion   c. opponent   d. rational statement

5. About child care Chisholm held __?__ .
   a. firm opinions   c. ideas based on no evidence
   b. conventional judgments   d. ideas based on evidence

6. __?__ were not part of Chisholm's political campaigns.
   a. Distracting ideas   c. False promises
   b. Sardines   d. Illogical statements

7. The dedicated politician could not be __?__ her opinions.
   a. changed from   c. deterred from
   b. aided in altering   d. informed about

8. Chisholm __?__ that she would win a seat in Congress.
   a. doubted   b. asserted   c. explained   d. predicted

9. Chisholm __?__ her claim that she would win the 1968 Congressional election.
   a. added to   b. debated   c. denied   d. made good

10. Her candidacy for the Presidency __?__ an old-fashioned idea.
    a. proved wrong   b. verified   c. validated   d. supported

1. _____
2. _____
3. _____
4. _____
5. _____
6. _____
7. _____
8. _____
9. _____
10. _____

Writing Assignment

Imagine that you are coaching someone who is about to participate in a debate. Using five words from the lesson, write a paragraph of instructions to this person, taking care to include debating strategies. Underline each vocabulary word.

Lesson 30

The Roots -gno- and -sci-

Gnōthi seauton — Know thyself! — thus read the inscription at the Delphic oracle in ancient Greece. The Greek root *-gno-* is common in words meaning "know" or "knowledge." Likewise, the Latin root *-sci-* is common in words with the same meanings. Both roots are found in English words, and in this lesson you will learn six words derived from *-gno-* and four more derived from *-sci-*.

WORD LIST
cognizant
connoisseur
conscientious
consciousness
diagnosis
notoriety
omniscient
prognosis
recognition
unconscionable

DEFINITIONS

After you have studied the definitions and example for each vocabulary word, write the word on the line to the right.

1. **cognizant** (kŏg′nĭ-zənt) *adjective* Aware; fully informed. (From the Latin word *cognoscere*, meaning "to learn")
   RELATED WORD   **cognizance** *noun*
   EXAMPLE   Paolo obviously was not *cognizant* of the consequences of his actions.

   1. _____

2. **connoisseur** (kŏn′ə-sûr′) *noun* One knowledgeable in any area, but especially in the arts or in matters of taste and discernment.
   EXAMPLE   Esther is a *connoisseur* of fine jewels.

   2. _____

3. **conscientious** (kŏn′shē-ĕn′shəs) *adjective* Thorough and attentive; careful; painstaking.
   RELATED WORDS   **conscientiously** *adverb*; **conscientiousness** *noun*
   EXAMPLE   *Conscientious* mechanics do their work quickly and efficiently.

   3. _____
   SEE *consciousness*.

4. **consciousness** (kŏn′shəs-nĭs) *noun* **a.** Awareness of one's thoughts and perceptions: *regaining consciousness after fainting*. **b.** The totality of attitudes or feelings held by a group: *national consciousness*. (From the Latin word *conscius*, meaning "knowing with others")
   RELATED WORDS   **conscious** *adjective*; **consciously** *adverb*
   EXAMPLE   Desiree lost *consciousness* when she was hit by the basketball.

   4. _____
   USAGE NOTE To be *conscientious* means "to be able to distinguish between right and wrong"; having *consciousness* means "having awareness of one's thoughts and perceptions."

Copyright © Houghton Mifflin Company. All rights reserved.

The Roots *-gno-* and *-sci-*   193

5. **diagnosis** (dī′əg-nō′sĭs) *noun* A critical analysis of the nature of something, particularly disease. (From the Greek word *diagnōsis*, meaning "discrimination")
   RELATED WORDS **diagnose** *verb;* **diagnostic** *adjective;* **diagnostician** *noun*
   EXAMPLE The doctor's *diagnosis* was a relief to the patient.

5. _____
SEE *prognosis.*

6. **notoriety** (nō′tə-rī′ĭ-tē) *noun* Fame of an unfavorable kind.
   RELATED WORDS **notorious** *adjective;* **notoriously** *adverb*
   EXAMPLE Joseph Stalin gained *notoriety* for his brutality.

6. _____

7. **omniscient** (ŏm-nĭsh′ənt) *adjective* Knowing all things; having total knowledge. (From the Latin words *omnis*, meaning "all" and *scire*, meaning "to know")
   RELATED WORDS **omniscience** *noun;* **omnisciently** *adverb*
   EXAMPLE Mrs. Papadopoulos seemed *omniscient* when speaking about the history of our town.

7. _____

8. **prognosis** (prŏg-nō′sĭs) *noun* **a.** A forecast of a probable result. **b.** The likelihood of recovery from a disease. (From the Greek word *prognōsis*, meaning "foreknowledge")
   RELATED WORD **prognosticate** *verb*
   EXAMPLE The *prognosis* for economic growth in the aircraft industry is encouraging.

8. _____
USAGE NOTE A *prognosis* usually comes after a diagnosis.

9. **recognition** (rĕk′əg-nĭsh′ən) *noun* **a.** Acknowledgment or attention; favorable notice. **b.** Awareness that something perceived has been perceived previously. (From the Latin word *recognitio*, meaning "investigation")
   RELATED WORDS **recognizable** *adjective;* **recognize** *verb*
   EXAMPLE Rosalinda Guerrero did not receive *recognition* as a great artist until after her death.

9. _____

10. **unconscionable** (ŭn-kŏn′shə-nə-bəl) *adjective* Unrestrained by conscience; unreasonable; unjust.
    EXAMPLE The mistreatment of the mentally ill in the past was *unconscionable*.

10. _____

Name _____ Date _____

Exercise 1   Completing Definitions

On the answer line, write the word from the vocabulary list that best completes each definition.

1. People who enjoy approval or favorable notice enjoy __?__ .
2. If you are aware of or fully informed about something, you are __?__ of it.
3. A critical analysis of the nature of something, such as a disease, is called a __?__ .
4. An unreasonable or unjust action is __?__ .
5. One who has total knowledge is __?__ .
6. The prediction of a likely result is called a __?__ .
7. If I am well qualified to judge things, especially in the arts, then I can be called a __?__ .
8. People who do their work carefully and well are __?__ .
9. When a criminal becomes well known, he achieves __?__ .
10. Awareness of one's thoughts and perceptions is __?__ .

1. _____
2. _____
3. _____
4. _____
5. _____
6. _____
7. _____
8. _____
9. _____
10. _____

Exercise 2   Using Words Correctly

Each of the following statements contains an italicized vocabulary word. Decide whether the sentence is true or false, and write *True* or *False* on the answer line.

1. One who steals from others without feeling guilty commits an *unconscionable* act.
2. For messages, one should keep a *notoriety* next to the phone.
3. A doctor who is analyzing tissue taken from a diseased organ is making a *diagnosis*.
4. If one feels guilty, one has a bad *consciousness*.
5. If you enjoy public *recognition*, the best way to get it is to become a hermit.
6. The more *cognizant* you are of a situation, the more you are likely to handle it appropriately.
7. A doctor who informs you what is likely to happen to you during the course of an illness has given you his or her *prognosis*.
8. A person who cannot tell the difference between representational and abstract painting is a true *connoisseur* of art.
9. *Conscientious* effort usually produces good results.
10. If I can correctly answer any question anyone could ask me, I am *omniscient*.

1. _____
2. _____
3. _____
4. _____
5. _____
6. _____
7. _____
8. _____
9. _____
10. _____

Copyright © 1988 Houghton Mifflin Company. All rights reserved.

The Roots *-gno-* and *-sci-*

Exercise 3 Choosing the Best Word

Decide which vocabulary word or related form best expresses the meaning of the italicized word or phrase in the sentence. On the answer line, write the letter of the correct choice.

1. Gangsters brought *unfavorable fame* to some places during the twenties.
   a. notoriety   b. connoisseur   c. recognition   d. diagnosis

2. Christina, my mechanic, has given me a *critical analysis of the nature* of the car's engine trouble.
   a. omniscience   b. prognosis   c. notoriety   d. diagnosis

3. Ebenezer Scrooge's methods of conducting his life and his business were *not controlled by conscience*.
   a. unconscionable   b. omniscient   c. recognizable   d. diagnostic

4. Because Genevieve was always *aware and informed* of her opponent's weaknesses, she usually won her tennis matches.
   a. prognosis   b. a connoisseur   c. cognizant   d. diagnostic

5. With *The Thumb of Zeno*, Jacqueline Potts has finally gained the *attention* that she deserves.
   a. omniscience   b. connoisseur   c. recognition   d. diagnosis

6. Because Henry is *one knowledgeable in the arts*, his friends took him along when they wanted to buy a Giacometti sculpture.
   a. a connoisseur   c. unconscionable
   b. a prognosis   d. omniscient

7. Even though Joel is not *all-knowing*, he seems to us to be pretty close to it.
   a. conscious   b. diagnostic   c. cognizant   d. omniscient

8. Tamara's *painstaking* effort to learn the sonata paid off in a first-class performance.
   a. recognition   b. conscientious   c. cognizant   d. conscious

9. The dietician's *forecast of a likely outcome* was a ten-pound weight gain in six weeks.
   a. omniscience   b. prognosis   c. consciousness   d. diagnosis

10. Charlene temporarily lost *awareness of everything* when she reached 17,000 feet.
    a. diagnosis   c. omniscience
    b. consciousness   d. conscientiousness

1. _____
2. _____
3. _____
4. _____
5. _____
6. _____
7. _____
8. _____
9. _____
10. _____

Exercise 4 Using Different Forms of Words

Decide which form of the vocabulary word in parentheses best completes the sentence. The form given may be correct. Write your answer on the answer line.

1. __?__ of one's mistakes is the first step toward correcting them. *(cognizant)*

2. Remember the __?__ saloon in old Dodge City? *(notoriety)*

3. On the first day of class, all students took a __?__ test so that the teacher would know how much they already knew. *(diagnosis)*

1. _____
2. _____
3. _____

196   The Roots *-gno-* and *-sci-*

4. Harriet studies fencing ? . (conscientious)

5. Alan ? a friend from camp whom he had not seen in fifteen years. (recognition)

6. The judge sentenced the woman to life imprisonment for her ? act. (unconscionable)

7. Should television networks continue to ? the outcome of elections prior to the closing of all polls? (prognosis)

8. Nell made a ? effort to speak slowly and clearly. (consciousness)

9. Let us try to look at the Bullocks Wilshire building as a ? of architecture would. (connoisseur)

10. The professor lectured ? about American literature of the 1840s. (omniscient)

Reading Comprehension

Each numbered sentence in the following passage contains an italicized vocabulary word. After you read the passage, you will complete an exercise.

Elizabeth Blackwell: America's First Woman Doctor

Elizabeth Blackwell was the first female doctor of medicine in the United States. Born in England in 1821, Blackwell came to the United States with her family when she was eleven. **(1)** Even at this early age, she was **cognizant** of a strong and growing interest in the healing arts.

When Mr. Blackwell died, six years after the family arrived in America, Mrs. Blackwell and her nine children started a boarding school for girls. **(2)** Elizabeth taught some of the girls, and in what little free time she had remaining, she became a **connoisseur** of medical textbooks, studying them carefully and mastering the information contained in them. **(3)** While she would not have claimed to be **omniscient** in medical matters, she did feel she had learned much and that she should go to medical school to pursue her interests.

She sent off her medical school applications, and all she received in return were rejections. **(4)** These rejections were not due to any lack of intelligence or ability on her part but rather to the **notoriety** attached to the idea of a woman's becoming a doctor in the mid nineteenth century. **(5)** (In the twentieth century, however, **consciousness** about such matters has changed.)

In 1847 the Medical College in Geneva, New York, admitted Elizabeth Blackwell. In two years she graduated and moved to Paris to work at La Maternité hospital. **(6)** This hospital made the **unconscionable** decision of refusing to recognize her medical degree and allowed her to work only as a midwife.

(7) The lack of **recognition** did not discourage Dr. Blackwell. **(8)** She remained **conscientious** in her duties. Several years later, she returned to New York, and again she was denied recognition by the medical establishment. She opened a clinic in the slums, and the poor and needy flocked to it. **(9)** After many a **diagnosis** of tuberculosis and other ailments, Blackwell worked for the improvement of the wretched living conditions of slum dwellers. As a result of her efforts, great improvements were made in sanitation and the maintenance of crowded urban tenements.

In 1857 Blackwell founded the New York Infirmary, a hospital for poor women and children, staffed entirely by women. The Infirmary developed a nursing school and, by 1868, a women's medical college as well. **(10)** In the years that followed, the **prognosis** for women entering the medical profession improved.

Please turn to the next page.

Reading Comprehension Exercise

Each of the following statements corresponds to a numbered sentence in the passage. Each statement contains a blank and is followed by four answer choices. Decide which choice fits best in the blank. The word or phrase that you choose must express roughly the same meaning as the italicized word in the passage. Write the letter of your choice on the answer line.

1. Even at eleven years old, Elizabeth Blackwell was __?__ of an interest in the healing arts.
   a. scared   b. thinking   c. aware   d. in awe

2. The future doctor became __?__ medical textbooks.
   a. an admirer of   c. one knowledgeable about
   b. a consumer of   d. a collector of

3. She would not have claimed to be __?__.
   a. all-seeing   b. all-feeling   c. all-powerful   d. all-knowing

4. __?__ was attached to the idea of a woman's becoming a doctor.
   a. Scandal   b. Unfavorable fame   c. Gossip   d. Happiness

5. In the twentieth century, __?__ changed.
   a. laws and regulations   c. sum and substance
   b. attitudes and feelings   d. customs and beliefs

6. The hospital in Paris made an __?__ decision.
   a. admirable   b. unreasonable   c. irritating   d. unwitting

7. The lack of __?__ did not discourage Dr. Blackwell.
   a. affection   b. protection   c. attention   d. money

8. She remained __?__ her duties.
   a. careless in   b. busy with   c. painstaking in   d. unaware of

9. Many a(n) __?__ tuberculosis was made.
   a. analysis of   b. prediction of   c. cure of   d. recovery from

10. The __?__ for women in medicine improved.
    a. pay   c. employment opportunities
    b. outlook   d. educational opportunities

1. _____
2. _____
3. _____
4. _____
5. _____
6. _____
7. _____
8. _____
9. _____
10. _____

Practice with Analogies

See page 79 for some strategies to use with analogies.

DIRECTIONS   On the answer line, write the vocabulary word that completes each analogy.

1. LUCK : MISFORTUNE : : fame : __?__
2. POWER : OMNIPOTENT : : knowledge : __?__
3. UNINFORMED : UNAWARE : : __?__ : mindful
4. CARELESS : IRRESPONSIBLE : : careful : __?__
5. FORECAST : SUNSHINE : : __?__ : recovery

1. _____
2. _____
3. _____
4. _____
5. _____

Name _____ Date _____

Reading Skills

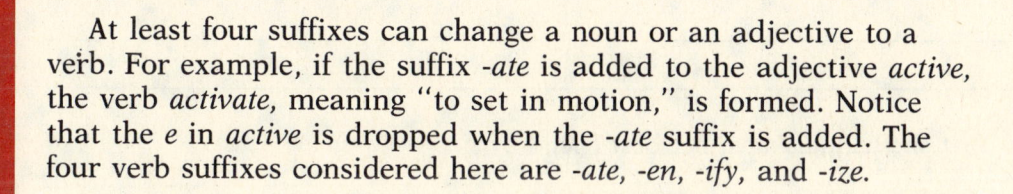

Four Verb Suffixes

At least four suffixes can change a noun or an adjective to a verb. For example, if the suffix *-ate* is added to the adjective *active*, the verb *activate*, meaning "to set in motion," is formed. Notice that the *e* in *active* is dropped when the *-ate* suffix is added. The four verb suffixes considered here are *-ate*, *-en*, *-ify*, and *-ize*.

SUFFIX MEANING	VERB	DEFINITION
1. *-ate:* to act upon in a specified manner	formulate	to state as a formula
2. *-en:* to cause to be, to become, or to have	deepen	to cause to become deep or deeper
3. *-ify:* to make; to cause to become	intensify	to make intense or more intense
4. *-ize:* to cause to be or to become; to cause to become like; to treat as; to subject to	dramatize Westernize	to adapt for presentation as a drama to convert to customs of the West

You can analyze the meaning of a word ending with one of these suffixes by putting together the meanings of the root and the suffix. Remember, though, that your definition will not be exact. You should check the meaning by using the dictionary.

Exercise Using Four Verb Suffixes

Each sentence in this exercise contains an italicized verb ending with the suffix *-ate*, *-en*, *-ify*, or *-ize*. *Step 1:* Write your own definition of the word. *Step 2:* Write the dictionary definition of the word. Choose the definition that best fits the way the word is used in the sentence. *Step 3:* Write a sentence of your own in which you use the word correctly.

1. Loretta laughed when she recalled that she *idolized* the rock star.

   YOUR DEFINITION _____

   DICTIONARY DEFINITION _____

   SENTENCE _____

2. The sound effects *heightened* the suspense of the radio drama.

   YOUR DEFINITION _____

   DICTIONARY DEFINITION _____

   SENTENCE _____

Please turn to the next page.

3. Louisiana's statutes were *codified* from French, not British, law.
   YOUR DEFINITION _____
   DICTIONARY DEFINITION _____
   SENTENCE _____

4. Liz was irritated with Leroy because he liked to *monopolize* the computer.
   YOUR DEFINITION _____
   DICTIONARY DEFINITION _____
   SENTENCE _____

5. Gwen failed to realize that she had *alienated* her best friend by her behavior.
   YOUR DEFINITION _____
   DICTIONARY DEFINITION _____
   SENTENCE _____

6. Wearing seat belts will *minimize* the chance of injury in an accident.
   YOUR DEFINITION _____
   DICTIONARY DEFINITION _____
   SENTENCE _____

7. Reaching the top of the mountain *gladdened* the spirits of the hikers.
   YOUR DEFINITION _____
   DICTIONARY DEFINITION _____
   SENTENCE _____

8. The actor felt *humiliated* when there was little applause for his performance.
   YOUR DEFINITION _____
   DICTIONARY DEFINITION _____
   SENTENCE _____

9. The owner had the fence repaired by hiring an ironworker to *replicate* the missing part.
   YOUR DEFINITION _____
   DICTIONARY DEFINITION _____
   SENTENCE _____

10. The plant engineer tried to *quantify* the changes that would be necessary to keep the plant competitive.
    YOUR DEFINITION _____
    DICTIONARY DEFINITION _____
    SENTENCE _____

Four Verb Suffixes

Copyright © 1988 Houghton Mifflin Company. All rights reserved.

LESSON 1 archaic	LESSON 1 jargon	LESSON 2 boycott	LESSON 3 bland	LESSON 3 epicure
LESSON 1 argot	LESSON 1 semantics	LESSON 2 galvanize	LESSON 3 culinary	LESSON 3 morsel
LESSON 1 connotation	LESSON 1 slang	LESSON 2 jovial	LESSON 3 delectable	LESSON 3 pungent
LESSON 1 denotation	LESSON 1 standard	LESSON 2 macadam	LESSON 3 devour	LESSON 3 quaff
LESSON 1 idiom	LESSON 1 vernacular	LESSON 2 maverick	LESSON 3 edible	LESSON 3 ravenous

| LESSON 2 mentor | LESSON 2 nemesis | LESSON 2 odyssey | LESSON 2 quixotic | LESSON 2 tantalize |

LESSON 1	LESSON 1	LESSON 2	LESSON 2	LESSON 3
archaic (är-kā′ĭk) *adj.* Referring to language that is now rarely used.	**jargon** (jär′gən) *n.* Specialized technical vocabulary.	**boycott** (boi′kŏt′) *tr. v.* To participate in an organized group refusal.	**mentor** (měn′tôr) *n.* A wise adviser or trusted counselor.	**bland** (blănd) *adj.* Mild; soothing; dull.
argot (är′gō) *n.* A secret language.	**semantics** (sĭ măn′tĭks) *n.* The study of changes in word meanings.	**galvanize** (găl′və-nīz′) *tr. v.* To stir to action or awareness.	**nemesis** (něm′ĭ-sĭs) *n.* Just punishment for wrongdoing.	**culinary** (kŭl′ə-něr′ē) *adj.* Pertaining to cooking or the kitchen.
connotation (kŏn′ə-tā′shən) *n.* Mental associations suggested by a word.	**slang** (slăng) *n.* Highly informal language.	**jovial** (jō′vē-əl) *adj.* Full of fun and good cheer; sociable.	**odyssey** (ŏd′ĭ-sē) *n.* An adventurous, wandering journey; a quest.	**delectable** (dĭ-lěk′tə-bəl) *adj.* Greatly pleasing to the taste.
denotation (dē′nō-tā′shən) *n.* The exact meaning of a word.	**standard** (stăn′dərd) *adj.* Conforming to established usage in speech or writing.	**macadam** (mə-kăd′əm) *n.* Paving material made of layers of small stones.	**quixotic** (kwĭk-sŏt′ĭk) *adj.* Full of impractical ideas.	**devour** (dĭ-vour′) *tr. v.* To eat up greedily; swallow; engulf.
idiom (ĭd′ē-əm) *n.* An expression that has a special meaning.	**vernacular** (vər-năk′yə-lər) *n.* Everyday spoken language of a region.	**maverick** (măv′ər-ĭk) *n.* An independent-minded person; a nonconformist.	**tantalize** (tăn′tə-līz′) *tr. v.* To tempt but deny satisfaction.	**edible** (ěd′ə-bəl) *adj.* Suitable for eating.

LESSON 3
epicure (ěp′ĭ-kyo͝or′) *n.* A person with refined taste in food or drink.
morsel (môr′səl) *n.* A bite or small amount of food.
pungent (pŭn′jənt) *adj.* Sharp; strong; penetrating.
quaff (kwŏf) *tr. v.* To drink heartily and deeply of.
ravenous (răv′ə-nəs) *adj.* Extremely hungry.

LESSON 4 devious	LESSON 4 hypocritical	LESSON 5 behold	LESSON 5 impressionistic	LESSON 6 cosmopolitan	LESSON 6 policy
LESSON 4 duplicity	LESSON 4 masquerade	LESSON 5 discernment	LESSON 5 insight	LESSON 6 geopolitics	LESSON 6 politico
LESSON 4 fictitious	LESSON 4 overt	LESSON 5 envision	LESSON 5 myopia	LESSON 6 impolitic	LESSON 6 suburban
LESSON 4 guileless	LESSON 4 reputable	LESSON 5 foresee	LESSON 5 perceptive	LESSON 6 megalopolis	LESSON 6 urban
LESSON 4 gullible	LESSON 4 veracity	LESSON 5 gape	LESSON 5 survey	LESSON 6 metropolitan	LESSON 6 urbane

LESSON 4	LESSON 4	LESSON 4	LESSON 4	LESSON 4
devious (dē′vē-əs) *adj.* Done in an underhanded manner; tricky.	**duplicity** (do͞o-plĭs′ĭ-tē) *n.* Deliberate deception.	**fictitious** (fĭk-tĭsh′əs) *adj.* Assumed in order to deceive; imaginary.	**guileless** (gīl′lĭs) *adj.* Free of slyness or craftiness; simple.	**gullible** (gŭl′ə-bəl) *adj.* Easily deceived or fooled.

LESSON 4	LESSON 4	LESSON 4	LESSON 4	LESSON 4
hypocritical (hĭp′ə-krĭt′ĭ-kəl) *adj.* Insincere.	**masquerade** (măs′kə-rād′) *intr. v.* To put on a deceptive appearance.	**overt** (ō-vûrt′) *adj.* Open and observable; apparent.	**reputable** (rĕp′yə-tə-bəl) *adj.* Having a good name; honorable.	**veracity** (və-răs′ĭ-tē) *n.* Honesty; conformity to truth.

LESSON 5	LESSON 5	LESSON 5	LESSON 5	LESSON 5
behold (bĭ-hōld′) *tr. v.* To gaze at; look upon.	**discernment** (dĭ-sûrn′mənt) *n.* Keenness in detecting or selecting.	**envision** (ĕn-vĭzh′ən) *tr. v.* To picture in the mind.	**foresee** (fôr-sē′) *tr. v.* To see or to know beforehand.	**gape** (gāp) *intr. v.* To stare open-mouthed in amazement.

LESSON 5	LESSON 5	LESSON 5	LESSON 5	LESSON 5
impressionistic (ĭm-prĕsh′ə-nĭs′tĭk) *adj.* Conveying a personal response.	**insight** (ĭn′sīt′) *n.* Ability to see the true nature of something.	**myopia** (mī-ō′pē-ə) *n.* Shortsightedness or lack of good judgment.	**perceptive** (pər-sĕp′tĭv) *adj.* Showing a keen awareness; knowing.	**survey** (sər-vā′) *tr. v.* To examine broadly; scrutinize.

LESSON 6	LESSON 6	LESSON 6	LESSON 6	LESSON 6
cosmopolitan (kŏz′mə-pŏl′ĭ-tn) *adj.* Internationally sophisticated.	**geopolitics** (jē′ō-pŏl′ĭ-tĭks) *n.* The relationship of geography and politics.	**impolitic** (ĭm-pŏl′ĭ-tĭk) *adj.* Unwise; not exhibiting good judgment.	**megalopolis** (mĕg′ə-lŏp′ə-lĭs) *n.* A unified urban region.	**metropolitan** (mĕt′rə-pŏl′ĭ-tən) *adj.* Pertaining to a major city.

LESSON 6	LESSON 6	LESSON 6	LESSON 6	LESSON 6
policy (pŏl′ĭ-sē) *n.* A general plan or course of action.	**politico** (pə-lĭt′ĭ-kō) *n.* An informal term for a politician.	**suburban** (sə-bûr′bən) *adj.* Pertaining to residential areas near cities.	**urban** (ûr′bən) *adj.* Characteristic of cities.	**urbane** (ûr-bān′) *adj.* Elegantly polite and sophisticated.

LESSON 7 comprehensive	LESSON 7 integral	LESSON 8 abnormal	LESSON 8 prevalent	LESSON 9 ambiguous	LESSON 9 intricate
LESSON 7 dearth	LESSON 7 paltry	LESSON 8 conventional	LESSON 8 prosaic	LESSON 9 baffle	LESSON 9 labyrinth
LESSON 7 deficient	LESSON 7 plethora	LESSON 8 idiosyncrasy	LESSON 8 quaint	LESSON 8 convoluted	LESSON 9 quandary
LESSON 7 deficit	LESSON 7 replenish	LESSON 8 orthodox	LESSON 8 rarity	LESSON 9 dilemma	LESSON 9 soluble
LESSON 7 exhaustive	LESSON 7 scant	LESSON 8 precedent	LESSON 8 singular	LESSON 9 enigma	LESSON 9 tactic

LESSON 7 **comprehensive** (kŏm′prĭ-hĕn′sĭv) *adj.* Covering completely or broadly.	LESSON 7 **integral** (ĭn′tĭ-grəl) *adj.* Essential for completeness; not fractional.	LESSON 8 **abnormal** (ăb-nôr′məl) *adj.* Not normal.	LESSON 8 **prevalent** (prĕv′ə-lənt) *adj.* Widespread; commonly occurring.	LESSON 9 **ambiguous** (ăm-bĭg′yōō-əs) *adj.* Having two or more meanings; unclear.	LESSON 9 **intricate** (ĭn′trĭ-kĭt) *adj.* Having a complicated structure; complex.
LESSON 7 **dearth** (dûrth) *n.* A scarcity or lack.	LESSON 7 **paltry** (pôl′trē) *adj.* Meager; insignificant; worthless.	LESSON 8 **conventional** (kən-vĕn′shə-nəl) *adj.* Customary; conforming to standards.	LESSON 8 **prosaic** (prō-zā′ĭk) *adj.* Ordinary; lacking in imagination.	LESSON 9 **baffle** (băf′əl) *tr. v.* To cause uncertainty in; puzzle.	LESSON 9 **labyrinth** (lăb′ə-rĭnth′) *n.* A confusing network of passages; a maze.
LESSON 7 **deficient** (dĭ-fĭsh′ənt) *adj.* Lacking an essential quality.	LESSON 7 **plethora** (plĕth′ər-ə) *n.* Superabundance; excess.	LESSON 8 **idiosyncrasy** (ĭd′ē-ō-sĭng′krə-sē) *n.* An unusual habit or mannerism.	LESSON 8 **quaint** (kwānt) *adj.* Charmingly old-fashioned.	LESSON 9 **convoluted** (kŏn′və-lōō′tĭd) *adj.* Coiled or twisted; complicated.	LESSON 9 **quandary** (kwŏn′də-rē) *n.* A state of uncertainty or doubt.
LESSON 7 **deficit** (dĕf′ĭ-sĭt) *n.* An amount by which something falls short.	LESSON 7 **replenish** (rĭ-plĕn′ĭsh) *tr. v.* To fill or make complete again.	LESSON 8 **orthodox** (ôr′thə-dŏks′) *adj.* Adhering to commonly accepted tradition.	LESSON 8 **rarity** (râr′ĭ-tē) *n.* Something special or uncommon, usually valued.	LESSON 9 **dilemma** (dĭ-lĕm′ə) *n.* Situation forcing a choice between alternatives.	LESSON 9 **soluble** (sŏl′yə-bəl) *adj.* Capable of being solved; dissolvable.
LESSON 7 **exhaustive** (ĭg-zô′stĭv) *adj.* Testing all possibilities; thorough.	LESSON 7 **scant** (skănt) *adj.* Being just short of full measure; inadequate.	LESSON 8 **precedent** (prĕs′ĭ-dənt) *n.* An action that serves as an example.	LESSON 8 **singular** (sĭng′gyə-lər) *adj.* Out of the ordinary; peculiar.	LESSON 9 **enigma** (ĭ-nĭg′mə) *n.* Something that is hard to figure out.	LESSON 9 **tactic** (tăk′tĭk) *n.* A method of achieving a goal; a strategy.

LESSON 10 broach	LESSON 10 convene	LESSON 10 debut	LESSON 10 embark	LESSON 10 generate
LESSON 10 incipient	LESSON 10 initiative	LESSON 10 innovation	LESSON 10 novice	LESSON 10 overture
LESSON 11 cessation	LESSON 11 commence	LESSON 11 deter	LESSON 11 hamper	LESSON 11 obstruction
LESSON 11 preclude	LESSON 11 procrastinate	LESSON 11 scuttle	LESSON 11 subside	LESSON 11 thwart
LESSON 12 composite	LESSON 12 disposition	LESSON 12 exponent	LESSON 12 impostor	LESSON 12 juxtaposition
LESSON 12 opposition	LESSON 12 proposition	LESSON 12 propound	LESSON 12 repository	LESSON 12 supposition

LESSON 10

broach (brōch) *tr. v.* To talk or write about for the first time.

convene (kən-vēn′) *intr. v.* To assemble or meet formally.

debut (dā-byōō′) *n.* The beginning of a career; a first public appearance.

embark (ĕm-bärk′) *intr. v.* To set out on a venture; commence.

generate (jĕn′ə-rāt′) *tr. v.* To cause or create.

incipient (ĭn-sĭp′ē-ənt) *adj.* In an early stage.

initiative (ĭ-nĭsh′ə-tĭv) *n.* The power to follow through with a plan.

innovation (ĭn′ə-vā′shən) *n.* A creative act; a change.

novice (nŏv′ĭs) *n.* A person new to a field or activity.

overture (ō′vər-chŏŏr′) *n.* An act that indicates readiness.

LESSON 11

cessation (sĕ-sā′shən) *n.* The act of ceasing or stopping; a halt.

commence (kə-mĕns′) *tr. v.* To begin; start; to come into existence.

deter (dĭ-tûr′) *tr. v.* To prevent from acting, as by means of fear.

hamper (hăm′pər) *tr. v.* To prevent the free movement of; limit.

obstruction (əb-strŭk′shən) *n.* An obstacle.

preclude (prĭ-klōōd′) *tr. v.* To make impossible or unlikely.

procrastinate (prō-krăs′tə-nāt′) *intr. v.* To put off doing something.

scuttle (skŭt′l) *intr. v.* To run hastily; scurry.

subside (səb-sīd′) *intr. v.* To sink to a lower or more normal level.

thwart (thwôrt) *tr. v.* To prevent from taking place.

LESSON 12

composite (kəm-pŏz′ĭt) *adj.* Put together from various parts.

disposition (dĭs′pə-zĭsh′ən) *n.* One's usual mood or temperament.

exponent (ĭk-spō′nənt) *n.* A person who speaks for something.

impostor (ĭm-pŏs′tər) *n.* A deceitful person who assumes a false identity.

juxtaposition (jŭk′stə-pə-zĭsh′ən) *n.* Placement side by side.

opposition (ŏp′ə-zĭsh′ən) *n.* The condition of being against.

proposition (prŏp′ə-zĭsh′ən) *n.* A plan suggested for acceptance.

propound (prə-pound′) *tr. v.* To offer for consideration.

repository (rĭ-pŏz′ĭ-tôr′ē) *n.* A place for safe storage; a source.

supposition (sŭp′ə-zĭsh′ən) *n.* An assumption.

LESSON 16 adept	LESSON 16 aptitude	LESSON 16 astute	LESSON 16 dexterity	LESSON 16 finesse
LESSON 16 inspiration	LESSON 16 precocious	LESSON 16 prodigy	LESSON 16 resourceful	LESSON 16 virtuoso
LESSON 17 arrogant	LESSON 17 diffident	LESSON 17 egocentric	LESSON 17 esteem	LESSON 17 gloat
LESSON 17 humility	LESSON 17 modest	LESSON 17 pompous	LESSON 17 swagger	LESSON 17 vaunt
LESSON 18 appraisal	LESSON 18 base	LESSON 18 candid	LESSON 18 criterion	LESSON 18 legitimate
LESSON 18 mediocre	LESSON 18 meritorious	LESSON 18 subtle	LESSON 18 truism	LESSON 18 validate

LESSON 16	LESSON 16	LESSON 16	LESSON 16	LESSON 16
adept (ə-dĕpt′) *adj.* Very skilled or capable.	**aptitude** (ăp′tĭ-tōōd′) *n.* A talent or natural ability.	**astute** (ə-stōōt′) *adj.* Shrewd in judgment; having a keen mind.	**dexterity** (dĕk-stĕr′ĭ-tē) *n.* Skill in using the hands, body, or mind.	**finesse** (fə-nĕs′) *n.* Delicacy and refinement of performance.

LESSON 16	LESSON 16	LESSON 16	LESSON 16	LESSON 16
inspiration (ĭn′spə-rā′shən) *n.* A creative stimulus for the mind.	**precocious** (prĭ-kō′shəs) *adj.* Having early intellectual development.	**prodigy** (prŏd′ə-jē) *n.* An unusually gifted young person.	**resourceful** (rĭ-sôrs′fəl) *adj.* Capable; effective.	**virtuoso** (vûr′chōō-ō′sō) *n.* One skilled in music.

LESSON 17	LESSON 17	LESSON 17	LESSON 17	LESSON 17
arrogant (ăr′ə-gənt) *adj.* Overbearingly proud; superior.	**diffident** (dĭf′ĭ-dənt) *adj.* Hesitant through lack of self-confidence.	**egocentric** (ē′gō-sĕn′trĭk) *adj.* Limited in outlook to one's own needs.	**esteem** (ĭ-stēm′) *n.* Favorable regard; respect.	**gloat** (glōt) *intr. v.* To feel triumphant, spiteful delight.

LESSON 17	LESSON 17	LESSON 17	LESSON 17	LESSON 17
humility (hyōō-mĭl′ĭ-tē) *n.* The quality of being humble.	**modest** (mŏd′ĭst) *adj.* Having a moderate estimation of one's abilities.	**pompous** (pŏm′pəs) *adj.* Making an exaggerated show of dignity.	**swagger** (swăg′ər) *intr. v.* To walk in a boastful manner; strut.	**vaunt** (vônt) *tr. v.* To call attention to, often boastfully.

LESSON 18	LESSON 18	LESSON 18	LESSON 18	LESSON 18
appraisal (ə-prā′zəl) *n.* An evaluation of the worth of something.	**base** (bās) *adj.* Mean or contemptible; inferior in quality.	**candid** (kăn′dĭd) *adj.* Without pretense or reserve; honest.	**criterion** (krī-tîr′ē-ən) *n.* A standard of judgment.	**legitimate** (lə-jĭt′ə-mĭt) *adj.* Authentic; genuine; lawful.

LESSON 18	LESSON 18	LESSON 18	LESSON 18	LESSON 18
mediocre (mē′dē-ō′kər) *adj.* Of moderate to low quality; average.	**meritorious** (mĕr′ĭ-tôr′ē-əs) *adj.* Having superior value.	**subtle** (sŭt′l) *adj.* Not immediately obvious.	**truism** (trōō′ĭz′əm) *n.* A statement of an obvious truth.	**validate** (văl′ĭ-dāt′) *tr. v.* To confirm or verify.

LESSON 19 circumlocution	LESSON 19 discourse	LESSON 19 euphemism	LESSON 19 falter	LESSON 19 literate
LESSON 19 prattle	LESSON 19 raconteur	LESSON 19 reiterate	LESSON 19 utterance	LESSON 19 verbose
LESSON 20 ascribe	LESSON 20 circumscribe	LESSON 20 inscribe	LESSON 20 nondescript	LESSON 20 prescribe
LESSON 20 proscribe	LESSON 20 scripture	LESSON 20 subscribe	LESSON 20 subscript	LESSON 20 transcribe
LESSON 21 aficionado	LESSON 21 bonanza	LESSON 21 bravado	LESSON 21 embargo	LESSON 21 flotilla
LESSON 21 hacienda	LESSON 21 junta	LESSON 21 peccadillo	LESSON 21 peon	LESSON 21 renegade

LESSON 19	LESSON 19	LESSON 19	LESSON 19	LESSON 19
circumlocution (sûr´-kəm-lō-kyōō´shən) *n.* A roundabout expression.	**discourse** (dĭs´kôrs´) *n.* Verbal expression in the form of speech or writing.	**euphemism** (yōō´fə-mĭz´əm) *n.* The substitution of an inoffensive term.	**falter** (fôl´tər) *intr. v.* To speak hesitatingly.	**literate** (lĭt´ər-ĭt) *adj.* Able to read and write; well-written.
© 1988 HMCo	© 1988 HMCo	© 1988 HMCo	© 1988 HMCo	© 1988 HMCo

LESSON 19	LESSON 19	LESSON 19	LESSON 19	LESSON 19
prattle (prăt´l) *intr. v.* To talk idly or meaninglessly; babble.	**raconteur** (răk´ŏn-tûr´) *n.* A skillful and witty storyteller.	**reiterate** (rē-ĭt´ə-rāt´) *tr. v.* To say over again; repeat.	**utterance** (ŭt´ər-əns) *n.* The act of expressing vocally.	**verbose** (vər-bōs´) *adj.* Using an excessive number of words.
© 1988 HMCo	© 1988 HMCo	© 1988 HMCo	© 1988 HMCo	© 1988 HMCo

LESSON 20	LESSON 20	LESSON 20	LESSON 20	LESSON 20
ascribe (ə-skrīb´) *tr. v.* To regard as caused by; attribute.	**circumscribe** (sûr´kəm-skrīb´) *tr. v.* To draw a line around; encircle.	**inscribe** (ĭn-skrīb´) *tr. v.* To engrave words or letters on a surface.	**nondescript** (nŏn´dĭ-skrĭpt´) *adj.* Lacking in distinctive qualities.	**prescribe** (prĭ-skrīb´) *tr. v.* To recommend the use of a remedy.
© 1988 HMCo	© 1988 HMCo	© 1988 HMCo	© 1988 HMCo	© 1988 HMCo

LESSON 20	LESSON 20	LESSON 20	LESSON 20	LESSON 20
proscribe (prō-skrīb´) *tr. v.* To prohibit; condemn.	**scripture** (skrĭp´chər) *n.* A sacred writing or book.	**subscribe** (səb-skrīb´) *intr. v.* To contract to receive and pay for something.	**subscript** (sŭb´skrĭpt´) *n.* Symbol written below and to the right of a letter, etc.	**transcribe** (trăn-skrīb´) *tr. v.* To make a written copy of.
© 1988 HMCo	© 1988 HMCo	© 1988 HMCo	© 1988 HMCo	© 1988 HMCo

LESSON 21	LESSON 21	LESSON 21	LESSON 21	LESSON 21
aficionado (ə-fĭsh´ē-ə-nä´dō) *n.* A fan; an enthusiastic admirer.	**bonanza** (bə-năn´zə) *n.* A source of wealth or luck; a rich mine.	**bravado** (brə-vä´dō) *n.* False bravery; swaggering courage.	**embargo** (ĕm-bär´gō) *n.* A government order prohibiting trade.	**flotilla** (flō-tĭl´ə) *n.* A small fleet.
© 1988 HMCo	© 1988 HMCo	© 1988 HMCo	© 1988 HMCo	© 1988 HMCo

LESSON 21	LESSON 21	LESSON 21	LESSON 21	LESSON 21
hacienda (hä´sē-ĕn´də) *n.* A large estate, ranch, or plantation.	**junta** (hŏon´tə) *n.* A group of rulers who seize power.	**peccadillo** (pĕk´ə-dĭl´ō) *n.* A small fault or transgression.	**peon** (pē´ŏn) *n.* An unskilled laborer; a farm worker.	**renegade** (rĕn´ĭ-gād´) *n.* A traitor or outlaw; a rebel.
© 1988 HMCo	© 1988 HMCo	© 1988 HMCo	© 1988 HMCo	© 1988 HMCo

LESSON 22 assert	LESSON 22 incisive	LESSON 23 arbitrary	LESSON 23 haphazard	LESSON 24 affectation	LESSON 24 factor
LESSON 22 dauntless	LESSON 22 outspoken	LESSON 23 coincidental	LESSON 23 intent	LESSON 24 beneficiary	LESSON 24 officiate
LESSON 22 ferocity	LESSON 22 temerity	LESSON 23 contrive	LESSON 23 premeditated	LESSON 24 defect	LESSON 24 officious
LESSON 22 flout	LESSON 22 vehement	LESSON 23 deliberation	LESSON 23 spontaneous	LESSON 24 efficacy	LESSON 24 prolific
LESSON 22 headstrong	LESSON 22 vibrant	LESSON 23 fortuitous	LESSON 23 unwitting	LESSON 24 faction	LESSON 24 suffice

LESSON 22	LESSON 22	LESSON 22	LESSON 22	LESSON 22
assert (ə-sûrt′) *tr. v.* To state positively or boldly; affirm.	**dauntless** (dônt′lĭs) *adj.* Not able to be discouraged; bold.	**ferocity** (fə-rŏs′ĭ-tē) *n.* Savagery; fierceness; barbarity.	**flout** (flout) *tr. v.* To show scorn or contempt for.	**headstrong** (hĕd′strông′) *adj.* Determined to have one's own way.

LESSON 22	LESSON 22	LESSON 22	LESSON 22	LESSON 22
incisive (ĭn-sī′sĭv) *adj.* Sharp; keen; perceptive.	**outspoken** (out-spō′kən) *adj.* Spoken without reserve; frank.	**temerity** (tə-mĕr′ĭ-tē) *n.* Foolish disregard of danger.	**vehement** (vē′ə-mənt) *adj.* Showing intense emotion; forceful.	**vibrant** (vī′brənt) *adj.* Pulsing with energy; lively.

LESSON 23	LESSON 23	LESSON 23	LESSON 23	LESSON 23
arbitrary (är′bĭ-trĕr′ē) *adj.* Based on whim rather than reason.	**coincidental** (kō-ĭn′sĭ-dĕn′təl) *adj.* Occurring together by chance.	**contrive** (kən-trīv′) *tr. v.* To plan cleverly; plot or scheme.	**deliberation** (dĭ-lĭb′ə-rā′shən) *n.* Careful thought in actions or decisions.	**fortuitous** (fôr-tōō′ĭ-təs) *adj.* Occurring unexpectedly; lucky.

LESSON 23	LESSON 23	LESSON 23	LESSON 23	LESSON 23
haphazard (hăp-hăz′ərd) *adj.* Lacking any definite order; random.	**intent** (ĭn-tĕnt′) *n.* An aim or purpose.	**premeditated** (prē-mĕd′ĭ-tā′tĭd) *adj.* Planned in advance.	**spontaneous** (spŏn-tā′nē-əs) *adj.* Happening without external cause.	**unwitting** (ŭn-wĭt′ĭng) *adj.* Not knowing; unaware.

LESSON 24	LESSON 24	LESSON 24	LESSON 24	LESSON 24
affectation (ăf′ĕk-tā′shən) *n.* Artificial behavior; pretense.	**beneficiary** (bĕn′ə-fĭsh′ē-ĕr′ē) *n.* One who receives funds.	**defect** (dē′fĕkt′) *n.* A flaw or imperfection.	**efficacy** (ĕf′ĭ-kə-sē) *n.* The power to produce a desired effect.	**faction** (făk′shən) *n.* A small group within a larger group.

LESSON 24	LESSON 24	LESSON 24	LESSON 24	LESSON 24
factor (făk′tər) *n.* Ingredient that helps bring about a result.	**officiate** (ə-fĭsh′ē-āt′) *intr. v.* To preside.	**officious** (ə-fĭsh′əs) *adj.* Very forward in offering advice.	**prolific** (prə-lĭf′ĭk) *adj.* Causing abundant growth.	**suffice** (sə-fīs′) *intr. v.* To meet present needs; be adequate.

LESSON 25 accolade	LESSON 25 adulation	LESSON 25 anathema	LESSON 25 commend	LESSON 25 eulogy
LESSON 25 extol	LESSON 25 homage	LESSON 25 laudable	LESSON 25 reproach	LESSON 25 reverence
LESSON 26 assess	LESSON 26 disregard	LESSON 26 enthrall	LESSON 26 heedless	LESSON 26 indifferent
LESSON 26 oblivious	LESSON 26 preoccupy	LESSON 26 receptive	LESSON 26 scrutinize	LESSON 26 vigilant
LESSON 27 contract	LESSON 27 detract	LESSON 27 distraction	LESSON 27 entreaty	LESSON 27 extract
LESSON 27 portray	LESSON 27 protracted	LESSON 27 retract	LESSON 27 tract	LESSON 27 trait

LESSON 25	LESSON 25	LESSON 25	LESSON 25	LESSON 25
accolade (ăk′ə-lād′) *n.* An expression of strong approval.	**extol** (ĭk-stōl′) *tr. v.* To praise highly.	**homage** (hŏm′ĭj) *n.* Particular respect or honor shown publicly.	**commend** (kə-mĕnd′) *tr. v.* To mention approvingly; praise.	**eulogy** (yōō′lə-jē) *n.* A speech or written tribute of praise.
adulation (ăj′ə-lā′shən) *n.* Enthusiastic or excessive praise.		**laudable** (lô′də-bəl) *adj.* Worthy of praise.	**reproach** (rĭ-prōch′) *tr. v.* To blame or criticize for something.	**reverence** (rĕv′ər-əns) *n.* A feeling of great respect; veneration.
anathema (ə-năth′ə-mə) *n.* A strong denunciation.				

LESSON 26	LESSON 26	LESSON 26	LESSON 26	LESSON 26
assess (ə-sĕs′) *tr. v.* To determine the importance of; evaluate.	**oblivious** (ə-blĭv′ē-əs) *adj.* Lacking conscious awareness.	**disregar** (dĭs′rĭ-gä...) pay little tion to.	**enthrall** (ĕn...) *tr. v.* To capt... hold spellboun... charm.	**heedless** (hēd′lĭs) *adj.* Unmindful; inattentive; careless.
	preoccupy (prē-ŏk′yə-pī′) *tr. v.* To hold the attention of.	**receptive** (rĭ-sĕp′tĭv) *adj.* Ready to receive something favorably.	**scrutinize** (skrōōt′n-īz′) *tr. v.* Pay close attention to detail.	**indifferent** (ĭn-dĭf′ər-ənt) *adj.* Marked by a lack of interest.
			vigilant (vĭj′ə-lənt) *adj.* Watchful; on the alert; wary.	

LESSON 27	LESSON 27	LESSON 27	LESSON 27	LESSON 27
contract (kŏn′trăkt′) *n.* Formal agreement between two parties.	**detract** (dĭ-trăkt′) *intr. v.* To take away something desirable.	**distraction** (dĭ-străk′shən) *n.* A diversion of attention.	**entreaty** (ĕn-trē′tē) *n.* An earnest request or plea.	**extract** (ĭk-străkt′) *tr. v.* To pull or draw out forcibly.
portray (pôr-trā′) *tr. v.* To make a likeness or representation of.	**protracted** (prō-trăk′tĭd) *adj.* Drawn out or lengthened in time.	**retract** (rĭ-trăkt′) *tr. v.* To draw back; withdraw.	**tract** (trăkt) *n.* A stretch of land.	**trait** (trāt) *n.* A distinguishing quality or feature.

LESSON 28 dogmatic	LESSON 28 pensive	LESSON 28 philosophy	LESSON 28 plausible	LESSON 28 ponder
LESSON 28 postulate	LESSON 28 rational	LESSON 28 reverie	LESSON 28 skeptical	LESSON 28 speculation
LESSON 29 apologist	LESSON 29 contend	LESSON 29 dissuade	LESSON 29 fallacy	LESSON 29 hypothesis
LESSON 29 indisputable	LESSON 29 inference	LESSON 29 red herring	LESSON 29 refute	LESSON 29 substantiate
LESSON 30 cognizant	LESSON 30 connoisseur	LESSON 30 conscientious	LESSON 30 consciousness	LESSON 30 diagnosis
LESSON 30 notoriety	LESSON 30 omniscient	LESSON 30 prognosis	LESSON 30 recognition	LESSON 30 unconscionable

LESSON 28	LESSON 28	LESSON 29	LESSON 29	LESSON 30	LESSON 30
dogmatic (dŏg-măt'ĭk) *adj.* Expressing a belief as if it were fact.	**postulate** (pŏs'chə-lāt') *tr. v.* To assume the truth without proof.	**apologist** (ə-pŏl'ə-jĭst) *n.* One who argues for an idea or cause.	**indisputable** (ĭn'dĭ-spyōō'tə-bəl) *adj.* Undeniable.	**cognizant** (kŏg'nĭ-zənt) *adj.* Aware; fully informed.	**notoriety** (nō'tə-rī'ĭ-tē) *n.* Fame of an unfavorable kind.
pensive (pĕn'sĭv) *adj.* Dreamily, and often sadly, thoughtful.	**rational** (răsh'ən-əl) *adj.* Based on reason; logical; sane.	**contend** (kən-tĕnd') *tr. v.* To maintain or assert.	**inference** (ĭn'fər-əns) *n.* A conclusion based on evidence.	**connoisseur** (kŏn'ə-sûr') *n.* One knowledgeable in any area.	**omniscient** (ŏm-nĭsh'ənt) *adj.* Knowing all things.
philosophy (fĭ-lŏs'ə-fē) *n.* Study of reality based on logic.	**reverie** (rĕv'ər-ē) *n.* The condition of being lost in thought.	**dissuade** (dĭ-swād') *tr. v.* To discourage from a course of action.	**red herring** (rĕd hĕr'ĭng) *n.* Something that draws attention away.	**conscientious** (kŏn'shē-ĕn'shəs) *adj.* Thorough and attentive.	**prognosis** (prŏg-nō'sĭs) *n.* A forecast of a probable result.
plausible (plô'zə-bəl) *adj.* Appearing true or reasonable.	**skeptical** (skĕp'tĭ-kəl) *adj.* Doubting; questioning.	**fallacy** (făl'ə-sē) *n.* An idea based on mistaken assumptions.	**refute** (rĭ-fyōōt') *tr. v.* To prove a person or idea to be wrong.	**consciousness** (kŏn'shəs-nĭs) *n.* Awareness of one's perceptions.	**recognition** (rĕk'əg-nĭsh'ən) *n.* Acknowledgment or attention.
ponder (pŏn'dər) *tr. v.* To think about carefully and at length.	**speculation** (spĕk'yə-lā'shən) *n.* Idea based on incomplete evidence; guess.	**hypothesis** (hī-pŏth'ĭ-sĭs) *n.* A theory that explains known facts.	**substantiate** (səb-stăn'shē-āt') *tr. v.* To support with proof; verify.	**diagnosis** (dī'əg-nō'sĭs) *n.* Critical analysis of a thing's nature.	**unconscionable** (ŭn-kŏn'shə-nə-bəl) *adj.* Unreasonable; unjust.

Lesson 10

Beginnings

Everything has a beginning. Our language supports this fact with a variety of words and expressions. How many of the following do you use to indicate the start of experiences in your life?

Make a fresh start
Dig in
Turn over a new leaf
Kick off
Break the ice
Get in on the ground floor
Get the show on the road
Start the ball rolling

The vocabulary words in this lesson describe different aspects of beginning. By studying these words, you will know which ones are appropriate substitutions for the informal expressions above.

WORD LIST
broach
convene
debut
embark
generate
incipient
initiative
innovation
novice
overture

DEFINITIONS

After you have studied the definitions and example for each vocabulary word, write the word on the line to the right.

1. **broach** (brōch) *trans. verb* To talk or write about for the first time; to bring up. (From the Old French word *broche*, meaning "piercing")
   EXAMPLE The ambassador to the United Nations *broached* the issue of world hunger.

2. **convene** (kən-vēn′) *intrans. verb* To assemble, usually for an official or public purpose; meet formally. *trans. verb* To cause to assemble. (From the Latin *com-*, meaning "together," and *venire*, meaning "to come")
   EXAMPLE Our club *convened* a half-hour early because of a long agenda.

3. **debut** (dā-byōō′, dā′byōō′) *noun* **a.** The beginning of a career or other course of action. **b.** A first public appearance, as of an actor on a stage. **c.** The formal presentation of a young woman to society. (From the French word *débuter*, meaning "to lead off in a game")
   RELATED WORD **debutante** *noun*
   EXAMPLE Hillary made her *debut* as an opera singer while she was still in high school.

1. _____

2. _____

3. _____

Copyright © 1988 Houghton Mifflin Company. All rights reserved.

4. **embark** (ĕm-bärk′) *intrans. verb* **a.** To set out on a venture; commence: *embark on a career.* **b.** To board a vessel, especially at the start of a journey. (From the Latin *in-*, meaning "in," and *barca*, meaning "boat")

   RELATED WORD **embarkation** *noun*

   EXAMPLE Robert Louis Stevenson *embarked* on a new life when he moved to an island in the Pacific.

   4. _____

5. **generate** (jĕn′ə-rāt′) *trans. verb* To cause or create. (From the Latin word *generare*, meaning "to produce")

   RELATED WORDS **generation** *noun;* **generator** *noun*

   EXAMPLE A good question *generates* lively discussion.

   5. _____

6. **incipient** (ĭn-sĭp′ē-ənt) *adjective* In an early stage; just beginning to exist or appear: *an incipient smile.* (From the Latin word *incipere*, meaning "to begin")

   RELATED WORDS **inception** *noun;* **incipiently** *adverb*

   EXAMPLE Belinda's *incipient* interest in photography lasted until she had her first roll of film developed.

   6. _____

7. **initiative** (ĭ-nĭsh′ə-tĭv) *noun* **a.** The power, ability, or instinct to begin or follow through with a plan or task; enterprise. **b.** A first step or opening move. **c.** The procedure by which citizens can propose a new law by petition and have it voted on. (From the Latin word *initium*, meaning "beginning")

   RELATED WORDS **initial** *adjective;* **initiate** *verb;* **initiation** *noun*

   EXAMPLE Because of John Roebling's *initiative* in 1867, the Brooklyn Bridge connects Brooklyn and Manhattan.

   7. _____

8. **innovation** (ĭn′ə-vā′shən) *noun* **a.** A creative act. **b.** Something begun or introduced; something that represents a change. (From the Latin word *innovare*, meaning "to renew")

   RELATED WORDS **innovate** *verb;* **innovative** *adjective;* **innovator** *noun*

   EXAMPLE Della's marketing *innovation* led to favorable publicity for her company.

   8. _____

9. **novice** (nŏv′ĭs) *noun* **a.** A person new to a field or activity; a beginner. **b.** A person who has entered a religious order but has not yet taken final vows. *adjective* Inexperienced. (From the Latin word *novus*, meaning "new")

   RELATED WORD **novitiate** *noun*

   EXAMPLE Brian was an expert cook but a *novice* at baking.

   9. _____

10. **overture** (ō′vər-cho͝or′) *noun* **a.** An act, offer, or proposal that indicates readiness to undertake a course of action. **b.** An instrumental composition that introduces an extended musical work. (From the Latin word *apertura*, meaning "an opening")

    EXAMPLE The new students welcomed their guides' *overtures* of friendship.

    10. _____

Name _____ Date _____

Exercise 1 Completing Definitions

On the answer line, write the word from the vocabulary list that best completes each definition.

1. To assemble or meet formally is to __?__ .
2. The beginning of a career or a first public appearance is a(n) __?__ .
3. The ability to begin or follow through with a plan is __?__ .
4. A creative act or something that represents a change is a(n) __?__ .
5. To talk or write about a topic for the first time is to __?__ it.
6. Something that is just beginning to exist is __?__ .
7. A person new to a field or activity is a(n) __?__ .
8. An act that indicates readiness to undertake a certain course of action is a(n) __?__ .
9. To set out on a venture or to board a vessel to start a journey is to __?__ .
10. To bring into existence or to cause is to __?__ .

1. _____
2. _____
3. _____
4. _____
5. _____
6. _____
7. _____
8. _____
9. _____
10. _____

Exercise 2 Using Words Correctly

Each of the following statements contains an italicized vocabulary word. Decide whether the sentence is true or false, and write *True* or *False* on the answer line.

1. You might cure an *incipient* cold by drinking fruit juice and getting more sleep.
2. Once the passengers *embark*, the empty ship floats higher in the water.
3. The power station at Hoover Dam *generates* electricity.
4. A lazy person often has much *initiative*.
5. A brainstorming session might produce ideas for *innovations*.
6. A *novice* at skiing may fall frequently.
7. After you have discussed a matter with friends several times, you might *broach* the subject to them.
8. Many school clubs *convene* after classes are over.
9. If its Broadway *debut* is successful, a play will close after opening night.
10. A snobbish attitude will generally be regarded as an *overture* of friendship.

1. _____
2. _____
3. _____
4. _____
5. _____
6. _____
7. _____
8. _____
9. _____
10. _____

Copyright © 1988 Houghton Mifflin Company. All rights reserved.

Beginnings

Exercise 3 Identifying Antonyms

Decide which word or phrase has the meaning that is opposite to that of the capitalized vocabulary word. Write the letter of your choice on the answer line.

1. EMBARK:
   a. travel   b. return   c. begin   d. encourage

2. BROACH:
   a. answer by guessing   c. avoid mention of
   b. announce   d. launch

3. NOVICE:
   a. beginner   b. sequel   c. ancient one   d. veteran

4. INITIATIVE:
   a. luck   b. enterprise   c. laziness   d. first step

5. INCIPIENT:
   a. beginning   b. final   c. upcoming   d. novel

6. DEBUT:
   a. retirement   b. beginning   c. deduction   d. debate

7. CONVENE:
   a. dismiss   b. gather   c. lose   d. meet

8. OVERTURE:
   a. assault   b. peace offering   c. finale   d. introduction

9. GENERATE:
   a. produce   b. stir up   c. cause   d. destroy

10. INNOVATION:
    a. procedure   b. representation   c. invention   d. tradition

1. _____
2. _____
3. _____
4. _____
5. _____
6. _____
7. _____
8. _____
9. _____
10. _____

Exercise 4 Using Different Forms of Words

Decide which form of the vocabulary word in parentheses best completes the sentence. The form given may be correct. Write your answer on the answer line.

1. Marie was selected by her friends to __?__ the subject of the skiing trip. *(broach)*

2. Our school will soon __?__ a computer course. *(initiative)*

3. For her introduction to society, the __?__ invited one hundred people to a dinner party. *(debut)*

4. The crew raised the gangplank after the __?__ of the last passenger. *(embark)*

5. The seminar participants did not __?__ in the afternoons. *(convene)*

6. The young man's __?__ at the monastery lasted one year. *(novice)*

7. __?__ new jokes is what keeps a comedy writer in business. *(generate)*

8. The Wright brothers were important __?__ in the field of aeronautics. *(innovation)*

1. _____
2. _____
3. _____
4. _____
5. _____
6. _____
7. _____
8. _____

64   Beginnings

Name _____ Date _____

9. The __?__ of our modern dictionary lies in the work of Dr. Samuel Johnson. *(incipient)*

9. _____

10. A sign on the door of the auditorium stated that no one would be seated during the __?__ . *(overture)*

10. _____

Reading Comprehension

Each numbered sentence in the following passage contains an italicized vocabulary word or related form. After you read the passage, you will complete an exercise.

Theodore Roosevelt: Twenty-Sixth President

Theodore Roosevelt was one of the most popular and effective Presidents in American history. **(1)** His colorful and forceful personality, his **innovative** policies, and his gift for phrase-making made "Teddy" or "T.R." a household name throughout the country.

Roosevelt was born on October 27, 1858. He was frail and sickly as a child, suffering from asthma. **(2)** When his father told him that he would need a strong body to give his mind the chance to develop fully, Roosevelt **embarked** on a regular exercise program. Horseback riding, swimming, and boxing helped him to overcome his asthma and build unusual physical strength.

After his graduation from Harvard College in 1880, Roosevelt began law school, but he did not like it. **(3)** When an acquaintance **broached** the idea of entering politics, Roosevelt welcomed the opportunity for public service. **(4)** He was elected assemblyman, and when the New York legislature **convened** in 1881, his intelligence and energy immediately won him the respect of his colleagues.

(5) He was regarded as an **incipient** leader of the Republican Party.

Between 1889 and 1895, Roosevelt served as the Civil Service Commissioner and as the Police Commissioner of New York City. With his usual energy, he began a campaign to rid New York of crime. **(6)** Although he accomplished little that was permanent, he did **generate** public support and added to his reputation as a champion of public decency.

Roosevelt became the Assistant Secretary of the Navy in 1897. Believing that the United States should declare war on Spain, he used his official position to prepare the Navy for the conflict. **(7)** On his own **initiative**, he organized a cavalry regiment composed mainly of cowhands and college athletes. He resigned as Assistant Secretary in 1898 so that he could be the commanding officer of his "Rough Riders." He emerged from the Spanish-American War as a national hero.

(8) When members of the Republican Party made **overtures** to him about running for Vice President in 1900, Roosevelt accepted the nomination and won the election. **(9)** Before he could tire of his limited duties as Vice President, Theodore Roosevelt made his **debut** as President on September 4, 1901, following the assassination of President William McKinley. **(10)** At the age of forty-two, Roosevelt was the youngest man to hold that office, but he was no **novice** in politics. His fifteen years of public service had prepared him well.

Please turn to the next page.

Copyright © 1988 Houghton Mifflin Company. All rights reserved.

Beginnings

Reading Comprehension Exercise

Each of the following statements corresponds to a numbered sentence in the passage. Each statement contains a blank and is followed by four answer choices. Decide which choice fits best in the blank. The word or phrase that you choose must express roughly the same meaning as the italicized word in the passage. Write the letter of your choice on the answer line.

1. Roosevelt's __?__ policies made his name a household word.
   a. stubborn   b. creative   c. traditional   d. indecisive

2. Roosevelt __?__ a regular exercise program.
   a. publicized   b. completed   c. worked at   d. began

3. An acquaintance __?__ the idea of entering politics to Roosevelt.
   a. brought up   b. indicated   c. vetoed   d. supported

4. When the New York legislature __?__ , Roosevelt won the respect of his colleagues.
   a. debated   b. retired   c. assembled   d. enacted bills

5. Roosevelt was a(n) __?__ leader of the Republican Party.
   a. reformed   b. important   c. strong   d. beginning

6. Roosevelt __?__ public support in his campaign to rid New York of crime.
   a. created   b. destroyed   c. lacked   d. encountered

7. Using __?__ , he organized a cavalry regiment.
   a. financial expertise   b. sincerity   c. enterprise   d. charm

8. When members of the Republican Party made __?__ to him about running for Vice President, Roosevelt accepted the nomination.
   a. proposals   b. objections   c. declarations   d. jokes

9. Roosevelt made his __?__ as President on September 4, 1901.
   a. reputation   c. first appearance
   b. first speech   d. last appearance

10. Although he was the youngest man to hold the office, Roosevelt was not a(n) __?__ in political affairs.
    a. expert   b. beginner   c. veteran   d. infant

1. _____
2. _____
3. _____
4. _____
5. _____
6. _____
7. _____
8. _____
9. _____
10. _____

Practice with Analogies

See page 79 for some strategies to use with analogies.

DIRECTIONS On the answer line, write the vocabulary word that completes each analogy.

1. AMATEUR : PROFESSIONAL : : __?__ : expert
2. ENGAGE : DISENGAGE : : __?__ : disembark
3. ENTRANCE : DEPARTURE : : __?__ : retirement
4. ASSEMBLE : GATHERING : : __?__ : meeting
5. LAZINESS : SLOTH : : enterprise : __?__

1. _____
2. _____
3. _____
4. _____
5. _____

66   Beginnings